Ministry in the Balance

Ministry in the Balance

by

Adrian DeVisser and Dave Sprowl

Contents

Dedications

By Adrian

THIS book is dedicated to Ophelia, who encourages me in believing what I do.

To my Son who practices the concepts that I have written.
To my daughter who helps me to hold a balance between writing and family life

By Dave

To Dale who makes my life a joy.

To Brooke, Barrett and Bayley who make me proud and assure me that something wonderful will live on after I am gone.

To Adrian, Ophelia, Prashan and Thelini, who have shown me how to live for God.

To Chris and KK, who let me be a part of something important and make it fun.

To Dave and Kandi, Doc and Lois, Kenton and Laurie and Gene and Kenette, who brought ministry to life for me.

Foreword by
Kenton Beshore

AS ministries move forward, they have never been so far off the map. The thinking in *Ministry in the Balance* brings navigational charts for the waters ahead. The insights in this book have come not from theory, reading or ideas; they are hard thought-out strategies by a person who has worked in leadership along side other people trying to figure out and find the course.

Dave Sprowl has the unique ability to bring great thinking and clarity to important issues facing ministries in the 21st century. With practical examples and stories, he gives insight to biblical principles and how they can be lived out in a complex world. Dave has a 360 degree view of the church and its ministries. His wealth of experience includes leading in church ministries for over 30 years, being in the marketplace, being on church boards, and serving on the staff of the church. His skill at synthesizing a vast amount of information and providing grounding foundational principles helps pastors and lay leaders plan and problem solve issues within their own ministries.

It is a gift to have a book that provides the strategic direction needed for the times ahead. We need powerful principles-biblical principles that help and guide us in the ministry opportunities that we face. Dave and Adrian provide principles, insights, and biblical wisdom which come from working in the church for many years. You will enjoy their clarity, insight and wisdom as well as practical ideas, helpful truths and how to think about the current state of ministries, how to implement a holistic ministry and how to face the future with optimistic enthusiasm. With these tools in hand, you can you achieve what God has given you to accomplish and keep your "ministry in the balance".

Kenton Beshore
Senior Pastor, Mariners Church

About this Book

In physics the tipping point is the point where a small change can make a balanced object topple. The ministry of Christ, as described in the gospel, exists at a tipping point. It requires a balance between the requirements of the great commission and great commandment. When these two dictates are in harmony, the ministry is healthy, vibrant, and productive. When they are out of balance it becomes unstable or unproductive.

This is a lesson for God's church. Just as He designed his creatures, God designed His church on earth to be rich in diversity and talent. But this richness must exist within God's basic blueprint. As the church celebrates its diversity and strives for relevance, it must take care to not abandon God's design. Otherwise it topples from the tipping point.

This book is designed to help the pastor or leader become free in his effort to be relevant and to celebrate the variety of gifts entrusted to him by reminding him of the basic boundaries and principles set by God's word. Secure in his knowledge of these principles, he may explore the richness and variety of God's resources while maintaining the equilibrium required by scripture. Ministry lies in the balance.

A WORD ABOUT VOICES

This book was written by two people, one a Pastor in Sri Lanka, the other a lawyer in California. Because of this, the perspective used may sometimes be confusing. At times the word "I" will obviously relate to the experiences of someone from the west, at other times from someone from the east. Other times "we" will be used. We ask forgiveness and for the reader to accept this as a consequence of the collaboration. Simply know that the comment is valid from the perspective of the particular writer. Also, to simplify we have used "he" rather than the "he or she" throughout this book.

Chapter 1

Holistic Ministry

The Nature of Holistic Ministry

A LL Christians would agree that believers, and the church that enriches them, are called to accomplish the mission of God. Despite this agreement the church has been divided by controversy. The rub lies in determining exactly what the "mission" is. Many believers, knowing that the only hope for mankind is to be born again, consider social betterment a waste of time and resources. Evangelism, for these Christians, is solely the preaching of the word. Hope lies in the next life. Others, promoting social justice, focus on God's role in improving the temporal life of man. Often this focus becomes a form of social political mantra almost divorced from the spiritual dimension. Holistic ministry attempts to find a balance by measuring our proper role in light of scriptural commands and examples.[1] It measures mission by the complete example of God's interaction with man, and the spiritual guidebook left us in the Bible.

The recent controversy of balancing spreading God's Word with serving God's people might suggest the concept of holistic ministry is new to the church. In fact, the concept is an old one. In his journal, dated May 7, 1741, John Wesley wrote:

I reminded the United Society, that many of our brethren and sisters

---

[1] Stott, J.R.W.(1975), *Christian Mission in the Modern World*, Downers Grove Intervarsity Press

had not needful food; many were destitute of convenient clothing; many were out of business, and that without their own fault; and many sick and ready to perish: That I had done what in me lay to feed the hungry, to clothe the naked, to employ the poor, and to visit the sick but was not, alone, sufficient for these things; and therefore desired all whose hearts were as my heart,

1. To bring what clothes each could spare, to be distributed among those that wanted most.

2. To give weekly a penny, or what they could afford, for the relief of the poor and sick. My design, I told them, is to employ, for the present, all the women who are out of business, and desire, it knitting.

To these we will first give the common price for what work they do; and then add, according as they need. Twelve persons are appointed to inspect these, and to visit and provide things needful for the sick. Each of these is to visit all the sick within their district, every other day: And to meet on Tuesday evening, to give an account of what they have done, and consult what can be done farther. [2]

As we will discuss, holistic ministry is as old as the Bible itself. Holistic ministry deals with both the spiritual and temporal needs of God's children, not because of political or social concerns, but because it is part of God's plan; His instructions to His believers. Paul wrote to the church at Galatia:

Do not be deceived, God is not mocked; for whatever a man sows, this he will also reap. For the one who sows to his own flesh shall from the flesh reap corruption, but the one who sows to the Spirit reap eternal life. And let us not lose heart in doing good, for in due time we shall reap if we do not grow weary. So then, while we have opportunity, let us do good to all men, and especially to those who are of the household of faith. [3]

Paul instructed us to consider our flesh as less important than our spiritual needs, but also to never tire of doing good. It was also Paul who discussed the needs of the body and the spirit in his benediction to the

[2] The works of John Wesley, vol. I, p. 309; Zondervan Publishing House
[3] Galatians 6:7-10, N.A.S.B.

church at Thessalonica, "Now may the God of peace Himself sanctify you entirely; and may your spirit and soul and body be preserved complete, without blame at the coming of our Lord Jesus Christ. Faithful is He who calls you, and He also will bring it to pass."[4]

Holistic ministry is a redemptive ministry which flows from the world view that God's rule extends to all of creation, which He desires to see returned to its rightful place under the Lordship of Christ. A holistic ministry seeks to exemplify the gospel in word and deed, to serve, not only "in word or speech, but [also] in truth and action" [5] Holistic ministry models the life and death of Jesus. It flows from the incarnation, where God's son became a man. As music stars Bono and B. B. King sang, *"That was the day when God came to town."* Having moved in, God embraced all facets of our plight on earth. He died to free us from sin, but lived in a way that modeled justice and compassion:

> The word compassion is derived from the Latin words *pati* and *cum* which put together mean "to suffer with." Compassion asks us to go where it hurts, to enter into places of pain, to share in brokenness, fear, confusion and anguish. Compassion challenges us to cry out with those in misery, to mourn with those who are lonely, to weep with those in tears. Compassion requires us to be weak with the weak, vulnerable with the vulnerable, and powerless with the powerless. Compassion means full immersion in the condition of being human.[6]

Jesus did not arrive like a messenger, deliver His thoughts and depart. He lived with us suffered with us, embraced the least of us. He fully immersed Himself in the human condition. Jesus Himself grew holistically - physically, mentally, spiritually and socially.[7] His life encompassed all that mankind experienced so that the message was more powerful. That is holistic ministry.

Holistic ministry is simply an acknowledgment that God's plan includes all; the spiritual and physical, the present and the future. Jesus demonstrates the importance of the present and the physical when he

---

[4] 1 Thessalonians 5:23-4, N.A.S.B.
[5] 1 John 3:18
[6] Henri Nouwen, as quoted from *CompassionCoalation.org* website
[7] Luke 2:42

exerts His power to heal, [8] to cast our demons and to feed the crowds.[9] God demonstrates the importance of the spiritual and the future in the fullness of the Kingdom that awaits us at the end of the age. This is when all matters are forever resolved with the separation of the righteous.[10] This is the renewal of all [11] where God's disciples celebrate.[12] Until that time we have work here on earth.

A holistic approach embraces the truth that all of mankind was created in the image of God and is entitled to the dignity that suggests. It dissolves the barriers between those serving and those being served, between the free and the enslaved, between the rich and the poor. All need God's plan, they simply suffer from different infirmaries:

> At the end of the day, the poverty of the non-poor is the same kind of poverty as the poor, only differently expressed. The poverty of the non-poor is fundamentally relational and caused by sin. The result is a life full of things and short on meaning. The non-poor simply believe in a different set of lies. The only difference is that the poverty of the non-poor is harder to change. "A bank account and abundant diet somehow (I cannot explain it quite satisfactorily) insulate man [sic] from coming to feel the primary truth of history" (citation omitted). This is what Jesus was trying to say when he compared a rich man getting into the kingdom as a camel trying to get through the eye of a needle. [13]

The internal needs of rich and poor are also the same. Apologist Ravi Zacharius noted that:

> One by one the generation that refused to be bound by the Pope, and refused to be bound by the Church, decided in an ecstasy of freedom that they would not be bound by anything–not by the Bible, not by conscience, not by God himself. From believing too much that never did have to be believed, they took to believing so little that for countless thousands human existence and the world itself no longer seemed to make any sense. Poets began talking about the 'wasteland'

---

[8] Matthew 4:23
[9] Matthew 12:28; Luke 11:20
[10] Matthew 13:40-43
[11] Matthew 19:28
[12] Luke 14:13
[13] Bryant Myers, *Walking with the Poor*, Orbis, 1999, p. 90

with "ghostly lives" as Stephen Spender put it, 'moving from fragmentary ruins which have lost their significance.' Nothingness became a subject of conversation, nihilism a motive, frustration and despair a theme for novelists and dramatists…yet all is not lost.[14]

Millions of people do not know who they are, nor that they have any significance or worth. Hence the urgent challenge to us to tell them who they are, to enlighten them about their identity, that is, to teach without compromise the full biblical doctrine of our human being–its depravity, yes, but also its dignity.[15]

A holistic ministry recognizes the inherent worthiness of being created in the image of God. It seeks the restoration of man's dignity that God intended and addresses the universal need for self worth. When humans, created in God's image, are devalued God is also devalued. It is like defacing a great work of art. Through scripture God has established that we should minister in the manner that Christ ministered, "As the Father has sent me, I am sending you"[16] and that the world should be conducted so that, "justice roll down like waters."[17] A holistic ministry seeks to bring those words to life on earth encapsulating all that God is, all that His mission for His believers on earth is:

…. Mission," simply put, is everything the church is sent to be and do in the world. This definition assumes that God initiated the mission of the church and continues to direct it. Likewise, this definition affirms that churches are sent, since the very word "mission" implies being dispatched or sent to perform a task or service. As Jesus was sent by God, so Jesus sent the disciples and followers who formed the church. As living embodiments of the living work of Christ, churches are to continue what Jesus began. The church, therefore, is by nature a sign and an agent of the kingdom of God here and now. Everything God rules is kingdom property. That includes everything the church is and does.... Mission involves everything the church does in response to God's creative and redemptive mandates. Evangelism and mission are not synonymous. Social action is not the same as mission. Discipleship, stewardship, and fellowship, like evangelism and social

---

[14] Zacharias, Ravi, Excerpts from: *Can Man Live Without God?*
[15] Stott, John, *The Contemporary Christian*
[16] John 20:21
[17] Amos 5:24

responsibility, deal with specific and concrete actions. Together these functions become the mission of the church.[18]

In short, God's mission is not what the church does, it is who God is. Mission involves "the complete dealing of the Triune God with the world". As David Bosch writes, "...mission is not primarily an activity of the church, but an attribute of God. God is a missionary God.... Mission is thereby seen as a movement from God to the world: the church is viewed as an instrument of that mission... There is church because there is mission, not vice versa."[19] A holistic approach to God's mission binds God's desire for man to be redeemed eternality to God's desire that mortal man live justly, reflecting the love of God, "He has told you, O man, what is good; And what does the LORD require of you But to do justice, to love kindness, And to walk humbly with your God?"[20]

Throughout history, the church, in accordance with God's instruction, has stepped forward to meet the needs of God's creation, establishing orphanages, feeding the hungry, clothing the naked. But the Bible is also clear that salvation is the most critical need of man, "I say to you, My friends, do not be afraid of those who kill the body and after that have no more that they can do. But I will warn you whom to fear: fear the One who, after He has killed, has authority to cast into hell; yes, I tell you, fear Him!"[21]

Both the actions of the church and the imperative of the gospel are in complete accord. God created man with both physical and spiritual needs. While the eternal needs are paramount, the physical needs may not be ignored. Indeed, meeting the spiritual needs is enhanced by tending to the physical concerns.[22] We are commanded to let our light shine before men[23] so that the glory of God is on display. Isaiah suggests the manner in which our light might shine:

If you spend yourselves in behalf of the hungry and satisfy the needs

---

[18] Ray Bakke and Sam Roberts, "The Expanded Mission of City Center Churches" (International Urban Associates, 1998), p. 85
[19] Transforming Mission: Paradigm Shifts in Theology of Mission, p. 390
[20] Micah 6:8
[21] Luke 12:4-5
[22] See e.g. Matthew 5:13-16
[23] Matthew 5:16

of the oppressed, then your light will rise in the darkness, and your night will become like the noonday. The Lord will guide you always; he will satisfy your needs in a sun-scorched land and will strengthen your frame. You will be like a well-watered garden, like a spring whose waters never fail.[24]

A further reason to meet the physical needs and lift the burdens on the oppressed is more straightforward; we are commanded to do so, "If anyone has material possessions, and sees his brother in need, but has no pity on him, how can the love of God be in him? Dear children, let us not love with words or tongue but with actions and in truth."[25] John's command is consistent with our duty to God's creation. In Romans eight Paul discusses this duty:

For I consider that the sufferings of this present time are not worthy to be compared with the glory that is to be revealed to us. For the anxious longing of the creation waits eagerly for the revealing of the sons of God. For the creation was subjected to futility, not willingly, but because of Him who subjected it, in hope that the creation itself also will be set free from its slavery to corruption into the freedom of the glory of the children of God. For we know that the whole creation groans and suffers the pains of childbirth together until now. And not only this, but also we ourselves, having the first fruits of the Spirit, even we ourselves groan within ourselves, waiting eagerly for our adoption as sons, the redemption of our body. For in hope we have been saved, but hope that is seen is not hope; for who hopes for what he already sees? But if we hope for what we do not see, with perseverance we wait eagerly for it. [26]

These verses make clear that the completion of God's creation waits for us, His children, to complete it. We as "the children of God", are the ones called to liberate the world from its groaning. The creation was not meant to groan and suffer but came to this state through the fall of man.[27] But as the sons of God we can restore it, we live in " in hope that the creation itself also will be set free from its slavery to corruption into

---

[24] Isaiah 58:10-11
[25] 1 John 3:17-18
[26] Romans 8:18-25
[27] Genesis 3:17

the freedom of the glory of the children of God." [28] God's desire for the restoration of creation was left in the hands of His church.[29] Jesus lived and died to reconcile both God's plan for man to be eternally saved and God's plan to restore the earth.[30]

Scripture is replete with examples of reconciling the fallen nature of God's creation with God's desire to see man in harmony with His wishes and Holiness. Beginning with God entrusting man with dominion over creation, his role in freeing the Israelites from the oppression of Egypt, the Leviticus laws protecting the poor, the cries of the prophets for justice and the healing and caring ministry of Christ, scripture is a symphony of God's desire for His children to care for each other in all their needs. Jesus was the personification of this concept:

> And the book of the prophet Isaiah was handed to Him. And He opened the book and found the place where it was written, "THE SPIRIT OF THE LORD IS UPON ME, BECAUSE HE ANOINTED ME TO PREACH THE GOSPEL TO THE POOR. HE HAS SENT ME TO PROCLAIM RELEASE TO THE CAPTIVES, AND RECOVERY OF SIGHT TO THE BLIND, TO SET FREE THOSE WHO ARE OPPRESSED, TO PROCLAIM THE FAVORABLE YEAR OF THE LORD." And He closed the book, gave it back to the attendant and sat down; and the eyes of all in the synagogue were fixed on Him. And He began to say to them, "Today this Scripture has been fulfilled in your hearing."[31]

The word and action carrying out the gospel are partners in God's plan. As we describe later in this work the Great Commission and the Greatest Commandment were meant to be in perfect harmony. The Lausanne Covenant, a manifesto issued by world Christian leaders, expresses the thought this way:

> We affirm that God is both the Creator and the Judge of all men. We therefore should share his concern for justice and reconciliation throughout human society and for the liberation of men and women from every kind of oppression. Because men and women are made in the image of God, every person, regardless of race, religion, colour,

---

[28] Romans 8:21
[29] Ephesians 1:22-23, Ephesians 3:9-10
[30] Colossians 1:18-20, see also Ephesians 1:9-10
[31] Luke 4:17-21

culture, class, sex or age, has an intrinsic dignity because of which he or she should be respected and served, not exploited. Here too we express penitence both for our neglect and for having sometimes regarded evangelism and social concern as mutually exclusive. Although reconciliation with other people is not reconciliation with God, nor is social action evangelism, nor is political liberation salvation, nevertheless we affirm that evangelism and socio-political involvement are both part of our Christian duty. For both are necessary expressions of our doctrines of God and man, our love for our neighbour and our obedience to Jesus Christ. The message of salvation implies also a message of judgment upon every form of alienation, oppression and discrimination, and we should not be afraid to denounce evil and injustice wherever they exist. When people receive Christ they are born again into his kingdom and must seek not only to exhibit but also to spread its righteousness in the midst of an unrighteous world. The salvation we claim should be transforming us in the totality of our personal and social responsibilities. Faith without works is dead.[32]

We are called to live our lives in a way that helps to transform the creation of God from its current troubled state. We do so by living in the way God calls us to live and by reflecting God's heart for the world. Holistic ministry calls for the healing of broken people, whatever the cause of the brokenness. Whatever the barriers separating them from God's mission, holistic ministry seeks to overcome those barriers.

Who should be the subjects of our ministry? The list is broad. First, we are responsible for our own family. "But if anyone does not provide for his own, and especially for those of his household, he has denied the faith, and is worse than an unbeliever."[33] Our church family comes next; they are our family in Christ, our brothers and sisters, "So then, while we have opportunity, let us do good to all men, and especially to those who are of the household of the faith." [34] Finally, as the verse above suggests, we are to care for "all men". The fact that scripture suggests greater attention be given to our biological and church family does not mean the instruction does not apply to "all men". Each command stands

---

[32] Lausanne Council for World Evangelism, *Lausanne Covenant*, Paragraph 5
[33] 1 Timothy 5:8, N.A.S.B.
[34] Galatians 6:10; N.A.S.B.

on its own as a requirement of God. Jesus made this clear in the story of the good Samaritan in Luke:

> And a lawyer stood up and put Him to the test, saying, "Teacher, what shall I do to inherit eternal life?" And He said to him, "What is written in the Law? How does it read to you?" And he answered, "YOU SHALL LOVE THE LORD YOUR GOD WITH ALL YOUR HEART, AND WITH ALL YOUR SOUL, AND WITH ALL YOUR STRENGTH, AND WITH ALL YOUR MIND; AND YOUR NEIGHBOR AS YOURSELF." And He said to him, "You have answered correctly; DO THIS AND YOU WILL LIVE." But wishing to justify himself, he said to Jesus, "And who is my neighbor?"

> Jesus replied and said, "A man was going down from Jerusalem to Jericho, and fell among robbers, and they stripped him and beat him, and went away leaving him half dead. "And by chance a priest was going down on that road, and when he saw him, he passed by on the other side. "Likewise a Levite also, when he came to the place and saw him, passed by on the other side. "But a Samaritan, who was on a journey, came upon him; and when he saw him, he felt compassion, and came to him and bandaged up his wounds, pouring oil and wine on them; and he put him on his own beast, and brought him to an inn and took care of him. "On the next day he took out two denarii and gave them to the innkeeper and said, 'Take care of him; and whatever more you spend, when I return I will repay you.' "Which of these three do you think proved to be a neighbor to the man who fell into the robbers' hands?" And he said, "The one who showed mercy toward him." Then Jesus said to him, "Go and do the same." [35]

When the lawyer asks, "who is my neighbor?" it is not an idle question. Jewish teachers of the time would most frequently use the term "neighbor" to apply to a fellow Israelite.[36] Jesus no doubt uses this example of a "good" Samaritan to give greater impact to the example. Samaritans were the offspring of Jewish women captured and impregnated by Israel's conquerors during the captivity. As such they were despised.

Jericho is at a lower elevation than Jerusalem. The route was a steep seventeen mile road that descended 3300 feet. It was a haven to robbers,

---

[35] Luke 10:25-37
[36] See e.g. Leviticus 19:18

and the man fell victim to these outlaws. The Pharisee, a priest, ignored the man. Priests were commanded to avoid the impurities associated with corpses, and the man appeared to be dead. Although also going down to Jericho and therefore not headed for temple duties, the priest decided to leave the matter to others. The Levite faced no such restrictions, but despite this passed by without any attempt to aid the fallen man. It was the despised Samaritan that acted, both to meet the immediate needs of the fallen man and to provide for his restoration. The lawyer would have hated the Samaritan, yet following the line of the story, he was forced to concede that it was the Samaritan who acted as a neighbor. The example is clear; we are to love each other without limit, and to meet needs without regard to race, wealth, position or social standing. We do so, because God has done so.

The connection between serving God's people and understanding the very heart of God is crystal clear in scripture:

But when the Son of Man comes in His glory, and all the angels with Him, then He will sit on His glorious throne. And all the nations will be gathered before Him; and He will separate them from one another, as the shepherd separates the sheep from the goats; and He will put the sheep on His right, and the goats on the left. Then the King will say to those on His right, 'Come, you who are blessed of my Father, inherit the kingdom prepared for you from the foundation of the world. For I was hungry, and you gave Me something to eat; I was thirsty, and you gave Me something to drink; I was a stranger, and you invited Me in; naked, and you clothes Me; I was sick and you visited Me; I was in prison, and you came to Me.' Then the righteous will answer Him saying, "lord when did we see You hungry, and feed You, or thirsty, and give You drink? And when did we see You a stranger, and invite You in, or naked, and clothe you? And when did we see You sick, or in prison, and come to You?' And the King will answer and say to them, 'Truly I say to you, to the extent that you did it to one of these brothers of Mine, even the least of them, you did it to Me." [37]

It is clear that those who do not understand the need to serve are far from God's heart. The marks of true faith and commitment to Jesus are abiding in Jesus' word, loving others and bearing fruit.[38]

[37] Matthew 25:31-40 N.A.S.B.
[38] John 8:31-32; John13:34-35; John 15:8.

THE HALLMARKS OF
HOLISTIC MINISTRY

Holistic ministry should address the needs of the individual by promoting evangelism, education, economics, and emotional and physical health. It should address the needs of the community though advocacy for justice and through the support of community development. It is important however, that these elements be kept in the proper context. They are done as a revelation of Christ's image and because they are part of God's plan, not as a separate adjunct to God's plan. To increase the material state of someone without meeting their eternal needs is like throwing someone a life preserver with no rope attached. They can stay afloat longer, but they remain lost.

In the process of creating holistic ministry several governing principles should be examined: freedom, restoration, transformation, integration and partnership.[39]

Freedom

Fundamentally our job as Christians is to engage in God's mission for us on earth. He calls on us to spread the good news of salvation. To do this we must free others from the constraints that separate them from God and interfere with receiving His love. We must enlist them as partners to continue to spread God's word. To hear the word and engage in the effort, people need to be delivered from the tyranny of poverty: material, social and spiritual.

Restoration

As creations of God all people must be restored to a position of dignity. They are entitled to basic necessities of life. They are entitled to enjoy their own culture and approach to worship where not prohibited by scripture. They are entitled to the support and resources necessary to allow them to participate in God's plan for the redemption of creation.

---

[39] Adapted from the works of Ted Yamamori

Transformation

Society falls short of the standards set by God. It needs to be transformed. We are called to bring about the transformation of society to meet God's model. We are the trustees of earth and must administer it in the manner that God has instructed. We can begin at the level of the community in which we serve, extending the influence of God by engaging our community, rather than cloistering ourselves inside our local church.

Integration

Our ministry must empower, dignify and integrate service and faith into the living of life. We need to be bold and creative, consistently seeking ways to become more credible witnesses for Christ. By relieving those in need of their burden we not only improve society, we build the individuals who become better witnesses and, having grown, serve others.

Partnership

Holistic ministry is the duty of the church, but it need not be done solely by the church. A believer cannot grow spiritually or effectively contribute his gifts to the body of Christ unless he belongs to a local church, but so long as para-church organizations work toward placing new believers in a local church there is no reason that they should not have an important role in ministry.

Holistic ministry is best served in partnership,[40] each partner lending his skills and resources to the other to achieve the common goal. This not only increases effectiveness, but the cooperation itself becomes a witness to others. We serve God when we put our talents in the service of others. We magnify our impact when we form partnerships with those who have other gifts.[41]

---

[40] See Chapter 6
[41] Extracted from various works of T. Yamamori

25

Characteristics

The implementation of these five principles will exhibit common characteristics adapted from the works of T Yamamori:

- Concern for the whole person
- Prophetic ministry that joins the worship of God and the work of justice for the needy
- Reflection of the ministry of Jesus through healing and meeting needs
- Programs that focus on the whole community
- Meeting the spiritual and physical needs of the person
- Participation between aid agencies and the local community
- Ministries reflecting cooperation between the churches and aid agencies
- Wide ranging Christian activities to serve the community
- Christian social transformation
- Integrated development

Our ministry will be effective if in includes these principles and characteristics and avoids the barriers which inhibit holistic ministry.

BARRIERS TO HOLISTIC MINISTRY

An Inaccurate View of Evangelism

Holistic ministry is inhibited by the widely held view that evangelism is the verbal spreading of the gospel message that Jesus died as payment for our sins. While this is true, it is also incomplete. Under this view one has been reached when was had heard the word of the Lord. Limiting the definition of evangelism in this way ignores that Christ brought not just the word, but the living word, "And the Word became flesh, and dwelt among us, and we saw His glory, glory as of the only begotten from the Father, full of grace and truth." [42]

The gospel was not only what Jesus said, it was how he lived and how he died. As John said, the Word became flesh. Jesus became one of us; he lived with us. He lived "full of grace and truth." Evangelism is importing that grace, truth and forgiveness into our lives. It necessarily involves incorporation into and transformation of a life.

Separating Material Needs from Spiritual Need

It is our tendency, especially in the west, to separate temporal and spiritual goals. For this reason it is difficult to think of meeting material needs as part of ministry. We think of the poor in economic terms. Individual decisions in a capitalist economy are directly influenced by self interest. This concept was made famous be world renowned economist Adam Smith in his maxim: "If each individual consumer, producer and supplier of resources pursues self-interest, he or she will, as if by an 'invisible hand,' be promoting the overall interests of society." Self interest is pursued by responding to a system of economic incentives. Positive economic incentives encourage economic decision makers and negative economic incentives discourage economic decision makers.[43] The poor have little impact on these incentives. This focus on self-interest is in direct opposition to the word of God. As Christians we do not look at self interest but at compliance with God's instructions:

> For I am not ashamed of the gospel, for it is the power of God for salvation to everyone who believes, to the Jew first and also to the Greek. For in it the righteousness of God is revealed from faith to faith; as it is written, "BUT THE RIGHTEOUS MAN SHALL LIVE BY FAITH."[44]

There is power in the word and that power extends, in part, from the "righteousness" of the word. We cannot separate the word from

---

[42] John 1:14, NASB

[43] From *Characteristics of Capitalism* as quoted from www.haywardecon.com

[44] Romans 1:16-17

the very righteousness it demands. By separating the word from the righteousness it demands, we fall prey to the economic self interest demanded by the standard of the world, "And do not be conformed to this world, but be transformed by the renewing of your mind, so that you may prove what the will of God is, that which is good and acceptable and perfect."[45] We can be successful by the standards of the world, but there is a better way, one that is "good and acceptable and perfect." That is the standard demanded of us.

Self-Denial and Protection

If one views reaching the lost solely as an exercise in communication, it is easy to avoid the harsher obligations of outreach. Those with this view are free to cloister themselves in the buildings of church and limit their contacts to fellow Christians. They may continue to study the Word for their own betterment content in the knowledge that people who seek God can simply choose to attend a church as they did. They are like a sports team that always trains but never takes the field. The problem is that this representation of grace robs it of its vigor. A true understanding of the word commands that the church live out the gospel in every aspect of its organization and work. The same duty applies to church members. We must strive to share God's grace and support His standard of righteousness to truly follow His word. God's grace, His command to see justice in the world he created, and his transformational power are welded together.

Organizational Inertia

Modern churches are organizations and carry with them the needs of any organization to compartmentalize to effectively manage and execute ministry in accordance with the resources at hand. Because of this and because of philosophical beliefs about ministry they tend to break God's plan into small pieces which can be more easily understood and managed. The result may be organizational inertia. When this occurs the church begins to think in terms of program rather than people.

---

[45] Romans 12:2

In 1994 a group of lay leaders from California, visited the New Life Church in Kiev, Ukraine. The short term mission trip included visits to orphanages and hospitals as well as a training conference for pastors. On one particular evening, leaders of women's ministries from our church met with their female counterparts in the high rise apartment of Nina, a board member of the church there. We worked with a translator, sat at a table, and each woman introduced herself in the circle. Part of the introduction included our ministry responsibilities at our respective churches. What we soon realized is that what we called "ministry" differed greatly from what they called "ministry". As the California women discussed their ministries, they spoke of Bible studies, small groups, Sunday school and Vacation Bible School for their own children. When the women of Kiev spoke about their ministries, they talked about visiting the elderly, serving them meals, after school programs for students in the neighborhoods, music and cultural lessons and additional care for orphans. What we quickly understood was that much of what our church called ministry much was internal support of our own people while the Ukrainian church their defined ministry as service in their city and neighborhoods, more of what we would call social work.

Let's take a closer look at institutional inertia. Many churches have commendably reached so many that they have grown to be very large institutions. This has tremendous potential for the Kingdom. It also carries with it certain pitfalls. In a large church, institutional factors can begin to govern decisions and influence the church. Specialists are hired to perform specific roles within the body of Christ. Separation into specific departments and ministries results in an environment in which calendar dates, budget, publicity, facility space, and perceived momentum determine success. This drives the church to competition rather than cooperation. This can occur despite the best intentions of the church if success is measured by numbers of participants, energy, excitement, momentum, and money rather than spiritual health. Even pastors are human, and in this environment they may seek greater power for their individual part of the church. This is a predictable trap and a ministry should create designs to prevent this effect.

Many of today's churches have a business/consumer relationship with their members. Those who attend focus primarily on their personal experience and well-being. Often the teaching is centered only on self-improvement and personal contentment. Worship, teaching, and participation in ministry are all centered on the effect and emotional satisfaction experienced by the participant. Treating evangelism and social aid as separate aspects of Christian duty allows Christians to avoid an aspect of ministry that stretches them. A holistic ministry resists this temptation and seeks to implement the entire gospel, forgiveness, conversion, physical well-being, equality in relationship, and resource equality into a single mission. It encompasses the word of Ephesians that Christ's redemptive work includes "far more than we can ask or imagine." [46]

A HOLISTIC APPROACH FITS WITH THE CULTURE OF THE THIRD WORLD

Asian, African, and South American cultures are community based. The emphasis is not on individualism, but on communal sharing of decisions and responsibilities. As a result they are by nature more integrated than Western culture. The models of evangelism and mission brought to them by the colonial powers that dominated them not only bear the stain of that oppression, they are unsuited to the cultures they serve. A holistic approach is better suited to these cultures which tend not to separate the sacred and secular. Because these cultures are more accepting of a holistic approach by their nature, not only will the impact of that approach be substantial, but they may also be a rich learning ground for the West, whose culture is less accepting of integrated approaches. In addition to fitting the culture there is another benefit. The approach provides protection to the persecuted church. In Sri Lanka attacks on the Christian church are common:

> Since late 2003, the country has witnessed a spate of attacks on Christian churches and sometimes pastors and congregants. Approximately 250 attacks have been alleged since 2003, with several dozen confirmed by the U.S. Embassy. In response, major political and religious leaders have publicly condemned the attacks, and police have arrested and prosecuted close to a dozen persons in

---

[46] Ephesians 3:20

connection with the incidents. Despite generally amicable relations among persons of different faiths, there has been an ongoing violent resistance by some Buddhists to Christian church activity, in particular that conducted by evangelical groups.[47]

The public benefit provided by the holistic approach often provides protection. For example, if a church as part of its ministry provides medical care, free pure water and care for local widows and orphans, the community is less likely to support or tolerate an attack on the church or its members. Any such attacks risk retaliation from the local community. This factor was confronted by the Pharisees in the time of Jesus:

> When He entered the temple, the chief priests and the elders of the people came to Him while He was teaching, and said, "By what authority are You doing these things, and who gave You this authority?" Jesus said to them, "I will also ask you one thing, which if you tell Me, I will also tell you by what authority I do these things.[48] "The baptism of John was from what source, from heaven or from men?" And they began reasoning among themselves, saying, "If we say, 'From heaven,' He will say to us, 'Then why did you not believe him?' "But if we say, 'From men,' we fear the people; for they all regard John as a prophet." And answering Jesus, they said, "We do not know." He also said to them, "Neither will I tell you by what authority I do these things.

Jesus responded to the priest's question with one of His own, a common rhetorical device in that time. By referring to John the Baptist, He implies to the crowd at large, that His authority, like John's, came from heaven. He is keenly aware that the priests were political figures who would not risk angering the crowd by denying John's authority. Here Jesus used John the Baptist's popularity as a shield for His own ministry. A holistic approach provides similar protection.

Better still, a holistic ministry can do more than offer protection from persecution, it can change the hearts of the persecutors. After the 2004 tsunami a monk stood in what was left of his temple when a group

---

[47] U.S. Department of State, *International Religious Freedom Report 2006,* Released by the Bureau of Democracy, Human Rights, and Labor
[48] Matthew 21:23-27, NASB

of young men came by and offered to help him rebuild. He gratefully accepted. They worked side by side for days until the building was whole again. On the last day he asked the young men where they came from. "We are from the Four Square Christian Church outside of Galle," they replied. The monk looked down mumbled a "thank you," turned and walked away. Several days later the young men were back at their church when they noticed the monk slowly walking toward them. Timidly he said, "Six months ago your church was burned down. That was done at my bidding. I am sorry, it will not happen again."

Another monk lost his computer, critical to his work, in the tsunami. The people from our church in Sri Lanka raised money to replace it. When I brought it to the monk, he opened a closet. Inside were 5,000 printed posters warning the people of Sri Lanka to beware of Christians who would use the tsunami to take advantage of them. "You may take these," the monk said, "I don't need them anymore."

HOLISTIC MINISTRY AND POLITICS

The responsibilities that flow from our obligation to serve mankind are many, and the task is immense. Despite this many Christians shy away from political involvement, considering it divorced from the spiritual world of Godly service. That view is not supported by Scripture. When we limit our action to the private sphere, we eliminate the ability of the public sphere to aid in our efforts. As noted above, until the return to fullness promised by the Lord, we are called to service and restoration. It was Jesus who called us to this service, and Jesus did not call for any separation from the political realm when it did not conflict with the laws of God:

> Every person is to be in subjection to the governing authorities. For there is no authority except from God, and those which exist are established by God. Therefore whoever resists authority has opposed the ordinance of God; and they who have opposed will receive condemnation upon themselves. For rulers are not a cause of fear for good behavior, but for evil. Do you want to have no fear of authority? Do what is good and you will have praise from the same; for it is a minister of God to you for good. But if you do what is evil, be afraid;

for it does not bear the sword for nothing; for it is a minister of God, an avenger who brings wrath on the one who practices evil. Therefore it is necessary to be in subjection, not only because of wrath, but also for conscience' sake. For because of this you also pay taxes, for rulers are servants of God, devoting themselves to this very thing. Render to all what is due them: tax to whom tax is due; custom to whom custom; fear to whom fear; honor to whom honor.[49]

We are called to submit ourselves to the authority of government:

Submit yourselves for the Lord's sake to every human institution, whether to a king as the one in authority, or to governors as sent by him for the punishment of evildoers and the praise of those who do right. For such is the will of God that by doing right you may silence the ignorance of foolish men. Act as free men, and do not use your freedom as a covering for evil, but use it as bondslaves of God. Honor all people, love the brotherhood, fear God, honor the king. [50]

Having been told to submit, it is hard to imagine that God did not want us to use these institutions to seek the justice He requires of His followers. We are called to serve our neighbors in every manner possible. There is no reason the political realm should be exempt. How we engage in the political realm is defined by scripture.[51] We know from scripture that the ills of the world have many parents. Social problems arise from sinful conduct for example.[52] Equally destructive are unjust systems implemented by authority. God abhors these systems:

They hate him who reproves in the gate, And they abhor him who speaks with integrity. Therefore because you impose heavy rent on the poor And exact a tribute of grain from them, Though you have built houses of well-hewn stone, Yet you will not live in them; You have planted pleasant vineyards, yet you will not drink their wine. For I know your transgressions are many and your sins are great, You who distress the righteous and accept bribes And turn aside the poor in the gate. Therefore at such a time the prudent person keeps silent, for it is an evil time. Seek good and not evil, that you may live; And

---

[49] Romans 13:1-7
[50] 1 Peter 2:13-17
[51] Timothy 3:16-17, See also Romans 15:4
[52] Proverbs 6:9-11

thus may the LORD God of hosts be with you, Just as you have said! Hate evil, love good, And establish justice in the gate! Perhaps the LORD God of hosts May be gracious to the remnant of Joseph.[53]

Unjust systems created by government are especially troubling, because they have wide effect, "Woe to those who enact evil statutes And to those who constantly record unjust decisions, So as to deprive the needy of justice And rob the poor of My people of their rights, So that widows may be their spoil And that they may plunder the orphans."[54]

By responsible engagement in politics, Christians can not only prevent unfair legislation but also support those policies supported by God's word, such as strengthening marriage or increasing universal opportunity. To be fully holistic we must work to transform both individuals and institutions. It is clear from Scripture that God cares deeply about a number of issues effected by government institutions: justice for the poor, equality of races, peace, care for the environment, which is God's creation, and protection of life.

We are commanded to resist government when it conflicts with God's law:

When they had brought them, they stood them before the Council. The high priest questioned them, saying, "We gave you strict orders not to continue teaching in this name, and yet, you have filled Jerusalem with your teaching and intend to bring this man's blood upon us." But Peter and the apostles answered, "We must obey God rather than men. "The God of our fathers raised up Jesus, whom you had put to death by hanging Him on a cross. "He is the one whom God exalted to His right hand as a Prince and a Savior, to grant repentance to Israel, and forgiveness of sins. "And we are witnesses of these things; and so is the Holy Spirit, whom God has given to those who obey Him." [55]

We are also commanded to obey government when not in conflict with God's law, "Remind them to be subject to rulers, to authorities, to be obedient, to be ready for every good deed."[56] It seems clear that

---

[53] Amos 5:10-15
[54] Isaiah 10:1-2
[55] Acts 5:27-32
[56] Titus 3:1, See also Matthew 22:15-22

the best way to serve God in harmony and effectively accomplish the tasks he has set for us is to work to assure government is not in conflict with the laws of God. Government also has been ordained by God. It co-exists with the institution of the church, each with its own responsibility.[57] To the extent these ordained entities exist in harmony, God's plan more easily succeeds.

Good government to the Christian is one that includes the hallmarks of holistic ministry: freedom, restoration, transformation, integration and partnership. In addition, good government is one that respects freedom of religion and the rights of the church to govern its own affairs:

> But while Gallio was proconsul of Achaia, the Jews with one accord rose up against Paul and brought him before the judgment seat, saying, "This man persuades men to worship God contrary to the law." But when Paul was about to open his mouth, Gallio said to the Jews, "If it were a matter of wrong or of vicious crime, O Jews, it would be reasonable for me to put up with you; but if there are questions about words and names and your own law, look after it yourselves; I am unwilling to be a judge of these matters." And he drove them away from the judgment seat. And they all took hold of Sosthenes, the leader of the synagogue, and began beating him in front of the judgment seat. But Gallio was not concerned about any of these things. [58]

Good government must work to protect the dignity of mankind as the object of the Lord's creation and give protection to the areas of society featured in the Bible. As we have been adopted into God's family,[59] we must work to protect God's value of family. We must work to preserve marriage as an institution of God,[60] as a symbol of God's relationship with His children.[61] Although government is not primarily responsible for the preservation of marriage and family, its dealings certainly have a profound impact. Easy divorce, drug and alcohol use, abortion,[62] child abuse, and gambling all impact the life God wants

[57] Romans 13:1-7
[58] Acts 18:12-17
[59] Romans 8:23
[60] Ephesians 5:22-33
[61] Jeremiah 3:20, Jeremiah 31:32
[62] See Psalms 139:13

for his children on earth. Labor practices, health care, education, and food distribution also have great impact. Governments have profound impact on wealth distribution, a primary concern of the Bible:

> Come now, you rich, weep and howl for your miseries which are coming upon you. Your riches have rotted and your garments have become moth-eaten. Your gold and your silver have rusted; and their rust will be a witness against you and will consume your flesh like fire. It is in the last days that you have stored up your treasure! Behold, the pay of the laborers who mowed your fields, and which has been withheld by you, cries out against you; and the outcry of those who did the harvesting has reached the ears of the Lord of Sabaoth. You have lived luxuriously on the earth and led a life of wanton pleasure; you have fattened your hearts in a day of slaughter. You have condemned and put to death the righteous man; he does not resist you.[63]

We are called upon to protect the vulnerable: the poor, women, children, the aged, immigrants, minorities, the persecuted, and prisoners. God measures societies by how they protect these people. He calls us to righteous and just societies.[64] Government, along with personal support, is an avenue to accomplish God's calling. Indeed, some issues such as the trafficking of women and children to sexual slavery almost require government action to be effective. Individual Christians or churches cannot control the borders nor punish the violator to effect deterrence. A Christian based foreign policy can go a long way toward meeting global issues such as HIV/AIDS and environmental issues. To accomplish God's goals, we must embrace and support[65] God's institution of government so long as it does not conflict with the laws of God.

---

[63] James 5:1-6
[64] See Isaiah 10:1-4; Isaiah 58:3-12; Jeremiah 5:26-29; Jeremiah 22:13-19; Amos 2:6-7; Amos 4:1-3; Amos 5:10-15
[65] 1 Timothy 2:1-2: "First of all, then, I urge that entreaties and prayers, petitions and thanksgivings, be made on behalf of all men, for kings and all who are in authority, so that we may lead a tranquil and quiet life in all godliness and dignity."

CONCLUSION

We do not own this world but have been given stewardship over it [66] and an obligation to restore it.[67] We are called to love and support one another regardless of standing or race, "For there is no distinction between Jew and Greek; for the same Lord is Lord of all, abounding in riches for all who call on Him; for "WHOEVER WILL CALL ON THE NAME OF THE LORD WILL BE SAVED." [68]

Jesus' life modeled and God's word supports a holistic approach; caring for both the spiritual and physical needs of our neighbors. As Jesus did, we must work to see all people own the dignity entitled to them as creations of God. Toward this end we should enlist the support of God's institution of government.

---

[66] Genesis 2:15
[67] Romans 8:18-23
[68] Romans 10:12

Chapter 2

Incarnational Ministry

The Incarnational Model of Jesus

IT is interesting to note that God never recommended a particular strategy, method of evangelism or program to reach the lost, but instead sent his Son to live among the people, to love them and show them the way, "The Word became flesh and made his dwelling among us. We have seen his glory, the glory of the One and only, who came from the Father, full of grace and truth."[69] Or as the Message translates this verse: "The word became flesh and blood, and moved into the neighborhood. We saw the glory with our own eyes, the one - of - a kind glory, like the Father, like son Generous inside and out, true from start to finish."[70] Two truths arise from Jesus' model of ministry; He identified with the people and lived among them, and he lived a life of grace coupled with speaking the truth in love.

This is the essence of the Biblical model of evangelism which we call "Incarnational."

Incarnation is a theological term describing God's Son entering the world as a human being. The term itself is not used in the Bible, but it is based on clear references in the New Testament to Jesus coming "in the flesh." [71] The word "flesh," as used in John 1:14 denotes "human nature" or "man."[72] The "Word" was made "man." This is commonly

---

[69] John 1:14, NIV
[70] Peterson, Eugene; The Message: The Bible in Contemporary Language
[71] John1:14, Romans 8:3; Ephesians 2:15; Colossians 1:22.
[72] Matthew 16:17; 19:5; 24:22; Luke 3:6; Romans 1:3; 9:5.

expressed by saying that he became "incarnate." When we say that a Jesus became "incarnate," we mean that one of a higher order than man, and of a different nature, became a man. What is meant here is that "the Word," or the second person of the Trinity, whom John had just proved to be equal with God, became a man, or was united with the man Jesus of Nazareth, so that it might be said that he "was made flesh."

The word in the original language denotes "dwelt; as in a tabernacle or tent." Some have supposed that John is saying that the human body was a tabernacle or tent for the Logos to abide in, an allusion to the tabernacle among the Jews, in which the *Shechinah*, or visible symbol of God, dwelt. This however, is not suggested by the context. The object of John was to prove that "the Word" became "incarnate." To do this he appeals to various evidences. One was that he "dwelt" among them; sojourned with them; ate, drank, slept, and was with them for years, so that they "saw him with their eyes, they looked upon him, and their hands handled him."[73] To "dwell in a tent with one" is the same as to be in his family; and when John says he "tabernacled" with them, he means that Jesus was with us as a friend or as one of a family, so that they had full opportunity of becoming acquainted with him, and could not be mistaken in supposing that "he was really a man."

Contrast this with the Old Testament relationship between God and man. Exodus clearly states no man may see God and live.[74] God dwells in unapproachable light.[75] God has now bridged this gap. He has come near in the person of Jesus.[76] He has taken on a form in which He can be seen, experienced and understood by us as human beings.[77] Jesus reveals God to us perfectly since in His human life He is the image of God,[78] exhibiting full likeness with the Father.[79] Jesus' Godhood in His manhood is the key to our intimate knowledge of God. Jesus became human, lived among us, cared for people and ministered to them with deep love. The four gospels provide us with ample evidence of his love. Having lived among people he commissions us to do the same, "Again

---

[73] 1 John 1:1
[74] Exodus 33:20
[75] 1 Timothy 6:16
[76] Matthew 1:23
[77] John 1:14, 18
[78] 2 Corinthians 4:4
[79] John 1:14

Jesus said, "Peace be with you! As the Father has sent me, I am sending you." [80]

In other words, as God sent me to preach, to be persecuted, and to suffer; to make known his will, and to offer pardon to men, so I send you. This is the design and the extent of the commission of the ministers of the Lord Jesus. He is their model; and they will be successful only as they study His character and imitate his example. This confirms this commission endowing them with the Holy Spirit:

> God invaded our planet and forever changed it. God became incarnate. He took on human flesh in a way that is shocking, concrete, raw, and physically tangible. God knew there was no better way to show human beings than by fully entering their world physically and emotionally. [81]

God took on skin and flesh for us. Ronald Rolheiser powerfully illustrates this point with a story:

> ... a four year old girl ... awoke on night frightened convinced that in the darkness around her there were all kinds of spooks and monsters. Alone, she ran to her parents' bedroom. Her mother calmed her down and, taking her by the hand, led her back to her own room, where she put on a light and reassured the child with these words: "You needn't be afraid, you are not alone here. God is in the room with you." The child replied, "I know that God is here, but I need some in this room who has some skin! [82]

Today God still has physical skin and can be seen, touched, heard, and tasted. How? Through his body, the church, in whom he dwells. We are called in the name of Jesus and by the indwelling Holy Spirit to be skin for people all around us. [83] St Basil, the Bishop of Caesarea in the fourth century, once wrote, "Annunciations are frequent, and incarnations are rare." [84] In other words, bold announcements of what

---

[80] John 20:21

[81] Barnes' Notes, Electronic Database Copyright © 1997, 2003 by Bible soft, Inc. All rights reserved

[82] The Emotionally Healthy Church by Peter Scazzero with Warren Bird, pg 175

[83] The Emotionally Healthy Church by Peter Scazzero with Warren Bird

[84] Ibid., pg 174

God is doing or saying are common. People who follow the humble way of Jesus are much more difficult to find.

THE DYNAMICS OF INCARNATIONAL LIVING

Incarnational living calls us out of our physical comfort zones to meet people where they are. Jesus left the glory of heaven and humbled himself to become man. Matthew Henry has a brief but excellent statement of the fact, "He emptied Himself, divested Himself of the honors and glories of the upper world and of His former appearance, to clothe Himself with the rags of human nature." [85]

Making incarnational ministry a priority disrupts the traditional church definition of success. It is no longer about doing more, fixing people, or arranging the world into something we consider God-Glorifying. It is about loving well. We must enter another world, love those in it completely, sacrifice for them while not losing ourselves in their world. Jesus modeled this for us:

> Therefore, since we have a great high priest who has gone through the heavens, Jesus the Son of God, let us hold firmly to the faith we profess. For we do not have a high priest who is unable to sympathize with our weaknesses, but we have one who has been tempted in every way, just as we are—yet was without sin. Let us then approach the throne of grace with confidence, so that we may receive mercy and find grace to help us in our time of need. [86]

When we choose incarnational ministry, we hang between our own world and the world of another person. We are called to remain faithful to who we are, not losing our essence, while at the same time entering into the world of another. We can be assured, however, that as Jesus' incarnation and death brought great life, so also will our efforts result in resurrection, life and fruit. This is the result of modeling Jesus' love. Throughout the New Testament the believers' love for their fellowmen is emphasized. This thought is particularly stressed in First John.

---

[85] Matthew Henry's Commentary, Vol.6, p.732f
[86] Hebrews 4:14-16

We understand the essence of love not through our love for God but through his love for us.[87] The love shown on the cross compels us to love one another.[88] In fact, John cannot recognize a love for God that is not shown in love for our fellow man.[89] It is God's commandment that the man who loves God also loves his brother.[90] Love to God, love to men and keeping of God's commandments are welded together.[91] Leon Morris explains it this way:

> Insistence on love for our fellowmen is a statutory reminder of what love means. Of course, we are all prepared to love God in a nebulous "Spiritual" way, other than ourselves. It is only as demanding as we are prepared to let it be, and it cannot be tested in practice. But our loves for our neighbor is quite another thing. [92]

Agape love produced in the heart of the believer through the work of the Holy Spirit, when combined with identification and Godly life, will help to break down the barriers that separate Christians from non Christians.

Amy Carmichael was a well-known missionary in India. She became a missionary at the Keswick Convention of 1887 when she heard Hudson Taylor describe his work. Three hundred girls lived in her rescue home and school. The girls had lived a hard life. Most were temple children; young girls dedicated to the gods and forced into prostitution to earn money for the priests. One girl wouldn't respond to the spirit of the rescuing institution. She was hard and rebellious. Miss Carmichael did everything she could to change her attitude. Finally, she took the girl into her room and bared her arm before the girl. " I am going to pierce my arm with a needle," she said. " It will hurt," said the girl. "Not nearly as much as you are hurting me," answered the missionary. "To let you know the pain in my heart, I am going to thrust this needle into my arm." She drove the needle into her arm until it bled. The rebellious girl began to weep, and through her tears

---

[87] 1 John 4:10

[88] 1 John 4:11

[89] 1 John 4:20

[90] 1 John 4:21

[91] 1 John 5:12

[92] Leon Morris, <u>Testaments of Love</u> (Grand Rapids: William B. Eerdmans Publishing Co., 1981), pp. 172-173.

she cried, '' I didn't know you love me like that.'' She was changed, changed through that blood.

A similar manifestation of *agape* love is found in the 1995 movie, *Dead Man Walking*. In this story Sister Helen Prejean is a nun living and working in the St. Thomas housing projects in New Orleans when she received an invitation to be a pen-pal with someone on death row. The condemned man, Matthew Poncelet, along with his friend, came across two beautiful teenagers, Loretta and David, in a lover's lane sugar field after a Friday night homecoming game. Loretta was raped. Both David and Loretta were left in the field, shot in the back of the head.

Sister Helen initially wondered if his claims to innocence might be true. Matthew argued that his partner actually committed the rape and murders. He does not ask her to be his spiritual director, but instead wants her to work on his behalf to prevent his execution. Sister Helen enters the ugly world of the condemned man. Matthew is not a lovable character. He is a racist, uses the "n" word, and talks of how well "Hitler got the job done." He refers to women as "bitches" and talks about how he wanted to blow up government buildings. Matthew informs Sister Helen that she missed out not being married and having sex. He does not evoke sympathy. Nonetheless, Sister Helen holds on to herself and her convictions. She repeatedly invites him to make himself right with God by confessing his sin. She encourages him to take responsibility for his actions but progress is slow, very slow.

Sister Helen also initiates a relationship with the grieving families of the victems. She enters their world of unfathomable loss and pain. The parents of the dead children are outraged, and pressures mount against Sister Helen to end her involvement with Matthew. They draw a line in the sand. "You can't befriend that murderer and expect to be our friend too," says the father of one as he asks Sister Helen to leave his house. "If you really care about this family, you'll want to see justice done."

Newspapers pick up Matthew's racist, pro-Nazi views and refer to Sister Helen in the same articles. Her colleagues at work complain she is neglecting her work, "You care more about him that your classes," they say. Sister Helen hangs between heaven and earth, in the raw, brute work of the incarnation. She is hanging between her world, the condemned killer's world, the parents of the murdered teens' world, and the world of her colleagues at work. When the male victim's father asks Sister Helen how she has the faith to act this way, she replies, "It's not faith , it's work." She does not give up. Over time Matthew begins to let down his defenses and reveal vulnerability. Finally at 11:38 p.m., only minutes before his execution at midnight, she asks him, "Do you take responsibility for both of their deaths?" Crying, he admits his guilt for the first time. A few minutes later, he says, "Thank you for loving me. I never had anybody really love me before."

Sister Helen recalls their walk together toward his execution. "That walk was the first time I had ever touched him. I looked down and saw his chains dragging across the gleaming tile floor. His head was shaved, and he was dressed in a clean, white T-shirt. When they took him into the execution chamber, I leaned over and kissed his back. "Matthew, pray for me." "Sister Helen, I will." When he is strapped to the chair to be injected with lethal solutions, she tells him to watch her face. "That way the last thing you will see before you die will be the face of someone who loves you." He heeds her advice and dies in love rather than in bitterness.[93] This kind of incarnation and sacrificial love is possible only when we have a deep walk with God.

THE BENEFITS OF INCARNATIONAL MINISTRY

Incarnational ministry breaks down the barriers between Christians and non Christians, allowing us to build bridges. In many third world nations, hostility towards Christianity is based on the views and interpretations of the Colonial rulers' behavior. The indigenous people are convinced that Christians are cruel people who promote foreign customs and are committed to destroying their religion and culture. These baseless accusations reflect real fears. Verbal denials in the face of historical precedent have little effect. Rather, a genuine identification with a person's life is necessary to breakdown the barriers and develop a mutual trust.

---

[93] The Emotionally Healthy Church,by Peter Scazzero with Warren Bird pp 189, 190, 191

Our Lord himself is the supreme example in this regard.[94] Though humans rebelled and were hostile to Him, He identified with our humanity. He identified with our poverty; He was born in a stable and had no place to lay his head. He identified with our toil; He worked at a carpenter's bench. He identified with our physical needs; He was often hungry and thirsty. He identified with our temptations; He was in all points tempted like as we are.[95] John the Baptist baptized him along with sinners. He paid for sin on our behalf and died on the cross between two thieves.

Paul also identified with the people whom he served. He described in detail the extent of his identification when writing to the Church of Corinth. We return once again to this important passage:

> Though I am free and belong to no man, I make myself a slave to everyone, to win as many as possible. To the Jews I became like a Jew, to win the Jews. To those under the law I became like one under the law (though I myself am not under the law), so as to win those under the law. To those not having the law I became like one not having the law. To the weak I became weak, to win the weak. I have become all things to all men so that by all possible means I might save some.[96]

Let us examine this more closely. In verse nineteen Paul shows that he has surrendered more than his right to personal subsistence. Though he was free from all men, not bound by the standards of fashions of others, he was prepared to make himself a slave to all and to conform to their standards. He relinquished his rights to win as many as possible to Christ. In accordance with this principle; Paul states in verse twenty that when he was with Jews, he acted as a Jew conforming to their customs under the Mosaic Law. In verse twenty-one, Paul shows that he was also ready to identify with those who were not bound by the Jewish law, that is the Gentiles. In verse twenty-two, Paul sums up his willingness to become all things to all men. This does not mean that he would act in an unprincipled manner or compromise any Christian principles. Instead Paul means he would sacrifice his own legitimate interests and preferences to save others.

---

[94] Philippians 2:6-8
[95] Hebrews 4:15
[96] 1 Corinthians 9:19-22, NIV

In verse twenty-three, Paul explains his reasons. He does this to share the gospel and to win the people of Corinth. Paul was willing to identify with others even at personal cost to himself. Charles Kraft comments:

> Identification is a difficult concept. And many people have the wrong impression of it. They think identifying with others is becoming fake. And some times it can be. But true identification is not being fake. It is not trying to be some one else it is rather taking the trouble to become more than what one ever was before by genuinely entering the life of the other people.

By entering the lives of other people we must become just as real in that context as we are in our normal lives. But to save the lost it is a small price to pay. Seamands in his book, Tell it Well, comments:

> In striving to identify ourselves with people, our aim is to achieve a feeling of togetherness or oneness. This is not simply a meeting of ideas but a meeting of persons. It is more than contact, it is communion. Identification does not come all at once. It must be developed and cultivated through actual participation in shared experience. By mingling with people, visiting their homes, making their friendships and being one with them in heart and mind. [97]

Such identification will provide our neighbors with an opportunity to watch our lives and evaluate them against the historical prejudices. They can then arrive at their own conclusions.

EFFECT ON STRATEGY

Our strategies must reflect these principles. We must reflect love and hospitality. Even though the bible has an emphasis on hospitality, the church has abandoned this strategy. I would strongly recommend hospitality as a key strategy for evangelism. Biblically, hospitality is so important that it is one of the prerequisites for elder qualification.

Here is a trustworthy saying: If anyone sets his heart on being an

---

[97] John T. Seamands, Tell it Well, (Kansas City: Beacon Hill Press, 1981). p. 94.

overseer, he desires a noble task. Now the overseer must be above reproach, the husband of but one wife, temperate, self-controlled, respectable, **hospitable**, able to teach, not given to drunkenness, not violent but gentle, not quarrelsome, not a lover of money. He must manage his own family well and see that his children obey him with proper respect. (If anyone does not know how to manage his own family, how can he take care of God's church?) He must not be a recent convert, or he may become conceited and fall under the same judgment as the devil. He must also have a good reputation with outsiders, so that he will not fall into disgrace and into the devil's trap.[98]

Hospitality played a very important role during the time of Christ and in the New Testament church, "...Offer hospitality to one another without grumbling."[99] Why would we find it to be less important now?

I am amazed how we have lived among people and continue to be blind to their needs. We have failed to develop relationships with our community. Despite this church leadership develops programs that keep the believers tied to the Church. We have failed to release people to go into the world to be the "salt" and "light" but expect the church to grow and to impact the community we live in. This is nothing but wishful thinking:

You are the salt of the earth. But if the salt loses its saltiness, how can it be made salty again? It is no longer good for anything, except to be thrown out and trampled by men. "You are the light of the world. A city on a hill cannot be hidden. Neither do people light a lamp and put it under a bowl. Instead they put it on its stand, and it gives light to everyone in the house. In the same way, let your light shine before men, that they may see your good deeds and praise your Father in heaven. [100]

Christians are called to be the salt of the earth and light of the world. Evangelism is not a special program of the Church, but rather a life we live. If we are to have the powerful influence God desires, we need to stop hiding our light and start sharing our lives with those who don't

---

[98] 1 Timothy 3:1-7, NIV
[99] 1 Peter 4:9, NIV
[100] Matthew 5:13-16, NIV

know Jesus. Personal contact is the only way non-Christians can come to understand our faith and believe it themselves.

Evangelism based on scripture is a life that touches the fives senses of a human being.

- To people's hearing, I am prepared to give a loving and well thought *audible* explanation of the hope that I have in Christ. [101]

- To people's *taste*, I am a salty Christian, a flavor enhancer who improves the quality of life of those around me.[102]
- To people's *sight*, I am the light of the world, a person who dispels the darkness. People see my good works and are directed to Jesus.[103]
- To people's sense of *touch*, I am the touch of Christ to needy people around me.[104]
- To people's sense of *smell*, a fragrance of the love and the life of Jesus Christ in my life lingers, inviting people to think about eternal realities.[105]

In short, we must stop witnessing and start loving. We start loving by becoming part of the life of others. In that role we need to model Godly living, "Live such good lives among the pagans that, though they accuse you of doing wrong, they may see your good deeds and glorify God on the day he visits us."[106] Here Peter was writing to the churches that were scattered throughout Pontius, Galatia, Capadocia, Asia, and Bithynia. These churches were persecuted by the cruel Emperor Nero. In verse eleven, Peter requests the believers to live "as aliens and strangers" on earth whose citizenship was in heaven. They were to be separated from the corruption of the world, not yielding to its sinful desires.

In verse twelve, we are told to live such exemplary lives that even those who wish to accuse us will see our deeds and see God glorified

---

[101] Romans 10:17
[102] Matthew 5:14
[103] Matthew 5:14-16
[104] Matthew 25:31-46
[105] 2 Corinthians 2:14-16
[106] 1 Peter 2:12, NIV

through those deeds. The Greek word translated as "see" refers to careful watching over a period of time. The pagan evaluation is not a snap judgment. We must always live so that others see Christ's love in our lives. In Titus 2:8, Paul urges Titus to show integrity, seriousness and soundness of speech, so that "those who oppose you may be ashamed because they have nothing bad to say about you."[107] Because of this advice people who evaluated Titus's life and teaching found no fault.

It is fascinating that Peter is writing to a church under severe persecution by Nero. Even though the church has suffered, his emphasis is not on the suffering, but on Godly living in the context of persecution, a powerful tool to counteract prejudice and hatred against Christians. As Brennan Manning notes, "The greatest single cause of atheism today is Christians who acknowledge Jesus with their lips then walk out the door and deny Him by their lifestyle. That is what an unbelieving world simply finds unbelievable."[108]

CARING

The Lausanne Committee for World Evangelization responding to the theological neglect of caring for those in need commented:

> We express penitence both for our neglect and for having sometimes regarded evangelism and social action as mutually exclusive. Although reconciliation with man is not reconciliation with God, nor is social action evangelism, nor is political liberation salvation, nevertheless we affirm that evangelism and socio-political involvement are both part of our Christian duty. [109]

As noted elsewhere in this book, churches are entrusted with both the Great Commission[110] and the great commandment.[111] There should be no issue. If we love our neighbor, we want him to learn of the saving grace of the Lord. If we love our neighbor, we also want to meets his needs. If we love our neighbor, serving them becomes natural, "If

---

[107] NIV
[108] Manning, Brennan; from *Free at Last: the Movie*
[109] The Lausanne, supra
[110] Matthew 28:18
[111] Matthew 22:36-40

anyone has material possessions and sees his brother in need but has no pity on him, how can the love of God be in him?" [112] How can a man love God who does not love those who bear his image? The meaning is plain; we cannot have evidence of piety unless we are ready to do good to others. The world is plagued with poverty and suffering so how can we ignore the needs of people and preach the gospel? How could we say we love them but do not care for their physical needs? This is inconsistent with love, yet to a certain degree the protestant church has distanced itself from the poor other than occasional acts of charity in the form of handouts. This behavior originates from a theological confusion.

Let us examine this confusion. After the Reformation the protestant Church began to focus on the theological truth that we are saved by grace. This truth is not in doubt, "For it is by grace you have been saved, through faith-- and this not from yourselves, it is the gift of God--not by works, so that no one can boast."[113] The emphasis brought freedom to many and a theological correctness within the church, but soon the church also abandoned good works, and caring for the poor was no longer an important ministry. Certainly salvation is by Grace, but those saved by His grace will conform to His nature through good works for those in need. Let us look at the verse that follows those quoted above, "For we are God's workmanship, created in Christ Jesus to do good works, which God prepared in advance for us to do."[114]

Some will argue that since the gospel brings eternal life, and this life is a time of preparation for heaven, our focus must be preaching and praying. They argue that we can never change this world and any attempt to do so is foolishness. This may be true, but Jesus does not say "My kingdom is not of this world, so therefore just sit around and wait for the next world" rather, He says, in effect, "My Kingdom is not of this world, so therefore go and fulfill the great commission and the great commandment, to love God and love your neighbor as yourself, and in doing so point the way to that kingdom."[115]

Church history, and the biographies of modern day Saints, show that they were looking to the next life but serving in this one. I agree

---

[112] 1 John 3:17
[113] Ephesians 2:8-9
[114] Ephesians 2:10
[115] Rumors of another world, Philip Yancey p 227

with C. S. Lewis who said "If you read history you will find out that the Christians who did most for the present world were precisely those who thought most of the next."[116] Keeping the unseen world in mind changes us in subtle ways so that we serve the kingdom of heaven while living on earth. Our point of view shifts, and we begin to see this planet as God's beloved work of art. From God's perspective after all, these are not two worlds, but one, and God's presence fills both. St Ignatius of Loyola pulled the two worlds together, he wrote:

> God freely created us so that we might know, love, and serve him in this life and be happy with him forever. God's purpose in creating us is to draw forth from us a response of love and service here on earth, so that we may attain our goal of everlasting happiness with him in heaven.[117]

All the things in this world are gifts of God, created for us, to be the means by which we can come to know Him better, love him more surely, and serve him more faithfully. As a result, we ought to appreciate and use these gifts of God to help us obtain our goal of loving service and union with God. Insofar as created things hinder our progress toward our goal, we need to let them go.[118]

In 316 A.D. in what we now know as Yugoslavia, a son was born to an unbelieving soldier in the Roman army. As a teenager, after becoming a Christian convert, Martin was forced to become a soldier himself. While on military duty in Northern Gaul on a cold winter day he came across a cold shivering beggar. Quickly the young Martin slashed his cloak in two with his sword and gave one half to the beggar. The next night Martin had a vision in which he saw Jesus, clothed in the half of the cloak which he had given away. He became known as Saint Martin of Tours. In his later life he was appointed a bishop, but kept his humble attitude. When his biographer, Sulpicius Severus, first met Martin of Tours, he was shocked. Martin did not live the usual palatial residence of a bishop, but in a small, cold monk's cell. More shocking, Martin washed Sulpicius' hands before dinner and his feet in the evening. Martin understood the need to model servanthood.

---

[116] Lewis, C.S. Mere Christianity

[117] Fleming, *Spiritual Exercises*

[118] Rumors of another world. Philip Yancey p 227

What we do to the least of our brethren we do unto him. We do not care for people or serve them with the intention of converting them, but to show God's nature. They have not seen God, but they have seen us. They have not yet experienced God's love, but they have seen an image of it through our good works. We must be afraid to love our people or do acts of kindness, just because there are a few extremists who may claim we are bribing people to accept our beliefs. If we fear their allegations and abandon good works, we would be failing our Lord.

TRUTH BEFORE GRACE

The Son of God who entered this world was full of Grace and truth, "The Word became flesh and made his dwelling among us. We have seen his glory, the glory of the One and only, who came from the Father, full of grace and truth."[119] The word "grace" means "favors, gifts, acts of beneficence." Jesus was kind, merciful, gracious, doing good to all, and seeking man's welfare by great sacrifices and love; so much so, that he could be said to "abounded" in favors to mankind. Jesus having become a man, constantly developed relationships with others. He cared for them. His approach to people was first "grace" followed by "truth." This approach is supported throughout scripture. Examine John 8:3-11:

> The teachers of the law and the Pharisees brought in a woman caught in adultery. They made her stand before the group and said to Jesus, "Teacher, this woman was caught in the act of adultery. In the Law Moses commanded us to stone such women. Now what do you say?" They were using this question as a trap, in order to have a basis for accusing him. But Jesus bent down and started to write on the ground with his finger. When they kept on questioning him, he straightened up and said to them, "If any one of you is without sin, let him be the first to throw a stone at her."

> Again he stooped down and wrote on the ground. At this, those who heard began to go away one at a time, the older ones first, until only Jesus was left, with the woman still standing there. Jesus straightened up and asked her, "Woman, where are they? Has no one condemned

---

[119] John 1:14

you?" "No one, sir," she said. "Then neither do I condemn you," Jesus declared. "Go now and leave your life of sin."[120]

Pay special attention to verse eleven, ""No one, sir," she said. "Then neither do I condemn you," Jesus declared, "Go now and leave your life of sin." Jesus said, "Neither do I condemn you," which is grace and then, "Go now and leave your life of sin," which is truth. Grace opens the door for truth. Jesus did not make a habit of condemning people. Instead he was very gracious, and by his graciousness he earned the right to address issues in the lives of people and lead them to trust in God.

In His encounter with Zaccheus, [121] Jesus invited himself for a meal; with the woman at the well[122], he requested water and engaged her in a discussion. He did not condemn the woman who was to be stoned. Instead, with great tenderness, he appealed her to give up the life of sin. He cared for the poor and the sinners so much that He became known as a friend of simmers. He built relationships with people and out of that caring relationship, he ministered to them. Jesus always earned the right to speak through grace. No wonder people listened to him.

The gospels mention eight occasions when Jesus accepted an invitation to dinner. Three of these: the wedding at Cana, the hospitality of Mary and Martha, and the interrupted meal in Emmaus after His resurrection, could be called normal social gatherings. The other five however, defy all social propriety. Those five served the purpose of manifesting grace. I believe prostitutes, tax collectors, and other sinners responded to Jesus because they felt comfortable in His presence. They felt comfortable because, though he knew no sin, he extended grace to those living in sin. Having extended grace the path to truth was clear. Let me highlight this principle using my own story of conversion.

I attended the Youth for Christ meetings when I was a teenager. The first thing that impressed me when I attended the meeting was the kindness extended to me. I was drawn to the people at the meetings because of their kindness. After I attended two meetings, I was invited to a camp. The thought of going on a camp for five days with a bunch of religious nuts scared the daylights out of me. I was also concerned

---

[120] NIV
[121] Luke 19:1-10
[122] Luke 19:1-10

because they were protestants. I had been taught that protestants had wandered away from the truth because some crazy king in England wanted to marry for the second time. My prejudice against them was high, yet I was drawn to them because of their kindness.

As the day of the camp drew closer, I lost my nerve and decided that I was not going to attend. But the leaders, Richard Brohier and Philip Sherherd, had been so kind to me I decided that I must not offend them. I decided to lie to avoid the camp but retain their acceptance. After the Saturday meeting, Richard and Philip both approached me about the camp with great enthusiasm. This was the time to employ my plan. I told them I could not go because my parents could not afford the cost. Much to my surprise, without discussion, both said that they would pay for me. I was shocked, ashamed and challenged; no one had ever extended such kindness to me.

That night I tried to discern the reason for such generosity. By morning I had lost courage again and came up with a better story. This time I met Phillip Sherrherd. I expressed my deep gratitude for their willingness to pay but declined the offer saying even if the camps fees were paid, I did not have adequate clothes to attend. Phillip, without batting an eyelid said, "I have sufficient clothes; I can share them with you." That day he earned the right to speak. I did not yet understand the truth but grace had opened the door.

GRACE AND TRUTH IN ASIA

We do not battle with atheists in Asia; the majority of our people are very religious and deeply committed to their religions. The problems we encounter arise out religious extremism. Because each person values and treasures his or her religion as precious, any attempt to share the gospel is seen as an attempt to undermine their religion and convert them. This is resented and opposed, sometimes very violently. This is the reality of Asia. We have not grappled with how to be relevant in this context; we have drifted away from biblical models and from the model of Jesus. Having abandoned these models, we gladly accepted successful strategies of evangelism developed in the West without any hesitation

Some religions see their god as a bookkeeper – one who maintains the account of ones' deeds on earth and rewards or punishment are based on this account. Thank God for Ephesians 2:8. We model grace because we have relieved it. Those who have experience the grace of God can be gracious to others. We must reflect God's grace in the home, in the church, and in the community. But to do this, we must avoid the thoughtless mimicking of western strategies. This is not because these strategies are not effective in the west, but because they are not effective in the rest of the world.

The western cultures are deeply committed to truth; they debate truth, uphold truth. The entire ethical system works on this concept. So naturally when it came to sharing the gospel they reversed the biblical order "Grace and Truth" to "Truth and Grace". As a result, presenting the truth is seen as more important than setting the stage through grace to share the truth. Western cultures are based on individualism. Individual freedom, individual rights, and isolation from the community are the norms. Christian leaders and strategists, recognizing this, developed methods of evangelism that suited their culture. Even though community living is more normal for us, we abandoned our understanding of community and sharing the gospel and instead copied strategies that spelled disaster for the church in Asia. Let me highlight a biblical strategy in the context of community living. To do this we must examine Acts chapter six:

> All the believers were one in heart and mind. No one claimed that any of his possessions was his own, but they shared everything they had. With great power the apostles continued to testify to the resurrection of the Lord Jesus, and much grace was upon them all. There were no needy persons among them. For from time to time those who owned lands or houses sold them, brought the money from the sales and put it at the apostles' feet, and it was distributed to anyone as he had need. [123]

For the purpose of showing how the gospel was shared in the context of the community, I will separate verse thirty-two from verses thirty-three and thirty-four, "All the believers were one in heart and mind. No one claimed that any of his possessions was his own, but they shared

---

[123] Acts 4:32-35, NIV

everything they had." [124] The believers lived in community and were of one mind. As a result of this community:

> With great power the apostles continued to testify to the resurrection of the Lord Jesus, and much grace was upon them all. There were no needy persons among them. For from time to time those who owned lands or houses sold them, brought the money from the sales.[125]

The apostles testified with great power, after assuring the community needs had been met. This is not an isolated example but is present throughout scripture.[126] Jesus modeled an incarnational approach when He became flesh and lived among us, participating in a particular time and culture. Incarnational ministry describes the method of identifying with a particular culture by living among the people, and understanding their culture. An incarnational approach is one that encourages ministry and action with the needy, not to the needy.

INCARNATIONAL MINISTRIES ARE MISSION FOCUSED

The Duke of Wellington, who defeated Napoleon at Waterloo, was asked whether Christians should be interested in missions or not. He responded with another question: "What has your commander-in-chief said about the matter?" The man answered: "Christ commanded us to go into the entire world and preach the gospel to every creature." The Duke said, "Well, then that settles the question. Now it is up to you to obey." Jesus "settled the question" in His last statement before ascension, "But you will receive power when the Holy Spirit comes on you; and you will be my witnesses in Jerusalem, and in all Judea and Samaria, and to the ends of the earth."[127]

As someone said, "His last command is our first concern."[128] The passage deserves further examination. At first blush Acts 1:8 may seem

---

[124] Acts 4:32
[125] Acts 4:33-34
[126] Acts 6:1-7, NIV
[127] Acts 1:8
[128] Navodaya Compendium p. 60

to be referring to a geographical location. However, a close examination reveals that the verse is referring more to a cultural distance:

1. *Jerusalem and Judea:* The majority of people in these communities were Jews. They adhered to the Law of Moses, and the prophetic writings, worshipping the only true God, and keeping the temple service, as prescribed in their law.
2. *Samaria:* The majority of people here were Samaritans, who worshipped the God of Israel in connection with other gods,[129] and who had no kind of religious connection with the Jews.
3. *To the Ends of the World:* This refers to the Gentiles, who lived through all other parts of the world, who were addicted to idolatry alone, and had no knowledge of the true God.

The progress of the Gospel also took place along cultural boundaries. First, "in Jerusalem, and in all Judea"; this is discussed in Acts 2 to Acts 8:4. Second, "in Samaria"; this is discussed in Acts 8:5, to Acts 11:25. Finally, "unto the uttermost part of the earth"; we have a beautiful anticipation of this in Acts 8:26 to the end, and the preparations for it in Acts 9 to Acts 12. Its execution is recorded in Acts 13 to the end of the book.[130] The focus of the local church must be missions. Emil Bruner reminds us that, "Mission work does not arise from any arrogance in the Christian Church; mission is its cause and its life. The church exists by mission, just as fire exists by burning. Where there is no mission, there is no church, and where there neither Church nor missions, there is no faith."

Today we neglect the Great Commission and the obligation imposed by Acts 1:8. We are reluctant to make the sacrifice required to effectively evangelize through incarnational ministry. We are reluctant to move outside the comfort of our own community to minister to others. Instead of reluctance, we should cry out to be sent:

Woe to me!" I cried. "I am ruined! For I am a man of unclean lips, and I live among a people of unclean lips, and my eyes have seen the King, the LORD Almighty." Then one of the seraphs flew to me with

---

[129] 2 Kings 17:5

[130] from Jamieson, Fausset, and Brown Commentary, Electronic Database. Copyright © 1997, 2003 by Biblesoft, Inc. All rights reserved

a live coal in his hand, which he had taken with tongs from the altar. With it he touched my mouth and said, "See, this has touched your lips; your guilt is taken away and your sin atoned for." Then I heard the voice of the Lord saying, "Whom shall I send? And who will go for us?" And I said, "Here am I. Send me!" He said, "Go and tell this people. [131]

We need to adopt the mentality of this verse. Hudson Taylor said "God's work done in God's way will never lack God's supply" while William Carey reminded us to, "Expect great things from God; attempt great things for God." This is the mindset we must have.

Reaching out to others is so important that Jesus repeated the great commission five times in the short period between the time of the resurrection and accession; in Matthew 28: 18-20, Mark 16:15-16, Luke 24:45-49, John 20:21, and Acts 1:8. Some scholars have concluded that it was a statement said once by Jesus that was repeated five times by the four evangelists. But if we study the great commission, we will recognize that they are different statements, with some common elements, but with different truths presented in each separate statement. Let us look at the elements of each statement.

In Matthew 28:18, the sovereignty of Christ is established, and then a goal is put in place, "making disciples of all nations." The verse next describes how it is to be done through, "baptizing and teaching." It concludes with the assurance of the presence of Jesus to the end of the age.

Mark 16:15-18, begins with a general statement, "To preach the Gospel to every creature." Next it speaks, "of the salvation that comes to those who believe and are baptized and the condemnation to those who don't." The passage in Mark ends with a description of the signs that will accompany those who believe.

Luke 24:45-49 begins by describing the Gospel that is to be preached, "the death and the resurrection of Christ and the repentance and forgiveness of the sins" and requires that, "it must go to all nations beginning at Jerusalem." They are told they are witnesses and given the power of power from on high.

John 20:21 records a simple statement of the fact that we are carrying through with what began with the incarnation; we are sent as Jesus was

---

[131] Isaiah 6:5-9

sent by the Farther. Acts 1:8 tells us that we are enabled by the Holy Spirit, which will make them witnesses, and then the geographical extent of the penetration of the Gospel is envisaged.

Based on their differences, we can conclude that five statements pertaining to the great commission was not one statement made by our Lord that the evangelists repeated five times, but rather, *Jesus repeated himself five times*. We might neglect the Great Commission, but Christ thought it important enough to repeat five times in a short time.

CONCLUSION

Incarnational ministry requires us to live in the world of those to whom we reach out. More than that, it requires us to live in a way that constantly demonstrates the *agape* love of the Lord. It is modeled both by the life of Jesus and the actions of the early church. We are required to manifest incarnational living across different cultures and across the world.

Vision

THE IMPORTANCE OF VISION

The word *vision* has been overused in the last few years. Most mission conferences will proudly begin with the slogan "Where there is no vision, the people will perish."[132] Management workshops place emphasis on developing a statement of purpose for the organization. Management consultants look at you oddly if you cannot recite your organization's purpose by memory and produce a printed card with your statement of purpose. Unfortunately, the average church will look at this as an unspiritual, non essential management technique.

Stephen Covey in his outstanding book, Seven Habits of Highly Effective People,[133] suggests that to accomplish anything significant we "begin with the end in mind." Imagine building a house. You plan every detail before you commence work on the physical house. You try to get a clear sense of what kind of house you want; you work with ideas until you get a clear image of what you want to build. Only then do you reduce it to blueprints and develop construction plans.[134] Without this planning, you can still build a house, but it will result in confusion, waste, and a series of moves from one idea to another. If you cannot communicate your dream to the contractor, you will be unable to estimate what it will cost or determine what it will look like. The

---

[132] Proverbs 29:18
[133] Steven Covey, 1989
[134] John Maxwell, Developing the Leader Within You, pg. 95

result will be chaos and confusion. You may have a house, but you may not wish to live in it.

This tragedy is repeated over and over in ministry. Some have plunged into church planting without a clear vision or dream. Plans have been made and remade on the run, generating activity without accomplishment. More troubling, the leaders are unable to evaluate the progress of the ministry, since they have no goals to measure against. These leaders wander from one strategy to another, and end up burned out and angry resenting the success of others.

Effective leaders have a vision of what they want to accomplish. That vision becomes the energy behind every effort and the force that pushes through all the problems. With a vision the leader is on a mission. The energy generated creates a contagious spirit felt among the crowd until others rise alongside. [135] Vision unites the community; long hours of labor are given gladly to accomplish the goal. Individual rights are set aside because the whole is more important than the part; commitment is the watchword. This is possible because people are following a leader with a vision. Helen Keller was asked, "What would be worse than being born blind?" She replied, "To have sight without vision."[136]

Sadly, too may people are placed in positions of leadership who have no vision for themselves, for the church, or for the organization they lead. No prophetic insight is needed to predict the future of these leaders or the future of the ministry they lead.

JESUS AND VISION

Jesus had a clear vision of his mission on earth:

THE SPIRIT OF THE LORD IS UPON ME, BECAUSE HE ANOINTED ME TO PREACH THE GOSPEL TO THE POOR. HE HAS SENT ME TO PROCLAIM RELEASE TO THE CAPTIVES, AND RECOVERY OF SIGHT TO THE BLIND, TO SET FREE THOSE WHO ARE OPPRESSED, TO PROCLAIM THE FAVORABLE YEAR OF THE LORD." And He closed the book,

---

[135] Ibid, p.139.
[136] Ibid, p.140.

gave it back to the attendant and sat down; and the eyes of all in the synagogue were fixed on Him. And He began to say to them, "Today this Scripture has been fulfilled in your hearing." [137]

Jesus clearly outlined his goals: "to preach good news to the poor, to proclaim freedom for the prisoners and recovery of sight for the blind, to release the oppressed, to proclaim the year of the Lord's favor." In fact, as we discuss in elsewhere in this book, Jesus repeated the great commission five times in the New Testament clearly establishing the vision in the hearts of his followers.

Jesus understood the importance of vision. Vision is the reason you exist - the *why* of your being. It is the concrete statement of your ultimate dreams for your work or for the world that you wish to impact. Your vision is part of the fabric of your company or life. It must be clearly understood, mastered until it is part of the DNA of your organization. Having a clear vision for yourself and ministry is critical. A well thought out vision brings many benefits for the organization its serves:

1. There is a clear defined purpose and direction for the movement.
2. The leader can communicate the God entrusted vision effectively and with deep clarity and conviction.
3. A clear vision makes it possible to constantly to determine whether one is on track with one's calling.
4. A clear vision assures commitment to specifics. So often in the name of ministry we drift from one idea to another without achieving anything significant for the Kingdom or the glory of God.
5. Vision will enable one to set goals, which will provide a measurable standard to determine whether one is successful.
6. Every option, no matter how noble and important it may look at first blush, can be measured against the vision. Based on that measurement, one can determine whether to focus time and effort there.
7. A clear vision makes it easy to communicate one's purpose to others. This makes partnership or support easier to obtain and thereby enhances the unity of the church.

[137] Luke 4:18-21, NASB

8. By communicating our vision, we enable the entire church or organization to live and minister with a purpose. It is not the vision of the pastor or executive director, but the responsibility entrusted to the organization by God, communicated by leadership, but owned and believed by all.

9. A group of people with a clear and compelling vision will not settle for anything less than their dream. They will work in the midst of opposition and difficulties and influence others to move in the same direction. They have seen the end product in their mind's eye.

Often the exhortation to create a cogent vision is not accompanied with advice on how to form a vision. This is a crucial question that demands an answer.

DEVELOPING A VISION

To develop a vision we must commence with the question, what is vision? Bill Hybels, Senior Pastor of Willow Creek Church suggests that, "Vision is a picture of the future that produces passion."[138] So what steps must be taken to discern this passionate future?

Look Up-Begin with God

It is helpful in forming your vision to remember some basic truths about your faith; God created you in His own image;[139] God loves you and was willing to die for you,[140] He has called you;[141] He has a purpose in calling you.[142] Based on these truths, we should begin our work by looking to Him in prayer. No vision is worthy of your life unless it fulfills your destiny, the purpose for which you were designed. Your vision must contribute to your destiny. For Christians that destiny is in the hands of God.

---

[138] Hybels, *Courageous Leadership*, page 32
[139] Genesis 1:27
[140] John 3:16
[141] Romans 1:1-6
[142] See e.g., Matthew 28:18-20

Look Within you-What
is your Passion

You can't borrow somebody else's vision. It must come from inside of you. It is the thing that ignites your passion. God called Dr. Billy Graham to bring the gospel to millions. This was his passion. Throughout his ministry, you could sense this passion. Mother Theresa's passion was to care for the poor. The sacrificial way she cared for the poor reflected the divine nature of God, as if God funneled his commitment for the poor into her heart. She said, "I am a little pencil in the hand of a writing God who is sending a love letter to the world." By her actions she exhibited the *Agape* love of God. How else could any human being love the poor with such passion and intensity?

Passion was the common thread that bound the lives of Hudson Taylor, Adonrian Judson and William Carey to their pioneering missions. They suffered, but would not give up their dreams because their passion within was greater than their suffering. Carey was captured by God's call to save the lost of the world. His vision was not without opposition. At a ministers' meeting in 1786, Carey raised the question of whether it was the duty of all Christians to spread the gospel throughout the world. J. R. Ryland, the father of John Ryland, is said to have retorted: "Young man, sit down; when God pleases to convert the heathen, he will do it without your aid and mine." (Some have disputed this statement was made).[143] Six years later in 1792 he published his groundbreaking missionary manifesto, "An Enquiry into the Obligations of Christians to use Means for the Conversion of the Heathens." In that same year Carey overcame the resistance to missionary effort and founded the Particular Baptist Society for Propagating the Gospel among the Heathen (now the Baptist Missionary Society).

True to beliefs, Carey journeyed to India with a British doctor, and spent years learning the language and raising support. Carey worked in an indigo plant for six years to generate funds for his effort. During these six years, he completed the first revision of his Bengali New Testament and began formulating the principles upon which his

---

[143] F. Deaville Walker, William Carey. Missionary Pioneer and Statesman (1925 ed.; repr. Chicago: Moody Press, n.d.), 54, n.1. See the recent discussion of this event by Brian Stanley, The History of the Baptist Missionary Society 1792-1992 (Edinburgh: T & T Clark, 1992), 6-7.

missionary community would be formed including communal living, financial self-reliance, and the training of indigenous ministers. His son Peter died of dysentery causing his wife Dorothy to suffer a nervous breakdown from which she never recovered. This forced Carey to minister while dealing with a wife who had become quite insane. Despite these hardships Carey remained true to his calling and to the vision he had developed over six long years working in the indigo plant. The result was the spread of the gospel throughout India. Vision has a power over adversity.

Look Behind you-What have you Learned?

> We know that all things work together for good for those who love God, who are called according to his purpose. For those whom he foreknew he also predestined to be conformed to the image of his Son, in order that he might be the firstborn within a large family. And those whom he predestined he also called; and those whom he called he also justified; and those whom he justified he also glorified.[144]

From this verse we have the assurance that we are "called" and that God is working for our good in "all things". Think of the freedom enclosed within that simple phrase. "All things" - all our afflictions and trials, all the persecutions and calamities to which we are exposed, all the time we expend the effort and see no measurable effect. All these frustrating life episodes are among the means that are appointed for our welfare. They "Work together for good"; they mutually contribute to our welfare. They teach us the truth about our frail, transitory and sinful condition; they lead us to look to God for support and to heaven for a final home; and they produce a subdued spirit, a humble temper, a patient, tender and kind disposition. This has been the experience of all saints. Consider Psalm 199:67, "Before I was afflicted I went astray, But now I keep Your word."[145] This same sentiment is echoed in Hebrews 12:11, "All discipline for the moment seems not to be joyful,

---

[144] Romans 8:28-29, NASB
[145] NASB

but sorrowful; yet to those who have been trained by it, afterwards it yields the peaceful fruit of righteousness."[146]

These assurances are available to those that love God. It is not that we take joy in the nature of suffering. It is that by understanding our role in God's mission and the importance of it we can see that the pain is worth it. Those who achieve this view are truly pious. To them, afflictions are a blessing. To others, they are seen as barriers or chastisements. They produce complaining, instead of peace; rebellion, instead of submission and anger; impatience and hatred, instead of calmness, patience and love. The devout Christian is made better by receiving afflictions as they should be received, in the context of God's overall plan. The sinner is made more hardened by resisting them and refusing to submit to their obvious intention and design.

Notice the phrase in verse twenty-eight, "…according to his purpose." It implies that God has a plan, or intention, for all who become Christians. We are not saved by chance or haphazardly. God does not convert people without design. Moreover, his designs are not new, but are eternal. What he does, he always meant to do. [147] Some of the difficulties we encounter are not only for the purpose of establishing character within us, but also for the purpose of preparing us for the future ministry. The life of Moses amplifies this truth perfectly.

Moses

In the time of Moses there was a king who tried to destroy God's people:

Then a new king, who did not know about Joseph, came to power in Egypt. "Look," he said to his people, "the Israelites have become much too numerous for us. Come, we must deal shrewdly with them or they will become even more numerous and, if war breaks out, will join our enemies, fight against us and leave the country."[148]

The king had a crafty plan, but God raised his servants to defeat his plan.

---

[146] NASB
[147] Barnes Notes, for Romans 28
[148] Exodus 1:8-10 (NIV)

The king of Egypt said to the Hebrew midwives, whose names were Shiphrah and Puah, "When you help the Hebrew women in childbirth and observe them on the delivery stool, if it is a boy, kill him; but if it is a girl, let her live." The midwives, however, feared God and did not do what the king of Egypt had told them to do; they let the boys live. Then the king of Egypt summoned the midwives and asked them, "Why have you done this? Why have you let the boys live?"

The midwives answered Pharaoh, "Hebrew women are not like Egyptian women; they are vigorous and give birth before the midwives arrive." So God was kind to the midwives and the people increased and became even more numerous. And because the midwives feared God, he gave them families of their own.[149]

Not only did God protect his children from the King's plan he used it to his advantage:

Now a man of the house of Levi married a Levite woman, and she became pregnant and gave birth to a son. When she saw that he was a fine child, she hid him for three months. But when she could hide him no longer, she got a papyrus basket for him and coated it with tar and pitch. Then she placed the child in it and put it among the reeds along the bank of the Nile. 4His sister stood at a distance to see what would happen to him.[150]

Notice how this desperate acts works to God's plan:

Then Pharaoh's daughter went down to the Nile to bathe and her attendants were walking along the river bank. She saw the basket among the reeds and sent her slave girl to get it. She opened it and saw the baby. He was crying, and she felt sorry for him. "This is one of the Hebrew babies," she said.

Then his sister asked Pharaoh's daughter, "Shall I go and get one of the Hebrew women to nurse the baby for you?"

"Yes, go," she answered. And the girl went and got the baby's mother. Pharaoh's daughter said to her, "Take this baby and nurse him for me, and I will pay you." So the woman took the baby and nursed him.

---

[149] Exodus 1:15-21 (NIV)
[150] Éxodus 2:1-4 (NIV)

When the child grew older, she took him to Pharaoh's daughter and he became her son. She named him Moses, saying, "I drew him out of the water." [151]

Although in God's hand, Moses grows impatient and tries to take control:

One day, after Moses had grown up, he went out to where his own people were and watched them at their hard labor. He saw an Egyptian beating a Hebrew, one of his own people. Glancing this way and that and seeing no one, he killed the Egyptian and hid him in the sand. The next day he went out and saw two Hebrews fighting. He asked the one in the wrong, "Why are you hitting your fellow Hebrew?"

The man said, "Who made you ruler and judge over us? Are you thinking of killing me as you killed the Egyptian?" Then Moses was afraid and thought, "What I did must have become known."

When Pharaoh heard of this, he tried to kill Moses, but Moses fled from Pharaoh and went to live in Midian, where he sat down by a well. Now a priest of Midian had seven daughters, and they came to draw water and fill the troughs to water their father's flock. Some shepherds came along and drove them away, but Moses got up and came to their rescue and watered their flock. [152]

While his hasty action demonstrates that God needs to prepare Moses to depend on Him, He deals with Moses very graciously. He provides him with a family, "Moses agreed to stay with the man, who gave his daughter Zipporah to Moses in marriage. Zipporah gave birth to a son, and Moses named him Gershom, saying, "I have become an alien in a foreign land."[153] Despite his lack of self-control God selects Moses for a mission. Listen to the conversation between God and Moses:

"Do not come any closer," God said. "Take off your sandals, for the place where you are standing is holy ground." Then he said, "I am the God of your father, the God of Abraham, the God of Isaac and the

---

[151] Exodus 2:5-10 (NIV)
[152] Exodus 2:11-17 (NIV)
[153] Exodus 2:21-22 (NIV)

God of Jacob." At this, Moses hid his face, because he was afraid to look at God.[154]

Please note very carefully, God's concern for the people and his intention to save them:

> The LORD said, "I have indeed seen the misery of my people in Egypt. I have heard them crying out because of their slave drivers, and I am concerned about their suffering. So I have come down to rescue them from the hand of the Egyptians and to bring them up out of that land into a good and spacious land, a land flowing with milk and honey—the home of the Canaanites, Hittites, Amorites, Perizzites, Hivites and Jebusites. And now the cry of the Israelites has reached me, and I have seen the way the Egyptians are oppressing them. So now, go. I am sending you to Pharaoh to bring my people the Israelites out of Egypt." [155]

God is acting, but summons Moses to be the human instrument. Actions, such as the king's desire to kill Israelite males, could not be seen by humans to lead to good. Despite this, God uses an unlikely circumstance and unlikely people, such as Moses, to bring his plans to fruition. It is this context that should occupy our thoughts when circumstances overwhelm us or when we fear are inadequacies will frustrate God's plan.

Hudson Taylor

Hudson Taylor, the famous missionary to China, had to look to his own adversity to become effective. Taylor found his calling early. At seventeen, after reading an evangelistic tract, he professed faith in Christ, and in December 1849, he committed to going to China as a missionary. He prepared himself as much as a man could. Taylor was able to borrow a copy of China: Its State and Prospects by Walter Henry Medhurst which he quickly read. He studied Mandarin, Greek, Hebrew and Latin. Fully committed, in 1851, he moved to a poor neighborhood in Kingston to be a medical assistant with Dr. William Hardey; he began

[154] Exodus 3:5-6 (NIV)
[155] Exodus 3:7-10 (NIV)

preparing himself for a life of faith and service, devoting himself to the poor and exercising faith that God would provide for his needs. He practiced distributing gospel tracts and open-air preaching to the poor. In 1852, he began studying medicine at the Royal London Hospital, as preparation for working in China.

Taylor left for China in 1853, and after a disastrous ocean voyage, arrived to find China in the midst of a civil war. Although well prepared and courageous, Taylor's eighteen preaching tours were poorly received even though he provided free medicine and medical aid at each tour stop. Feeling that he had wasted all his efforts he, "looked behind him" to see what God was telling him. He realized that although he had worked to make himself better able to convey God's message, he had not worked to make the Chinese better able to receive it. By learning from the failures of his effort, he built toward successes in the future. Made strong by adversity and determined not to waste his preparation, Taylor looked to his history to determine where he had failed.

He realized that he was evangelizing as he would have in England, rather than as he should have in China. He made a decision to adopt the native Chinese clothes and Queue (pigtail) with shaven forehead, and was then able to gain an audience without creating a disturbance. He accustomed himself to the Chinese culture without sacrificing the purity of the Word. Learning from his past, he held firm to his new method of implementing his vision of reaching China. While other missionaries sought to preserve their British ways, Taylor was convinced that the gospel would only take root in Chinese soil if missionaries were willing to affirm the culture of the people they were seeking to reach. He argued, paraphrasing the Apostle Paul, "Let us in everything not sinful become like the Chinese, that by all means we may save some."

Hardened by his initial trials Taylor was resolute, he wrote of his commitment, "If I had a thousand pounds China should have it- if I had a thousand lives, China should have them. No! Not China, but Christ. Can we do too much for Him? Can we do enough for such a precious Savior?" By the end of his service Taylor had spent fifty-one years in China. The China Inland Mission, which he founded, was responsible for bringing over eight hundred missionaries who began 125 schools in the country,[156] as well as establishing more than three hundred stations

---

[156] The Educational Directory for China (1905), p. 43

of work with more than five hundred local helpers. His ministries were located in all eighteen provinces.[157]

Look Around you-Listen to your Community

We are the family of God:

But you are a chosen people, a royal priesthood, a holy nation, a people belonging to God, that you may declare the praises of him who called you out of darkness into his wonderful light. Once you were not a people, but now you are the people of God; once you had not received mercy, but now you have received mercy. [158]

We belong to God and to one another. Community can and must be involved in helping us know God's leading.

Do Not Determine your Vision based on the Resources at Hand

Let's return to the example of Moses. We have discussed his commissioning by God through the burning bush. Take a moment to consider the task set for him. Moses, a single man, and a refugee at that, was given the task of delivering an entire ethic group from the most powerful nation on the earth. We should consider Moses when the task before us appears to be to large. His only encouragement was an instruction, "God said to Moses, "I Am who I Am"; and He said, "Thus you shall say to the sons of Israel, 'I Am has sent me to you.'"[159] However, God supplied what was needed. God next gave Moses a partner, Aaron, to serve as his spokesman:

Then the anger of the LORD burned against Moses, and He said, "Is there not your brother Aaron the Levite? I know that he speaks fluently. And moreover, behold, he is coming out to meet you; when

[157] Christian Literature Society for China (1911), 281-282
[158] 1 Peter 2:9-10 (NIV)
[159] Exodus 3:14 NASB

he sees you, he will be glad in his heart. You are to speak to him and put the words in his mouth; and I, even I, will be with your mouth and his mouth, and I will teach you what you are to do. Moreover, he shall speak for you to the people; and he will be as a mouth for you and you will be as God to him.[160]

To enhance his credibility, He gave Moses the staff of power for working wonders.[161] When he set out on his task, Moses was unaware that God would provide for him. Look at his reaction when first given his mission, "But Moses said to God, 'Who am I, that I should go to Pharaoh, and that I should bring the sons of Israel out of Egypt?'" [162] In response God provided nothing specific, just an assurance that he would be with Moses in the future, "And He said, 'Certainly I will be with you, and this shall be the sign to you that it is I who have sent you: when you have brought the people out of Egypt, you shall worship God at this mountain.'" [163]

God called Moses without clarity as to method, but with clarity of vision. He gave him a partner to support him and sufficient power to accomplish his goal. As a result, the Israelites were freed. Can we find this faith when God calls us to less daunting missions?

Joshua's life is also instructive. Joshua established his faith early on. His was one of the twelve spies sent to the Promised Land. Ten of the twelve were impressed with the defenses they faced, and forgetting that God had commissioned them, argued that the mission should be abandoned. Only Joshua and Caleb recommended that the Israelites follow God's instructions.[164] The others so completely terrorized the people that they not only refused to conquer the Holy Land, they attempted to stone Joshua and Caleb.[165] As we will see, Joshua's dedication to mission has profound results later, while those who fled from God's mission were punished. The remaining ten spies perished immediately,[166] while the Israelites were sentenced to wander in the wilderness for forty years, one year for every day that the spies were in

---

[160] Exodus 4:14-16
[161] Exodus 4:17
[162] Exodus 3:11 NASB
[163] Exodus 3:12
[164] Deuteronomy 1:22-46
[165] Numbers 14:10
[166] Numbers 14:36

Palestine.[167] Joshua and Caleb were exempted from exclusion from the Promised Land.[168]

Joshua, having established his willingness to follow God, was selected by God for more powerful missions. We are all familiar with the account of when Joshua was confronted with the walls of Jericho, a fortress of incredible strength:

> But the Lord said to Joshua, "Jericho and its king and all its mighty warriors are already defeated, for I have given them to you! Your entire army is to walk around the city once a day for six days, followed by seven priests walking ahead of the Ark, each carrying a trumpet made from a ram's horn. On the seventh day you are to walk around the city seven times, with the priests blowing their trumpets. Then, when they give one long, loud blast, all the people are to give a mighty shout, and the walls of the city will fall down; then move in upon the city from every direction."[169]

Joshua followed the Lord's leading. The result was exactly as captured in the song, "the walls came tumbling down." Moses could not have foreseen visitation of the plagues, the gift of the staff of power, or the parting of the Red Sea when he undertook his mission. Joshua could not have predicted the world's mightiest fortress would fall at the attack of shouting and trumpets. God called them. They obeyed. God provided all the resources to fulfill their destiny. God will not let you down. If God called you for a purpose, He will also provide. It remains only for us to step out in faith.

Notice that Moses and Joshua, unaware of how God would provide, could have focused on the barriers they faced or waited until God laid out precisely how they would accomplish His plan, but they did not. Unfortunately, negative attitudes may afflict church leaders. The scripture is clear-it is not enough to posses a clear vision, one must have the courage to act on it. Without this courage we can fall into traps:

1. Having established our vision, we wait for something to happen instead of causing it to happen.
2. We can focus on the obstacles we face and being thus distracted

---

[167] Numbers 14:29; 26:64 f; 32:11 ff
[168] Numbers 14:24, 30, 38; 26:65; 32:12; Deuteronomy 1:25 ff
[169] Joshua 6:2-5

fail to see the opportunities. In this case, we may abandon the vision without ever seeking to obtain it.

To avoid these traps we must see beyond the problems, envision the opportunities and resolve to act. When we do this, we have the privilege of seeing the impossible happen. Many obstacles may stand between our vision and achieving it, but armed with faith we can overcome these barriers. As Konrad Advenauer put it, "We all live under the same sky, but we don't all have the same horizon".[170] Certain we are serving the Lord we have the strength to endure. Adoniran Judson, the missionary who served Burma so faithfully, was captured by the Burmese, imprisoned and hung by his thumbs. They taunted him asking, "Now what of your plans to win the heathen to Christ?" Judson replied, "My future is as bright as the promises of God!" [171]

I received a personal example from a friend who works in Zimbabwe. Her mother used herbs in an attempt to abort her on five occasions. Unsuccessful, she gave birth to her in the African bush and left her to die. She was discovered by old women seeking firewood. She became a worker for the village, shuttled from hut to hut trading work for scraps of food. Later she became the victim of sexual abuse at the hands of a man in the village. Nevertheless, she found the Lord, and he called her to work with children. This is the message the Lord gave her, "Do not look in your pockets for you will say I have no money. Do not look in your pot for you will say, I have no food. Rather, look only to me." Heeding this call, she followed. She now runs four Christian orphanages and provides for six thousand orphans in Zimbabwe.

Remember, your vision will not be accomplished overnight. You will encounter many difficulties. Your commitment to your vision must give you the capacity to hang in there in the midst of these difficulties. Remember also, since God called you and entrusted this vision to you, you can trust Him and seek Him and His Grace. He is faithful, and He can be trusted.

Automobile genius Henry Ford once came up with a revolutionary plan for a new kind of engine. We know it today as the V-8. Ford was eager to get his great new idea into production. He had some men

---

[170] Developing the Leader Within You, p.141.
[171] Bayer, Chip, *Church amid 32 covered bridges presents God's recipe for salvation,* the Baptist Press, November 6th, 1998

draw up the plans and presented them to the engineers. One by one the engineers came to the same conclusion. Their visionary boss just didn't know much about the fundamental principles of engineering. He'd have to be told gently—his dream was impossible. Ford said, "Produce it anyway."

They replied, "But it's impossible." "Go ahead," Ford commanded, "and stay on the job until you succeed, no matter how much time is required." For six months they struggled with drawing after drawing, design after design. Nothing. Another six months. Nothing. At the end of the year Ford checked with his engineers, and once again they told him that what he wanted was impossible. Ford told them to keep going. They did. And they discovered how to build a V-8 engine. Henry Ford and his engineers both lived under the same sky, but they didn't all have the same horizon.

In *A Saviour for All Seasons*, William Barker tells the story of a bishop from the East Coast who many years ago paid a visit to a small, Midwestern religious college. He stayed at the home of the college president, who also served as professor of physics and chemistry. After dinner the bishop declared that the millennium could not be far off, because just about everything about nature had been discovered and all inventions conceived. The young college president politely disagreed and said he felt there would be many more discoveries. When the angered bishop challenged the president to name just one such invention, the president replied he was certain that within fifty years men would be able to fly. "Nonsense!" sputtered the outraged bishop. "Only angels are intended to fly." The bishop's name was Wright, and he had two boys at home who would prove to have greater vision than their father. Their names were Orville and Wilbur. The father and his sons both lived under the same sky, but they didn't all have the same horizon.

When God calls someone to serve him, He also gives them all the grace that is needed to get the job done. Some trust Him and venture out to achieve the impossible while others see all of the problems and give up even before attempting the task. These may be referred to as reactive leaders. Think back to our study of Joshua. Moses entrusted his mission of spying on Palestine to twelve leaders. Upon their return, ten lost their courage,[172] and only Joshua and Caleb kept faith.[173] Contrast

---

[172] Numbers 13:17-20
[173] Numbers 13:30-33

God's response to the group that lost their courage[174] with his response to those who kept it. [175] Keep in mind that among those who lost their courage were those who had seen the Red Sea part at God's command. Even great signs and wonders will not help the reactive to believe. After the Israelites courage failed, Lord responded:

> Then the Lord said to Moses and to Aaron, "How long will this wicked nation complain about me? For I have heard all that they have been saying. Tell them, 'The Lord vows to do to you what you feared: You will all die here in this wilderness! Not a single one of you twenty years old and older, who has complained against me, shall enter the Promised Land. Only Caleb (son of Jephunneh) and Joshua (son of Nun) are permitted to enter it.'" [176]

God punished those sent on the mission who lost heart and rewarded those who kept their faith. It is the way of the world that there will be fewer people who have the courage to move toward vision than those who those who will be frightened to move forward. Remember, Joshua and Caleb were leaders in their community. Not only could they not convince others, the community almost decided to stone them.

Although we can count on the Lord to develop the character of those who move forward to accomplish His vision, we must encourage them to make the journey. Share your vision with the leaders of the community; do not frighten them off by unrealistic goals. Remember you are trying to make them believe in something they have not seen. God may well accomplish miracles but we should not promise them. Remember, only a few will embrace the vision. Many will wait to see how others react, and join with those who reject it. Our attitude to their response is very important. Carefully weigh their opinions. Through them you may discover some concerns that you have overlooked, that you are straying away from God will, or that you have stretched yourself beyond your ability.

Even if you encounter men and women of little faith, do not ridicule or belittle their point of view; you may be lose them forever. After examining yourself, prayerfully move forward. It will be foolish to imagine that everyone will hail you as a hero and immediately accept

---

[174] Numbers 14:1-4
[175] Numbers 14:6-10
[176] Numbers 14:26-30

your vision. People will want to determine whether God is with you. Share honest testimonies of God's blessing and His leading to fulfill your vision. Do this with the intention of honoring God, encouraging believers, and as a testimony that God is blessing the vision.

Make sure you stick by your vision, do not drift from one idea to another. Shortly after the 2004 tsunami, I walked up a beach from a ruined fishing village on the southwestern part of the island. I came upon the remains of a home, only the foundation left amid a pile of soggy rubble. I asked the young man standing near it if it belonged to him. It did. He told me that when the wave came he ran to save his two sons, a three year old and an eighteen month old. He grabbed each under an arm and ran. The waters caught him and pushed him against a fence. There the pressure became too much and his youngest son was wrestled from him, carried away, and drowned. He asked me if I could help him and his remaining son.

The question put me in agony. Before the trip, we had committed that no one from the team would give an individual gift. We wanted to make sure that what we did had the largest impact possible, both for those suffering from the tsunami and for the kingdom. I said no and walked back up the beach to meet the team. It was a difficult walk. Surely, I thought, God was telling me through the emotions I experienced to help this man. At the end of the walk, I noticed that my hand had involuntarily moved to clasp the top of the money belt I carried, as if telling me to return to the man and ease his pain.

Later that night the team met to decide what our initial help should be. We had learned that a fishing boat with nets would provide permanent employment for its operator and also feed ninety people in the village for each boat purchased. We had enough funds for two. The village had over seven hundred people in it. We found several respected elders of the village, men too old to fish themselves, and asked them to determine the two most worthy men and have them come to the church of our local partner that Sunday. We would be leaving in a few days and we wanted the gift to come from a local pastor. When Sunday arrived, the two selected men appeared at the church. One was my friend from beach. It was one of the happiest moments of my life. God had told me directly to honor the prayerfully considered plans and strategy developed by the leaders, and to trust Him for the result. Many leaders have lost their credibility because they are not fully committed to the vision they promote.

Vision helps you with the big picture, but it is your core values that will help reflect your character and organizational culture – the *who* and *how* of what you do. They are your convictions on how your organization functions and how people are treated; the inside and outside your organization. To effectively establish values, we must recognize and hold in tension dependence on God and human responsibility. The common error is the failure to hold the tension, resulting in the church moving to one or the other extreme. I will identify these extremes as practical humanism and pious irresponsibility. Both are fatal for a Christian organization.

PRACTICAL HUMANISM

"The Lord has entrusted me with the responsibility of the church. I do it for the Lord." Few Christian leaders would say this but our practices may reflect it. When we fall into this trap our focus is on our particular institution rather than God's church. The emphasis is on an efficient organization, a balanced budget, and an appealing program. Travailing prayer is not a common occurrence; it is a human effort that occasionally looks to God to bless the plans we humans have made. It is not "Thy will be done", but rather let our will be done, and God, be kind enough to bless our efforts. The psalmist has a warning against this way of thinking, "Unless the LORD builds the house, its builders labour in vain. Unless the LORD watches over the city, the watchmen stand guard in vain." [177]

The emphasis is placed upon the futility of human effort without God's help. Man's utter dependence on God is illustrated by reference to basic human endeavors. Building a house and watching over a city cannot succeed (according to divine standards of success) if God is not included in man's plans and efforts. Even the diligent man who works from early morning until late evening cannot hope for success without God's sanction. Consider the teaching of Acts:

So in the present case, I say to you, stay away from these men and let

---

[177] Psalms 127:11 (NIV)

them alone, for if this plan or action is of men, it will be overthrown; but if it is of God, you will not be able to overthrow them; or else you may even be found fighting against God [178]

Consider the difference when the author of the plan is the Lord, "And I tell you that you are Peter, and on this rock I will build my church and the gates of Hades will not overcome it." [179]

This verse makes clear that although man is central to the accomplishment of God's mission, God builds the church. In his first epistle to the church in Corinth, Paul deals with a dispute due to church believers focusing on Paula and Apollos as leaders. The preference for Paul or Apollos is causing dissent in the church. Paul, while careful to respect both his own efforts and those of Apollos, points out that it is God who is in control:

I planted the seed, Apollos watered it, but God made it grow. So neither he who plants nor he who waters is anything, but only God, who makes things grow. The man who plants and the man who waters have one purpose, and each will be rewarded according to his own labour. For we are God's fellow-workers; you are God's field, God's building. [180]

If we lose focus on God, we cannot expect God to lend his strength to the effort. We will find our efforts full of activity but lacking in accomplishment. If the Lord does not build the house, we labor in vain. Even Jesus emphasized the importance of reliance on God.

Jesus gave them this answer: "I tell you the truth, the Son can do nothing by himself; he can do only what he sees his Father doing, because whatever the Father does the Son also does. For the Father loves the Son and shows him all he does. Yes, to your amazement he will show him even greater things than these. [181]

We are the children of God. As such we should only do what our Father calls us to do and be obedient to his instruction. "For the Father

[178] Acts 5:38-39
[179] Matthew 16:18, NIV
[180] 1 Corinthians 3:6-9 NIV
[181] John 5:19-20 NIV

loves the Son and shows Him all He does. Yes, to your amazement he will show him even greater things than these."[182] Jesus would not do anything without consulting the Father.

> For just as the Father raises the dead and gives them life; even so the Son gives life to whom he is pleased to give it.[183]

***

> By myself I can do nothing; I judge only as I hear, and my judgment is just, for I seek not to please myself but him who send me.[184]

In his ministry Jesus modeled how to remain focused on God. The key is consistent prayer. Examine his actions; he commenced His ministry with fasting and prayer, "Jesus, full of the Holy Spirit, returned from the Jordan and was led by the Spirit in the desert, where for forty days he was tempted by the devil. He ate nothing during those days, and at the end of them he was hungry."[185]

He selected his apostles after a night of prayer, "And it came to pass in those days, that he went out into a mountain to pray, and continued all night in prayer to God. And when it was day, he called unto him his disciples: and of them he chose twelve, whom also he named apostles;"[186]

He spends the whole night with the Father before he went to the cross:

> On reaching the place, he said to them, "Pray that you will not fall into temptation." He withdrew about a stone's throw beyond them, knelt down and prayed, "Father, if you are willing, take this cup from me; yet not my will, but yours be done." An angel from heaven appeared to him and strengthened him. And being in anguish, he prayed more earnestly, and his sweat was like drops of blood falling to the ground. When he rose from prayer and went back to the disciples, he found

---

[182] NIV
[183] John 5:19-21 NIV
[184] John 5:30 NIV
[185] Luke 4:1-2 NIV
[186] Luke 6:12-13 (KJV)

81

them asleep, exhausted from sorrow. "Why are you sleeping?" he asked them. "Get up and pray so that you will not fall into temptation." [187]

Finally Jesus prayed for the Apostles, before leaving them.

I pray for them. I am not praying for the world, but for those you have given me, for they are yours.[188]

***

I will remain in the world no longer, but they are still in the world, and I am coming to you. Holy Father, protect them by the power of your name-- the name you gave me-- so that they may be one as we are one.[189]

***

My prayer is not that you take them out of the world but that you protect them from the evil one.[190]

***

"My prayer is not for them alone. I pray also for those who will believe in me through their message." [191]

The key to avoiding practical humanism is focus on vision and prayer.

PIOUS IRRESPONSIBILITY

Pious irresponsibility is the opposite of practical humanism. It rejects plans or strategies; the common reason is "We will wait till the Lord does it." I call this pious irresponsibility because, though the statement looks sound, it is flawed. Let's seek biblical counsel. Once again we return to the life of Joshua. God said to him:

---

[187] Luke 22:40-46 (NIV)
[188] John 17:9 (NIV)
[189] John 17:11. (NIV)
[190] John 17:15 (NIV)
[191] John 17:20 (NIV)

Moses My servant is dead; now therefore arise, cross this Jordan, you and all this people, to the land which I am giving to them, to the sons of Israel. "Every place on which the sole of your foot treads, I have given it to you, just as I spoke to Moses. "From the wilderness and this Lebanon, even as far as the great river, the river Euphrates, all the land of the Hittites, and as far as the Great Sea toward the setting of the sun will be your territory. "No man will be able to stand before you all the days of your life. Just as I have been with Moses, I will be with you; I will not fail you or forsake you. "Be strong and courageous, for you shall give this people possession of the land which I swore to their fathers to give them. "Only be strong and very courageous; be careful to do according to all the law which Moses My servant commanded you; do not turn from it to the right or to the left, so that you may have success wherever you go. "This book of the law shall not depart from your mouth, but you shall meditate on it day and night, so that you may be careful to do according to all that is written in it; for then you will make your way prosperous, and then you will have success. "Have I not commanded you? Be strong and courageous! Do not tremble or be dismayed, for the Lord your God is with you wherever you go.[192]

God promises the land. The promise is followed by the condition upon which the Lord would fulfill His word. Joshua was to be firm and strong, well-assured, courageous, not alarmed.[193] In the first place, he was to rely firmly upon the Lord and His promise, as Moses and the Lord had already told him;[194] second,[195] he was to strive to attain and preserve this firmness by a careful observance of the law.[196] We "wait on the Lord" for results, not to act.

Let me provide a personal example. I was asked to serve on a team to evaluate mission partnership opportunities in Asia. The team leader did not schedule any meetings before we left. I was not concerned; we had a long flight to discuss matters. On the flight, I asked what framework we should apply in evaluating opportunity. Where was the focus of our sending organization, so that we could discuss our goals with our overseas partner and see where the two meshed? I was met

---

[192] Joshua 1:2-9
[193] Deuteronomy 31:6
[194] Deuteronomy 31:7 and 23
[195] Ibid. vs.7, 8
[196] See also Matthew 28:18-20.

with a scornful reply, "This is ministry," I was told "We don't need a strategy, we will simply look at the country and God will speak to us." This, of course, is nonsense. Not that God does not speak to us, He certainly does. He does not, however, ask us to put aside our intelligence and effort until He has a hosted a private conversation.

It is true that God often leads us in ways we do not anticipate, and we need to be open to His leading. This openness should not be confused with vacancy. God gave us a heart to speak to but also two arms to work with and a brain to think with. He desires our best efforts,[197] effective service and an evaluation of how to do so as well as our own commitment:

> For which one of you, when he wants to build a tower, does not first sit down and calculate the cost to see if he has enough to complete it? "Otherwise, when he has laid a foundation and is not able to finish, all who observe it begin to ridicule him, saying, 'This man began to build and was not able to finish.' "Or what king, when he sets out to meet another king in battle, will not first sit down and consider whether he is strong enough with ten thousand men to encounter the one coming against him with twenty thousand? "Or else, while the other is still far away, he sends a delegation and asks for terms of peace."[198]

God desires that we share our gifts by planning to serve Him.[199] His word renders no support for spiritualizing each opportunity as a method of avoiding hard work and planning. Too often I have heard persons who adopt this approach say that they are "waiting on the Lord." Once again this is a misapplication of a valid Biblical concept. Through His word God has called us to active service, not to pious waiting. We serve the Lord with vigor and wait upon Him to learn how he will bless our actions. We do not wait to serve.

Clarence Jordan, the founder of Koinonia, a Christian community in Georgia, planted pecan trees in the fields that Koinonia owned. Pecan trees do not produce a harvest for many years. Jordan was asked, "Why do you plant these trees that won't bear fruit for many years?"

---

[197] See e.g., Exodus 23:19
[198] Luke 14:28-32, NASB
[199] See e.g., Proverbs 15:22, "Without consultation, plans are frustrated, But with many counselors they succeed." NASB. See also Proverbs 21:5 and the authorities cited in the chapter on partnership.

He answered that he was being faithful in planting them for future generations. Johnson acted to serve and "waited on the Lord" for the fruits of service, trusting his faithfulness would be rewarded, whether he witnessed the result or not.

Being faithful means trusting that others will continue the work and that God will see it through. Some of the things we do may not produce fruit for many years. Some ideas we celebrate now may come to nothing, others that we feel have little chance of success may astound us. God controls the outcome, and that is what frees us to celebrate the effort.[200] But without the effort there is nothing to celebrate, no act of obedience to the Lord's calling. We must never assume that we should wait upon the Lord to act. He has all ready called us to action through the scripture. God entrusts us with a responsibility, promises help, but calls us to act in confidence. It is dependence and action; the action is based on his revelation. We act with dependence on God, strategize based on his revelation and minister within the cultural context.

GOD-DEPENDENCE AND HUMAN ACTION

In 2 Chronicles 20:1-12, the people of Judah faced invasion by a powerful enemy. In their faith, they turned to God:

> Now it came about after this that the sons of Moab and the sons of Ammon, together with some of the Meunites, came to make war against Jehoshaphat. Then some came and reported to Jehoshaphat, saying, "A great multitude is coming against you from beyond the sea, out of Aram and behold, they are in Hazazon-tamar (that is Engedi)." Jehoshaphat was afraid and turned his attention to seek the Lord, and proclaimed a fast throughout all Judah. So Judah gathered together to seek help from the Lord; they even came from all the cities of Judah to seek the Lord.

> Then Jehoshaphat stood in the assembly of Judah and Jerusalem, in the house of the Lord before the new court, and he said, "O Lord, the God of our fathers, are You not God in the heavens? And are You

---

[200] Proverbs 16:9, "The mind of man plans his way, But the LORD directs his steps." NASB

not ruler over all the kingdoms of the nations? Power and might are in Your hand so that no one can stand against You. "Did You not, O our God, drive out the inhabitants of this land before Your people Israel and give it to the descendants of Abraham Your friend forever? "They have lived in it, and have built You a sanctuary there for Your name, saying, 'Should evil come upon us, the sword, or judgment, or pestilence, or famine, we will stand before this house and before You (for Your name is in this house) and cry to You in our distress, and You will hear and deliver us.' "Now behold, the sons of Ammon and Moab and Mount Seir, whom You did not let Israel invade when they came out of the land of Egypt (they turned aside from them and did not destroy them), see how they are rewarding us by coming to drive us out from Your possession which You have given us as an inheritance. "O our God, will You not judge them? For we are powerless before this great multitude who are coming against us; nor do we know what to do, but our eyes are on You." [201]

Christians often find themselves in the same position; we seem to be over matched. Much of the world is unreached; it lacks adequate churches, adequate training schools, adequate financial support, or sufficiently equipped workers to reap the harvest, "But our eyes are on the Lord." Because of his focus on the Lord, King Jehoshaphat's faith was rewarded:

Then in the midst of the assembly the Spirit of the LORD came upon Jahaziel the son of Zechariah, the son of Benaiah, the son of Jeiel, the son of Mattaniah, the Levite of the sons of Asaph; and he said, "Listen, all Judah and the inhabitants of Jerusalem and King Jehoshaphat: thus says the LORD to you, 'Do not fear or be dismayed because of this great multitude, for the battle is not yours but God's. 'Tomorrow go down against them. Behold, they will come up by the ascent of Ziz, and you will find them at the end of the valley in front of the wilderness of Jeruel. 'You need not fight in this battle; station yourselves, stand and see the salvation of the LORD on your behalf, O Judah and Jerusalem.' Do not fear or be dismayed; tomorrow go out to face them, for the LORD is with you."[202]

With the Lord's support, we can ignore the size of our opposition;

---

[201] NASB
[202] 2 Chronicles 20:14-17 (NIV)

"For the battle is not yours, but God's." The battle to reach all the nations for Jesus Christ is not ours - it is God's. He is more than up to it; there is nothing to be afraid of, no reason to be discouraged. We need only to take our position at the feet of the Lord and act based on his leading.

King Jehoshaphat and his people expressed their confidence in the Lord. They were not passive spectators but rather active participants in the battle; they were active in worshiping, and boldly proclaiming the goodness of the Lord, "After consulting the people, Jehoshaphat appointed men to sing to the LORD and to praise him for the splendor of his holiness as they went out at the head of the army, saying: "Give thanks to the LORD, for his love endures forever."[203]

When we keep our eyes on God the result is overwhelming, "When they began singing and praising, the LORD set ambushes against the sons of Ammon, Moab and Mount Seir, who had come against Judah; so they were routed."[204] Often we battle for the Lord, to be effective we must allow the Lord battle for us. Remember the words of the Lord to Zerubbabel in Zechariah 4:6,"So he said to me, 'This is the word of the LORD to Zerubbabel': 'Not by might nor by power, but by my Spirit,' says the LORD Almighty." [205]

VISION MUST BE MONITORED

While as Christian leaders we adhere strongly to a Godly vision, this does not mean we do not adapt. While the over arching vision may not change, the methods for accomplishing it may be altered. We have discussed the need to be relevant to culture. Culture is not fixed in time. As the culture changes with the time so must the methods. Let us look at one example, the experience of the American Medical Charity, The March of Dimes.

Poliomyelitis, commonly known as polio, killed thousands of Americans during the first half of the twentieth century. On January 3rd 1938, the "National Foundation for Infantile Paralysis" was founded. The president at the time, Franklin D Roosevelt was suffering from

---

[203] 2 Chronicles 20:21-24 (NIV)
[204] 2 Chronicles 20:22 NASB
[205] NIV

what was then believed to be polio. The foundation was established to raise funds to research a cure for the disease and care for its victims. Its fundraising concept was to ask for everyone in the nation to give one dime to the cause. The appeal was named the "March of Dimes" by popular entertainer and movie star Eddie Kantor.[206] The organization was widely supported. President Roosevelt was so closely associated with it that after his death, he was portrayed on the U.S. dime. Over the years, the name "March of Dimes" became synonymous with that of the charity and was officially adopted in 1979.

The organization was so successful that it faced a crisis. It successfully supported the development to two vaccines for the disease[207] which eradicated the illness in the western world. What then of the organization? Its leadership anticipated that its work would be successful, and as the results showed its prediction to be true, it shifted its goals and used its charitable infrastructure to serve mothers and babies by preventing premature birth, birth defects and infant mortality. The leadership was able to predict the need to change their direction and adapt, keeping well ahead of the S-curve (See below). They never abandoned their overall vision of dealing with childhood illnesses, but they adapted to be relevant to the present. This is a challenge for all leaders.

A friend of mine who is a runs an evangelical foundation offered some wisdom about keeping organizations on track. He said the life of any organization follows a pattern of successive S-curves, as pictured below:

---

[206] Helfand, William H.; Jan Lazarus and Paul Theerman (August 2001). ...So That Others May Walk": The March of Dimes. American Journal of Public Health 91 (8): 119
[207] Both Jonas Salk's and Albert Sabin's research were partly funded by the March of Dimes

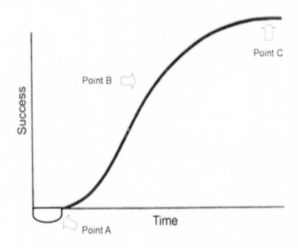

At the birth of any organization, there is generally a period of chaos while training, instilling vision and mastering roles and responsibilities takes place. This time is illustrated at point A of the drawing in the area where the success measurement dips below the baseline. As time goes on, a well-run organization will become more successful, as illustrated at point B. But as success grows, a number of factors take hold. The environment can change, methods to achieve the vision may no longer be relevant, and leadership may become complacent. Also, institutional factors can control where the members work mostly to secure their place within an organization rather than advance its cause. This occurs at point C. If leadership does not quickly and effectively respond at point C or before, the organization will steeply drop down the success measurement line. Leadership must constantly be on guard to assure that their present approaches have not been "overtaken by events."

A Case Study

Shortly after the 2004 Tsunami, a group from American visited Sri Lanka to see if it was possible to help. Several among them were impassioned and felt called by God to help. The question was how? "Looking up," they began with God. They spent time meeting together in fellowship. They spent independent time in prayer. Looking within themselves, they identified in their past a passion for the most vulnerable and a history of service. "Looking behind", they felt they had learned that local leadership was most effective at dealing with local issues and that they needed to move beyond viewing mission as a series of trips. Instead they should look at it as they would a key venture in their own country and identify the needs, find extraordinary leadership and determine what they could contribute. "Looking around", listening to the local leaders, they learned what was needed and learned how to work effectively. After this preparation, it was simply a matter of recognizing what they could contribute and finding others to fill the gaps.

Instead of limiting their vision to their own resources, they looked upon their deficiencies as a challenge to partner with others where their own resources were not enough. They listened to both the community in Sri Lanka and their local community through meetings with leaders experienced in the areas where advice was needed. As a part of the process they developed a vision statement to be used to assure that they stayed on track, and that any changes were conscious ones, not simply due to lack of steadfastness. They then worked to simplify that statement so that it could be remembered and communicated effectively. The result appears below:

MISSION	To follow God's call by contributing our gifts and resources toward the accomplishment of Revelation 11:15
VISION	To support gifted leaders in holistic ministry with resources and expertise, paying special regards to the needs of widows, orphans and society's victims.
VALUES	To achieve our vision we use these values as guides

Ideas	We are looking for creative approaches to problems. Ideas that consider the special circumstance and culture involved.
Ideals	We work with those who understand that God controls the result. We require the highest ethics and commitment to scripture.
Impact	We work with those who have a proven record of accomplishment.
Intimacy	We work with those who are open and honest; who understand partnership involves the review of successes and mistakes with the goal of constant improvement.
Indigenous	We work with local leaders with a demonstrated knowledge of the culture they serve.
Integration	We work with leaders who take a holistic approach to ministry.
Infrastructure	We seek to avoid dependence and therefore look to support specifically defined projects rather than supporting continuing obligations. We provide training and capital improvement that do not require continuing support.

This simple statement keeps the group focused, and allows others to know if they have compatible views. More importantly, the exercise of creating the vision statement forced a thorough review of the goals of the group. Forming, following and adapting the methods to achieve one's vision is a key to successful ministry. We seek God's leading, and then move forward with courage.

CONCLUSION

God has called us to His service and given us the talents to effectively serve. To do so we must be set a vision which is in line both with scripture's commands and our own culture. The resulting vision should be faithfully pursued. We must be active in accomplishing our vision while avoiding the traps of pious inactivity and human dependence.

CHAPTER 4

Working Among
the Poor

A DEEPENING CRISIS

TECHNOLOGY has advanced at an unparalleled rate in the past few decades. This celebrated achievement in electronic and computer science has disguised a devastating regression in social science. As we marvel at what we are able to do, we fail to notice what we refuse to do. We are living Thoreau's quote, "Our inventions are wont to be pretty toys, which distract our attention from serious things. They are but improved means to an unimproved end, an end which it was already but too easy to arrive at." [208]

Consider the following facts: Half the world—nearly three billion people—live on less than two dollars a day.[209] The combined wealth of the world's three richest persons is more than the Gross Domestic Product of the poorest forty-eight nations, which make up one quarter of the world's countries.[210] Twenty per cent of the population in developed nations consumes 86% of the world's goods. A few hundred millionaires now possess[211] as much wealth as the world's poorest 2.5 billion people.[212] The combined wealth of the world's two hundred

[208] Henry David Thoreau, Walden (1854), p. 42

[209] Innacio Ramonet, The Politics of Hunger, Le Monde Diplomatique, Novemebr 1998

[210] ibid

[211] 1998 Human Development Report, United Nations Development Programma

[212] Economic Forever: Building Sustainability into Economic Policy. PANOA Briefing 38, March 2000

richest people equaled one trillion dollars in 1999; while the combined incomes of the 582 million people living in the forty-three least developed countries is only $146 billion.[213]

More ominously, the numbers are trending toward increased disparity between the wealthy and destitute. An analysis of long term trends shows that the ratio between the rich and poor countries was three to one in 1820, thirty-five to one in 1950 and seventy- two to one in 1992.[214] The numbers are more disturbing when brought from a global perspective to a human one. Nearly a billion people entered the twenty-first century unable to read a book or sign their names.[215] According to UNICEF, thirty thousand children die each day due to the effects of poverty. Thirty thousand per day equals 210,000 children each week or nearly eleven million children each year.[216] To place this number in context, the Holocaust, perhaps the greatest single manifestation of evil in history, took the lives of six million persons over several years.[217] Arguably, the horror of the Holocaust was unknown until the latter stages of the war. The deaths of these children are known, but ignored. They "die quietly in some of the poorest villages on earth, far removed from the scrutiny and the conscience of the world. Being meek and weak in life makes these dying multitudes even more invisible in death." [218]

Clean water, vaccinations and public health services, commodities that the western world takes for granted, are scarcities in much of the rest of the world. Some 1.1 billion people in developing countries

---

[213] Human Development Report 2000, p82, United Nations Development Programme.

[214] 1999 Human Development Report, United Nation Development Programme.

[215] The State of the world Children, 1999. UNICEF.

[216] Progress of Nations 2000, UNICEF, 2000, Robert E. Black, Saul S. Morris, Jennifer Bryce, Where and why are 10 million children dying every year?, The Lancet, Volume 361, Number 9376, 28 June 2003. (Note: Although the title mentions 10 million children the body of the paper refers to 10.8 million.) State of the World's Children, 2005, UNIFEF (Citing the number as 10.6 million.)

[217] nNiewyk, Donald L. The Columbia Guide to the Holocaust, Columbia University Press, 2000, p.45: "The Holocaust is commonly defined as the murder of more than 5,000,000 Jews by the Germans in World War II." Also see "The Holocaust," Encyclopaedia Britannica, 2007: "the systematic state-sponsored killing of six million Jewish men, women and children, and millions of others, by Nazi Germany and its collaborators during World War II

[218] Progress of Nation, 2000, supra.

have inadequate access to water, and 2.6 billion lack basic sanitation. The impact is staggering. 1.8 million children die each year as a result of diarrhea. 2.2 million children die each year because they are not immunized. Another fifteen million are orphaned due to HIV/Aids.[219] Collectively 443 million school days are lost by these children each year due to water-related illness.[220] Nearly half of all people in developing countries who suffer from health problems can trace the cause to water and sanitation deficits.[221]

These conditions build upon each other in a cycle of hopelessness. In Sri Lanka, a country where forty percent of the people live in poverty,[222] its demands require children to refrain from school to help meet the needs of their families.[223] Fifty percent of Sri Lankan children drop out of school between the ages of fifteen and eighteen. Twelve percent of young children between five and fourteen have never attended.[224] "This situation leads to the perpetuation of poverty because such children will have no access to jobs and will acquire no skills."[225] International programs designed to relieve these conditions have, in many cases, made them worse. The developing world now spends thirteen dollars on debt repayment for every one dollar it receives in grants.[226]

These facts only constitute a small portion of the statistics of despair in "The Third World."[227] The "Third World" itself is a troubling name. It suggests that this portion of our world community is severable, remote from us. Most people feel that due to our industrial advances, the world is shrinking. Despite this awareness, they ignore the obvious conclusion: as the world grows smaller, we face a choice. Will we partner with our less fortunate brothers to solve the problems they face, or do nothing and inherit these problems as they spill across the rapidly condensing barriers that protect us? As Christians we are not allowed the choice of waiting. Rather the Lord calls us to act and to act effectively. To do so,

---

[219] The State of the world's Children, 1999. UNICEF

[220] 2006 United Nations Human Development Report

[221] Ibid, pp 6,7 , 35

[222] Department of Census and Statistic, Sri Lanka

[223] UNICEF 1998, *The Annual State of the Worlds Children.*

[224] Ibid.

[225] Quoted from Professor Swarna Jayaweera, head of the Centre for Women's Research in Sri Lanka.

[226] Global Development Finance World Bank, 1999.

[227] For further evidence please refer to Appendix 1.

we must understand both the nature of the problem and the nature of our obligation as Christians.

UNDERSTANDING OUR OBLIGATION AS CHRISTIANS

Overview of the Poor in the Bible

God chose the manner of his son's birth. Jesus was born to poor parents, He was born in a stable, and His birth was announced by shepherds who the society held in low esteem. On the eighth day after Jesus' birth, Joseph and Mary made the offering of the poor demonstrating their poverty.[228] Our Savior, being born into poverty, proclaimed that there is no dishonor in being poor. No station is dishonorable if God has placed us there.

Serving the poor was key to Jesus' ministry. Jesus, quoting Isaiah 61:1, said His mission was "to preach good tidings to the poor,"[229] As proof that he was the Messiah, Jesus offered the fact that "the poor have the gospel preached to them."[230] Poverty was a constant subject in His teachings. He advised the rich young ruler to give to the poor.[231] He advised his followers to invite the poor, the crippled, the lame and the blind to dine with them at banquets.[232] Jesus took special notice of the poor widow's contribution.[233]

When we serve the poor, Jesus considers it as service to him. When we fail the poor, we have failed Him. Consider Matthew 25:31-40:

> When the Son of Man comes in his glory and all the angels are with him, he will sit on his glorious throne. All the nations will be assembled in front of him, and he will separate them from each other

---

[228] Luke 2:22-24 See also Lev. 12:6,8
[229] Luke 4:18 NIV
[230] Matthew 11:5; Luke 7:22.
[231] Matthew 19:21, Mark 10:21; Luke 18:22
[232] Luke 14:13-14
[233] Luke 21:3.

as a shepherd separates the sheep from the goats. He will put the sheep on his right but the goats on his left.

Then the king will say to those on his right, 'Come, you who have been blessed by my Father, inherit the kingdom prepared for you from the foundation of the world. For I was hungry, and you gave me something to eat. I was thirsty, and you gave me something to drink. I was a stranger, and you welcomed me. I was naked, and you clothed me. I was sick, and you took care of me. I was in prison, and you visited me.'

Then the righteous will say to him, 'Lord, when did we see you hungry and give you something to eat, or thirsty and give you something to drink? When did we see you as a stranger and welcome you, or naked and clothe you? When did we see you sick or in prison and visit you?' The king will answer them, 'Truly I tell you, in that you did it for one of the least important of these my brothers, you did it for me.'

Then he will say to those on his left, 'Get away from me, you who are accursed, into the eternal fire that has been prepared for the devil and his angels! For I was hungry, and you gave me nothing to eat. I was thirsty, and you gave me nothing to drink. I was a stranger, and you didn't welcome me. I was naked, and you didn't clothe me. I was sick and in prison, and you didn't visit me.'

Then they will reply, 'Lord, when did we see you hungry or thirsty or as a stranger or naked or sick or in prison and didn't help you?' Then he will say to them, 'Truly I tell you, in that you did not do it for one of the least important of these, you did not do it for me.' These people will go away into eternal punishment, but the righteous will go into eternal life.

By ignoring the poor and needy, the stranger and the prisoner, we show that we do not have Christ's spirit and we are unfit for His kingdom. The source of condemnation is not improper action, but a failure to act at all; a neglect of duty. Christ, through His actions on earth and His holy word, has left his imperative that we reach out in love and grace to the poor. We must decide how to respond.

Much of the present day church is locked in debate on whether to focus on social ministry or evangelism. By implying the concepts are severable, the church does an injustice to the gospel. Two of the best known verses the Bible are the great commission and the greatest commandment. The great commission is found in Matthew 28:16-20:

> The eleven disciples went into Galilee to the hillside to which Jesus had directed them. When they saw him, they worshiped him, though some had doubts.
>
> Then Jesus came up and said to them, 'All authority in heaven and on earth has been given to me. Therefore, as you go, disciple all the nations, baptizing them in the name of the Father, and of the Son, and of the Holy Spirit, teaching them to obey all that I have commanded you. And remember, I am with you every day until the end of the age.'

The greatest commandment is found in Matthew 22:36-40:

> 'Teacher, which is the greatest commandment in the Law?' Jesus said to him, 'You must love the Lord your God with all your heart, with all your soul, and with all your mind.' This is the greatest and most important commandment. The second is like it: 'You must love your neighbor as yourself.' All the Law and the Prophets depend on these two commandments.

Despite the importance of these verses, much of the church fails to see the need to integrate them when determining actions. The great commission leads us in the direction of evangelism and the great commandment makes it imperative that we love people who are created in the image of God. There is no biblical evidence that argues in favor of one over the other. On the contrary, Biblical evidence suggests that those saved by grace will respond with good works. Consider theses verses from Ephesians:

> For it is by grace you have been saved, through faith-- and this not from yourselves, it is the gift of God-- [234]

***

---

[234] Ephesians 2:8 N.I.V

For we are God's workmanship, created in Christ Jesus to do good works, which God prepared in advance for us to do.[235]

Emphasis on salvation by grace should not take away our responsibility of caring for the poor. Those saved by grace are called do good works. Indeed the Bible suggests emptiness where Christian words are not matched by Christians acts. James 2:15-17:

If a brother or sister is without clothing and in need of daily food, and one of you says to them, "Go in peace, be warmed and be filled," and yet you do not give them what is necessary for their body, what use is that? Even so faith, if it has no works, is dead, being by itself.[236]

James connects true religion with taking care of widows and orphans in their distress,[237] urges the church to avoid favoring the rich over the poor,[238] and charges them to take care of those who need help as indications of one's faith being authentic.[239] James urges the wealthy in the church not to use their wealth or position to take advantage of the vulnerable.[240]

The early church understood the need to integrate evangelism and social care. Acts 6:1-7 states:

In those days when the number of disciples was increasing, the Grecian Jews among them complained against the Hebraic Jews because their widows were being overlooked in the daily distribution of food. So the Twelve gathered all the disciples together and said, "It would not be right for us to neglect the ministry of the word of God in order to wait on tables. Brothers, choose seven men from among you who are known to be full of the Spirit and wisdom. We will turn this responsibility over to them and will give our attention to prayer and the ministry of the word." This proposal pleased the whole group. They chose Stephen, a man full of faith and of the Holy

---

[235] Ephesians 2:20 N.I.V.
[236] NASB
[237] James 1:27
[238] James 2:1-7
[239] James 2:15-17. This is echoed in 1 John where John connects a heart for the poor with the love of God being within us. (1 John 3:17-18)
[240] James 5:1-6

Spirit; also Philip, Procorus, Nicanor, Timon, Parmenas, and Nicolas from Antioch, a convert to Judaism. They presented these men to the apostles, who prayed and laid their hands on them. So the word of God spread. The number of disciples in Jerusalem increased rapidly, and a large number of priests became obedient to the faith.

Note that the apostles did not say that their prayer and preaching of the word of God meant that food should not be served to the hungry. Rather they understood the requirement of such service and that it needed to be performed despite all other demands on their time and therefore assured that Godly men performed this duty. The verses contain five important truths:

1. It is the responsibility of the Church to care for the poor.
2. The church looked for wise men filled with the Holy Spirit to take care of the poor.
3. The work of caring for those in need is not secondary to other obligations.
4. Apostles laid hands on and commissioned the chosen candidates as representatives of the church.
5. As a result of these actions, the gospel spread.

Although the apostles delegated the responsibility to serve the poor, they assured the obligation stayed within the church and was accomplished by those anointed with the Holy Spirit. This illustrates the caution that must be shown by the church in meeting the requirement of providing for the poor. Para-church organizations can increase the church's impact by providing additional resources or needed, but scarce, expertise. However, such groups, no matter how valuable, cannot excuse the church from its obligations. These groups are also bound by scripture and must follow scripture by ministering through those filled with the Holy Spirit and commissioned by the church. Simply put, one cannot expect someone to receive evidence of the works of the Holy Spirit from a person who does not possess it.

Just as this service cannot be delegated outside of the church, it cannot be limited within it. The work cannot be confined to the missions or social justice committees. It must be vibrant within the church body before leadership can be satisfied. The Bible suggests that concern for the poor is both required to be integrated into one's daily life and a necessary predecessor for the effective sharing of the word.

Old Testament Lessons

In Old Testament communities, God's law was also society's law for the Jews. In that time provision for the poor was incorporated into all aspects of society. God set up Israel under the Mosaic Law with rules and structures in place to protect the vulnerable. Society was structured to prevent exploitation. Traditions such as the law of gleaning[241] , the year of Jubilee, the obligation of land redemption [242] and laws about loans to the poor [243] protected the poor from those who would take abuse them. Israelites were not to take economic advantage of the poor. This is one of primary components of Israel being a "kingdom of priests" and a "holy nation" set apart for God.[244] Israel did not so much have a social ethic, as they were a social ethic. The way they lived in a just society was a testimony to their neighbors of the reality of God in their midst.[245]

The year of the Jubilee provided that every fifty years the land was to be returned to the original owner, while the law of the sabbatical year provided for the liberation of slaves and debtors every seven years.[246] The principle of gleaning required one-tenth of all farm produce, whether animal, grain or wine, to be set aside as a tithe. "At the end of every three years you shall bring forth all the tithe of your produce in the same year.... and the Levite.... And the sojourner, the fatherless, and the widow, who are within your towns, shall come and eat and be filled; that the Lord your God may bless you." [247]

This principle is best illustrated by the story of Ruth. This poor widow was able to survive because of the law of gleaning. When she and Naomi returned to Bethlehem penniless, the grandmother of King

---

[241] Deuteronomy 24: 19-22

[242] Leviticus 25

[243] Deuteronomy 24:10-18

[244] Exodus 19: 5-6

[245] This paragraph is taken from a Mariners Church report on Social Justice with permission of one of its authors. (Mariners Paper)

[246] Exodus 23:10-12

[247] Deuteronomy 14:28-29; see also Lev. 27:30-32; Deut. 26:12-15; Num. 18:21-32

David went into the fields at harvest time and gathered the stalks of grain dropped by the gleaners.[248] She could do that because God's law decreed that farmers should leave some of the harvest, including the corners of grain fields, for the poor. Grapes that had been dropped accidentally were to be left.

"You shall leave them for the poor and sojourner: I am the Lord your God."[249] The law of gleaning was one of several established methods for preventing debilitating poverty among the people of God and sojourners in the land.

1. Every third year a tithe was to be given "unto the Levite, to the sojourner, to the fatherless and to the widow" that Yahweh might bless them.[250]
2. The poor were to have the free use of all that grew spontaneously in field or vineyard during the Sabbatical year.[251]
3. The corners of fields were to be left for the poor, and if a sheaf was forgotten it should remain.[252]
4. Fruit and ripe grain in a field might be eaten by any hungry person, but none should be carried away. [253]

It is God's nature to be concerned for the poor. Therefore this concern must be manifest in those who love him. This is a constant theme in the Old Testament. In the Psalms, God is repeatedly portrayed as the rescuer of the oppressed, weak and poor—that is fundamentally who He is.[254] This is why the proverb can make the claim that "whoever oppresses the poor shows contempt for their Maker, but he who is kind to the needy honors God."[255] The way the Israelites lived was to be a testimony to their neighbors of the reality of God in their midst.

The prophets routinely admonished the people and leadership to defend the cause of the poor. This mandate is often linked to fundamental

---

[248] Ruth 2

[249] Leviticus 19:9-10

[250] Deuteronomy 14:28-29; 26:12

[251] Exodus 23:10 f; Lev 25:5-6

[252] Leviticus 19:9-10; 23:22; Deut 24:19

[253] Deuteronomy 23:24-25

[254] Psalm 10:16-18; 35:10, 72: 12-14; 82: 2-4; 103:6; 140:12, 146: 5-9, see also Jer. 20:13

[255] Proverbs 14:31, this paragraph is from the Mariners paper

aspects of our life with God and doing what is right[256]—linked to doing right[257]—linked with true religious observance[258]—linked with knowing God[259]—linked with being a light to the gentiles.[260] Justice is also connected with the coming of the Messiah and His kingdom.[261]

Injustice against the vulnerable and failure to advocate for them also characterizes a society that has gone spiritually astray.[262] Micah, for example, condemns those who use their power to exploit the poor. Such injustice is considered a primary identifying characteristic of a community that has gone spiritually astray and according to the prophets, is a cause of God's judgment.[263] Micah points out what should be obvious to the people—that God requires those who follow Him to act justly (literally, "do justice"), love mercy and walk humbly with God.[264] This is in contrast to the empty religious ritual so prevalent in Old Testament Israel. God desires justice more than religious ritual. Zechariah called the people to repentance, a part of which is a call to promote compassion and justice for the poor and vulnerable.[265] Malachi echoed this call, by putting a lack of concern for justice toward the poor on the same level with those who engaged in false religion and sexual sin.[266]

The effects and consequences of disregarding the poor are demonstrated in Amos.

During this time, Judah and Israel enjoyed heights of prominence second only to Solomon's golden age. The kingdom grew economically while it expanded its borders. Unfortunately, disobedience to God's covenants led to an internal moral decay. God's word required loyalty to God's love for one's fellow man. Instead, idolatry, pagan worship and sexual immorality were prevalent throughout the country. The

---

[256] Isaiah 1: 11-17
[257] Isaiah 58: 5-8
[258] Jeremiah 22: 13-17
[259] see also Proverbs 28:5; Isa. 42:6-7
[260] Isaiah 42:1-4, Isa. 61: 1-2
[261] Ibid. Portions from Mariners Paper.
[262] Isaiah 1:21-23, Jer. 5:26-29, Ezekiel 22:6-13, 29
[263] Micah 2: 1-3, 3:1-4, 9-12
[264] Micah 6:6-8
[265] Zechariah 7:8
[266] Mal. 3:5

culture tried to integrate these perversions into the practice of keeping God's commands.[267]

Ritual prostitution and the worship of warlike gods had pervaded the society. The erosion of Israel's social structure showed itself in a cleavage between the rich and the poor. The improved economic situation in Israel led to an increase of the wealthy, who neglected the poor and used them to further increase their wealth. The social concern inherent in the structure of the law was forgotten. God's will, as it applied to the nation of Israel, was ignored; and this spurred the eighth-century prophets to action. Though their protest was largely ignored[268] the prophets preserved faith by assuring the people that God had not forsaken his promise. They saw emerging from their fallen society a kingdom different from any other: an ideal kingdom headed by the messianic King whose rule would be completely just.[269] God's judgment was manifest. According to Amos 2:6-8:

> Thus says the LORD, "For three transgressions of Israel and for four I will not revoke its punishment, because they sell the righteous for money and the needy for a pair of sandals. These who pant after the very dust of the earth on the head of the helpless Also turn aside the way of the humble; And a man and his father resort to the same girl in order to profane My holy name."

In one breath God condemns both sexual misconduct and legalized oppression of the poor. Sexual sins and economic injustice are equally displeasing to God. The lack of concern for justice permeated the community. Amos 5:11-13 says:

> Therefore because you impose heavy rent on the poor And exact a tribute of grain from them, Though you have built houses of well-hewn stone, Yet you will not live in them; You have planted pleasant vineyards, yet you will not drink their wine. For I know your transgressions are many and your sins are great, You who distress the righteous and accept bribes And turn aside the poor in the gate.

Not content merely to take advantage of the poor, cheating them was also prevalent. Amos 8:4-6 states:

---

[267] See Barnes Notes on the Old Testament, "Introduction to Amos"
[268] 2 Kings 17:13-14
[269] The Expositor's Bible Commentary. Frank E. Gaebelein. p. 269-270

Hear this, you who trample the needy, to do away with the humble of the land, saying, "When will the new moon be over, So that we may sell grain, And the Sabbath, that we may open the wheat market, To make the bushel smaller and the shekel bigger, And to cheat with dishonest scales, So as to buy the helpless for money And the needy for a pair of sandals, And that we may sell the refuse of the wheat?"

As a result of these actions, God judged the community harshly:

"Behold, days are coming," declares the Lord GOD, "When I will send a famine on the land, Not a famine for bread or a thirst for water, But rather for hearing the words of the LORD. People will stagger from sea to sea And from the north even to the east; They will go to and fro to seek the word of the LORD, But they will not find it." [270]

The bitterness of the punishment has increased the Lord's withdrawal of His word from them. As proclaimed by the prophets those who will not now hear this word will endure the greatest longing for it.[271]

New Testament Lessons

Jesus continued the Old Testament theme of caring for the poor and expected His followers to do the same.[272] Here the command to care for the poor is connected to a person's commitment to Jesus himself, echoing Proverbs 14:31: "Whoever is kind to the needy honors God." Jesus was well known for his relationships with the marginalized, including foreigners, women, children and the poor. Jesus intervened aggressively to correct an injustice when He cleansed the temple. He threw out the moneychangers, who were using a religious cloak to oppress the poor.[273] He rebuked the religious leaders for neglecting justice, which Jesus called one of the "weightier matters of the law" in favor of empty religious rituals. [274] Though it might not look like Jesus confronted societal injustice, remember that the political and religious

---

[270] Amos 8:11-12
[271] Keil & Delitzsch, Commentary on the Old Testament
[272] Matthew 25: 31-46
[273] John 2:12-17
[274] Luke 11:42

systems in first century Israel were virtually identical. The religious leaders were also the political leaders, holding political power under the Romans. Thus when Jesus attacked the religious status quo, He was also confronting the social-economic-political status quo.

The early church followed this example, in fulfillment of the great commission. That is, combating injustice is part of the final command Jesus left to His disciples ("teaching them to observe all that I have commanded you".)[275] In Acts, one of the clearest identifying marks of the church's "growth" is their commitment to the poor, even though the majority of early believers were poor themselves. Two of the three early snapshots of life in the early church concern taking care of the poor.[276] From these Old and New Testament examples, there is little doubt that care for the poor and oppressed is a fundamental duty of the church and its members, which must be integrated into all aspects of a believer's life.

As mentioned above, in issuing the great commission, Christ admonished his disciples to spread the gospel not simply by proclaiming the good news, but also by "teaching them all that I have commended you."[277] By examining Christ's own actions, we can see that He included service to the poor as part of effective witnessing. We have already noted that Jesus began his ministry by referencing care for the poor. Jesus consistently preceded the proclamation of the good news by service to the disadvantaged. Mathew 4 speaks of this service as a reason for the spread of knowledge of Jesus:

> Then he went throughout Galilee, teaching in their synagogues, proclaiming the gospel of the kingdom, and healing every disease and every illness among the people. 24His fame spread throughout Syria, and people brought to him all who were sick—those afflicted with various diseases and pains, the demon-possessed, the epileptics, and the paralyzed—and he healed them. Large crowds followed him from Galilee, the Decapolis, Jerusalem, Judea, and from across the Jordan.[278]

At the completion of his first long message Jesus again established a

---

[275] Matthew 28:19-20
[276] Acts 2:42-47, Acts 4:32-37
[277] Matthew 28:19-20
[278] Mathew 4:23-25

foundation for his teaching by serving. Mathew 8 records His healings of many afflicted by disease. As He expounds upon the charter of God and His kingdom He continues to serve.[279] After appointing the twelve apostles, He instructs them to make service an element of their witness, "As you go, proclaim, 'The kingdom of heaven is near!' Heal the sick, raise the dead, cleanse lepers, drive out demons. Without payment you have received; without payment you are to give."[280]

This picture of fortifying the gospel with acts of compassion is repeated through His ministry.[281] Christ used concrete manifestations of God's compassion as a necessary part of effective witnessing, even to the extent that someone unwilling to serve was not qualified to receive the message:

> As Jesus was setting out on a journey, a man ran up to him, knelt down in front of him, and asked him, "Good Teacher, what must I do to inherit eternal life?" Jesus said to him, "Why do you call me good? Nobody is good except for one—God. You know the commandments: 'Never murder.' 'Never commit adultery.' 'Never steal.' 'Never give false testimony.' 'Never cheat.' 'Honor your father and mother.'" The man replied to him, "Teacher, I have kept all of these since I was a young man." Jesus looked at him and loved him. Then he told him, "You're missing one thing. Go and sell everything you own, give the money to the destitute, and you will have treasure in heaven. Then come back and follow me." But the man was shocked at this statement and went away sad, because he had many possessions.[282]

Jesus exemplified grace and care for the poor throughout his time on earth. In meeting Zaccheus He formed a relationship by staying at his home. Zaccheus, upon meeting Christ and gaining understanding of His nature, sold half of his possessions and gave them to the poor.[283] Jesus spoke to the Samaritan women who, in that culture, would have been shunned by the Jews.[284]

His ministry demonstrated that grace opens the door for truth:

---

[279] see Mathew 8,9.
[280] Mathew 10:7-8
[281] See e.g. Luke 6-11
[282] Mark 10:17-22
[283] Luke 19:1-10
[284] John 4:7-10

For by grace you have been saved through faith; and that not of yourselves, it is the gift of God; not as a result of works, so that no one may boast. For we are His workmanship, created in Christ Jesus for good works, which God prepared beforehand so that we would walk in them.[285]

Martin Luther, in his protest against the Catholic Church, emphasized the grace described in verse eight. However, the Protestant church should not forget the tie between verses eight and verse ten: by grace we are saved and created for good works. The two concepts are not severable:

And the Word became flesh, and dwelt among us, and we saw His glory, glory as of the only begotten from the Father, full of grace and truth. John testified* about Him and cried out, saying, "This was He of whom I said, 'He who comes after me has a higher rank than I, for He existed before me.'" For of His fullness we have all received, and grace upon grace."[286]

If we refuse to care for those who need it and instead restrict ourselves to teaching, we have elevated truth above grace. The early church made no such error. Michael Green, in Evangelism in the Early Church, points out that even enemies of the church such as Celsus and Julian the Apostate mentioned the extraordinary conduct of early Christians as a major factor in winning converts.[287] As Bosch notes, "In the final analysis it was not the miracles on the itinerant evangelists and the wandering monks-miracle workers were a familiar phenomenon in the ancient world-but the exemplary lives of ordinary Christians."[288]

It is this incorporation of faith, the Word and acts of compassions that distinguishes the New Testament from the Old. The New Testament brings the word to life, as Christians reflect the nature of God's love in their lives as part of an incarnational theology. The early church understood that to separate truth and grace was to show an incomplete picture of God. It is this presentation of the total nature of God that served as the bona fides of the church, proving the gospel of love is

---

[285] Ephesians 2:8-10, NASB
[286] John 1:14-16, NASB
[287] (1970) 178-193
[288] exemplary lives of ordinary Christians

real, "Be careful how you live among your unbelieving neighbors. Even if they accuse you of doing wrong, they will see your honorable behavior, and they will believe and give honor to God when he comes to judge the world." [289]

Service to the poor and oppressed is required of all believers. Unless we can loosen the chains that bind us tightly to our own resources enough to care for others, we will be missing one thing. The Bible contains a sobering message for the churches that ignore this duty in Luke:

> Once there was a rich man who used to dress in purple and fine linen and live in great luxury every day. A beggar named Lazarus, who was covered with sores, was brought to his gate. He was always craving to satisfy his hunger with what fell from the rich man's table. In fact, even the dogs used to come and lick his sores.

> One day the beggar died and was carried away by the angels to Abraham's side. The rich man also died and was buried. In hell, where he was in constant torture, he looked up and saw Abraham far away and Lazarus by his side. So he shouted, 'Father Abraham, have mercy on me! Send Lazarus to dip the tip of his finger in water and to cool off my tongue, because I am suffering in this fire.' But Abraham said, 'My child, remember that during your lifetime you received blessings, while Lazarus received hardships. But now he is being comforted here, while you suffer. Besides all this, a wide chasm has been fixed between us, so that those who want to cross from this side to you can't do so, nor can they cross from your side to us.'

> The rich man said, 'Then I beg you, father, send him to my father's house—for I have five brothers—to warn them, so that they won't end up in this place of torture, too.' Abraham said, 'They have Moses and the Prophets. They should listen to them!' But the rich man replied, 'No, father Abraham! Yet if someone from the dead went to them, they would repent.' Then Abraham said to him, 'If they do not listen to Moses and the Prophets, they will not be persuaded, even if someone rises from the dead.'"[290]

The single purpose of this story is to warn those with wealth against

---

[289] 1 Peter 2:12
[290] Luke 16:19-31

ignoring the poor. Despite the dire consequences suffered by the rich man, Jesus did not charge him with any crime. He did not say that the man had acquired this property by dishonesty. The specific words used add clarity to the story. Although translated as "beggar" the word used actually is better translated as "poor man." The name Lazarus is Hebrew, and means a man destitute of help: a needy, poor man.

Lazarus was "covered with sores." He was afflicted not only with poverty, but with loathsome and offensive ulcers, which often accompany poverty and want. These images are designed to show how different his condition was from that of the rich man. He was clothed in purple; the poor man was covered with sores. The rich man fared sumptuously; the poor man was dependent even for the crumbs that fell from the rich man's table.

Lazarus' condition was so miserable that even the dogs, as if moved by pity, came and licked his sores in kindness to him. These circumstances are very touching and his condition, contrasted with that of the rich man is striking. Although the verses note that the rich man was buried, this cannot be said of Lazarus. Burial was thought to be an honor, and funerals were often expensive, splendid, and ostentatious. This is said of the rich man showing he had every earthly honor and all that the world calls desirable.

As a result of his actions, the rich man was consigned to hell. The word "hell" here means a dark, obscure and miserable place far from heaven, where the wicked shall be punished forever. The rich man's only observable crime was failure to care for the poor. He lived a selfish life and paid a heavy penalty. [291]

UNDERSTANDING POVERTY

It is apparent that the church must take its obligations to the poor very seriously. To do so, we must begin by understanding the poor. Often churches err because they believe that "the poor" are one homogeneous group and treat them as a single entity. This is not true. Let us consider some of the roots of poverty.

---

[291] See also Matthew 25:32-46

Roots of Poverty

Political Mismanagement

This is the curse that has plagued most African, Asian and Latin American countries. Bribery, corruption, selfishness and lack of accountability have ruined countries. As stated by Makoba and Wagona in their article "Rethinking explanations of political changes in Sub-Saharan Africa":

> .... Africa's economic decline may be attributed to a combination of several factors including: lack of organizational and managerial skills; inadequate know-how and insufficient resources; accumulation of vast foreign debts; and poor terms of trade. However, it is economic mismanagement and widespread corruption that led to the severe economic decline experienced throughout the 1980s. Such economic mismanagement and corruption have afflicted virtually all African countries regardless of their ideological inclination [292]

Acceptance of these conditions is often made easier by the worldview of the country's population, whose religious beliefs may include the appeasement of gods by the offer of gifts in exchange for the granting of one's wishes. Where these beliefs exist the concept of bribery may be seen as normal. In fact, the concepts have become so related that in India the celebration of Diwali, a Hindu religious festival which includes gift giving, has been used to disguise bribery of government officials.[293]

Human Failure

The Bible identifies human failure as one of the main reasons for poverty. Proverbs 6:6-11 states:

> Take a lesson from the ants, you lazy fellow. Learn from their ways and be wise! For though they have no king

[292] Journal of Third World Studies, Fall 1999
[293] "Damali Highlights Indian Bribery", BBC News, October 23, 2003

to make them work, yet they labor hard all summer, gathering food for the winter. But you—all you do is sleep. When will you wake up? "Let me sleep a little longer!" Sure, just a little more! And as you sleep, poverty creeps upon you like a robber and destroys you; want attacks you in full armor[294]

Where human failure is the cause of poverty, handouts from the church cannot help. As noted by William Easterly[295] in his *Los Angeles Times* article, "The handouts that feed Poverty": [296]

.... FOREIGN AID today perpetrates a cruel hoax on those who wish the world's poor well. There is all the appearance of energetic action—a doubling of foreign aid to Africa promised at the G-8 summit last July, grand United Nations and World Bank plans to cut world poverty in half by 2015 and visionary statements about prosperity and democracy by George W. Bush, Tony Blair and Bono. The economist Jeffrey Sachs even announced the "end of poverty" altogether by 2025, which he says will be "much easier than it appears.

No doubt such promises satisfy the urgent desires of altruistic people in rich countries that something be done to alleviate the grinding misery of the billions who live in poverty around the world. Alas, upon closer inspection, it turns out to be one big Potemkin village. These grandiose but unreal visions sadly crowd out better alternatives to give real help to real poor people.

***

What are the better alternatives? If the aid agencies

---

294 See also; Proverbs 10:4(NIV) Proverbs 12:24, (NIV), Proverbs 13:4 (NIV), Proverbs 14:23(NIV), Proverbs 20:13 (NIV), Proverbs 13:18 (NIV), Proverbs 21:5 (NIV), Proverbs 21:17 (NIV), Proverbs 23:21 (NIV). Proverbs 28:19 (NIV)
295 William Easterly is a professor of economics at New York University and the author of "The White Man's Burden: How the West's Efforts to Aid the Rest Have Done So Much Ill and So Little Good."
296 April 30, 2006

passed up the glitzy but unrealistic campaign to end world poverty, perhaps they would spend more time devising specific, definable tasks that could actually help people and for which the public could hold them accountable.

As Easterly observes, handouts without accountability and absent measurable steps toward progress are not only ineffective, but also damaging. Massive programs have little hope of meeting the human and spiritual needs of the individual. Unfortunately, many large organizations do not have the ability to develop specific, definable goals because their size and vision keeps them remote from the persons who need the help. One cannot set effective goals for an individual one does not know, nor can progress be measured by those who leave when the handouts have been dispensed.

Lack of Resources

In many parts of the world, people live in areas that cannot support them. Lack of water for crops and livestock and inability to control damaging insects or clear disease ridden areas may hold people in a condition of poverty. Poverty in such areas is beyond the ability of local inhabitants to control. For example, nearly half of Ethiopia's sixty-eight million people have experienced some degree of malnutrition over the last few decades due to draught. Millions more face hunger in Eritrea, Somalia, and the Sudan.[297]

Conflict

Much of Africa and Asia is torn by violent conflicts. These conflicts strike at all aspects of a community's economy. Fighting leads to death and disability, damage to educational institutions and erosion of medical capacity. Financial resources are drained and investments scared away. It also disrupts relationships and impacts trust and the ability to work together toward goals. Management of natural resources becomes subservient to the need of the conflict and at the same time, the infrastructure is destroyed. These different sources of poverty cannot

---

[297] *Ending Famine in the Horn of Africa*, White House Press Release, June 10, 2004

be treated as if there is only one cause. The want of resources cannot be handled in the same manner as human failure, political corruption or conflict. The cure must match the cause.

Identifying Barriers

In addition to determining the cause of poverty one must identify the barriers to effectively deal with the problem. Often those you are seeking to help are subject to conditions that block the very help they need.

Fatalistic World View

Many areas of the world have a tradition of *Karma*, the view that present circumstances are determined by past actions, often those which occurred in a prior life. Those who subscribe to a belief in *Karma* believe it has rule over their life:

> I am the owner of my karma.
> I inherit my karma.
> I am born of my karma.
> I am related to my karma.
> I live supported by my karma.
> Whatever karma I create, whether good or evil, that I
> shall inherit.[298]

These cultures tend to be reactive and believe that little can be done to change their circumstances.

Subsidy Mentality

Third World governments often come to power by promising subsidies. Even in established countries, policies enacted with the best of intentions can result in harming those they are seeking to support. This issue is being examined in Malaysia where the Bumiputeras, an ethnic group entitled to special privileges and subsidies, is being held back by

---

[298] The Budha, Anguttara Nikaya V.57- Upajjhatthana Sutta

the entitlement programs.[299] Based on experience, persons accustomed to subsidies may expect the church to be an agent of subsidy. Rather than asking the question; "What can I do for the church and others?" instead they ask; "What can the church do for me?"

Dependent Attitude

In many cultures children remain dependent on parents until marriage or later. Often this limits their desire to provide for others and inhibits the conduct of their lives. This attitude may develop into a personality disorder with severely damaging effects. The dependent personality disorder is described in DSM-IV-TR, a widely used manual for diagnosing mental disorders,[300] as a "pervasive and excessive need to be taken care of that leads to submissive and clinging behavior and fears of separation, beginning by early adulthood and present in a variety of contexts..."

Persons suffering from this disorder have difficulty making everyday decisions without an excessive amount of advice and reassurance from others and also need others to take responsibility for their own lives. They have difficulty expressing disagreement with others because of fear of loss of support and fail to initiate projects because of low self-confidence. They may go to excessive lengths to obtain nurturance and support from others, to the point of volunteering to do things that are unpleasant. They are uncomfortable alone and urgently seek relationships as a source of support.[301] These characteristics limit the ability of a person to advance from his state of poverty and honestly embrace a relationship with the Lord.

Fighting dependency is a tricky issue for a Christian leader. New believers both seek and need mentors for guidance. Often the Bible refers to new believers as infants or children.[302] This time of dependence is necessary as the believer bonds to the new Christian community.

---

[299] "Get away from subsidy mentality", NSTONLINE, October 11, 2007
[300] Diagnostic and Statistical Manual of Mental Disorders (Fourth Edition)
[301] Ibid.
[302] 1 Corinthians 14:20; 2 Corinthians 6:13; Ephesians 4:14.

Leaders must gauge when it is time for the believer to move from this developmental stage.

Emotional Hurts

The greatest pain of poverty is not hunger, but rejection and the hurts that accompany it. As Proverbs 14:20 states "The poor is hated even by his neighbor, but those who love the rich are many."[303] If you desire to help the poor you must grapple with this issue. Consider the impact of poverty upon the poor and their children:

> Children in low income families are prone to low self-esteem and associated mental health difficulties. Depression, frustrations and anger are frequent emotions and consequences to mental health that families living in poverty experience. Research has consistently shown that recipients of social assistance suffer from dramatically higher levels of depression, and other mental health problems, than the general population (Workfare Watch: 1999).[304]

The poor often feel rejected and mistrusted. They have to deal with the stress of constant want. Their condition may expose them to ridicule and limit their social connections. They may feel that fate has preferred others opening them to feelings of envy. These feelings can lead them to be angry at their parents and with God. As a result they may lose their feeling of self-worth and with it their motivation. Man without motivation, will always complain, but never work towards improvement. He will blame anything and anyone other than himself, offer every possible excuse and live in self-pity. Self-pity kills faith and cripples any creative initiative. A person who has given into self-pity will always blame his external circumstances. If the poor are to be developed with dignity and self-respect, one should not begin with economic liberation, but with emotional liberation. They will need assistance to live, but will need emotional recovery to thrive.

To achieve emotional liberation, the mind must be reprogrammed to

[303] N.A.S

[304] "The Impact of Poverty on the Health of Children and Youth", by Robin Singer.

think about oneself and the world biblically. This can be accomplished by counseling coupled with behavioral modification through mentoring. This is no easy task. In Sri Lanka there is an elephant orphanage that holds several hundred elephants. To train them, while they are young, they are chained to a concrete pillar. They will fight against the chain for many days, but they soon learn they cannot overcome it. Later, as fully grown elephants weighing several tons, they could easily snap the chain, but they never attempt the task. A stronghold in their mind, their previous learning, tells them they cannot break free.

This is also true of individuals. They learn to accept limitations. Through counseling we can help them break free these strongholds of the mind and disprove the lies that individuals grow to accept. Once the strongholds have been conquered, they are free to accept their new position in Christ. With that new position, self worth is restored. A person with self worth and dignity, who accepts and believes that God cares for him, will work towards self-improvement. As they learn the character of God, they will learn to depend on Him, that He cares for them and can help them. The Lord's plans are for the betterment of his people, "'For I know the plans I have for you,' says the LORD. 'They are plans for good and not for disaster, to give you a future and a hope.'" [305]

Stephen R. Covey in his outstanding book, The Seven Habits of Highly Effective People uses the term "proactivity" to define the attitude that must be achieved for the individual to make progress, Covey writes, "It means more than merely taking initiative. It means that as human beings, we are responsible for our own lives. Our behavior is a function of our decisions, not our conditions. We can subordinate feelings to values. We have initiative and responsibility to make things to happen." [306]

This principle is illustrated by the story of Victor Frankl, a Jewish psychologist imprisoned in a German concentration camp. In the German death camp he experienced acts that were so repugnant to one's sense of decency that they should not be repeated. His parents,

---

[305] Jeremiah 29:11
[306] Covey, Stephen, The Seven Habits of Highly Effective People, pg. 70

his brother, and his wife died in the camps, sent to the gas ovens. Except for his sister, his entire family perished. Frankl himself suffered torture and indignities, never knowing from one moment to the next if his path would lead to the ovens or if he would be among the "saved" who would remove the bodies or shovel out the ashes.

One day, naked and alone in a small room, he became aware of what he later called, "the last of the human freedoms," the freedom his Nazi captors could not take away. They could control his entire environment, they could do what they wanted to his body, but Victor Frankl himself was a self-aware being who could look as an observer at his own fate. His basic identity was intact. He could decide within himself how all of this was going to affect him. Between what happened to him, or the stimulus, and his response to it, was his freedom or power to choose that response.

In the midst of his experiences, Frankl envisioned himself in different circumstances, such as lecturing to his students after his release from the death camps. He would picture himself in the classroom in his mind's eye, and lecture on the lessons he was learning during his torture. Through a series of such disciplines, he exercised his small, embryonic freedom until it grew larger and larger, until be had more freedom than his Nazi captors. They had more liberty, more options to choose from in their environment; but he had more freedom, more internal power to exercise his options. He became an inspiration to those around him, even to some of the guards. He helped others find meaning in their suffering and dignity in their prison existence.

In the most degrading circumstances imaginable, Frankl used the human endowment of self-awareness to discover a fundamental principle about the nature of man; between stimulus and response, man has the freedom to choose. Without this recovery of the ability to see the possibilities one's life holds, there can be no effective recovery from poverty. C. Nabukeer, a Ugandan native, writes in his essay on poverty reduction:

> ... the poor in Uganda need much more than material
> wealth. We have psychological and emotional needs as

well. We have been traumatized by a succession of brutal regimes for the last 41 years. We watch as our land is appropriated, we watch the killing of our relatives, the raping and mutilation of our children; we are ill and diseased. We need 'health' as a resource so that we can engage in productive activities. For successful poverty reduction interventions, we need to restore "hope" as a starting point. [307]

The term that Covey uses as "proactive" in the context of management, I will call "faith" in the context of the church. Faith is not accepting the inevitable, but changing the impossible situations, into possible situations by the grace of God. One can chose to believe change is impossible and give up, or one can act now, based on your confidence that God will see you through. With this belief comes "hope," a commodity as scarce as wealth in the poor areas of the world.

A MODEL FOR WORKING
WITH THE POOR

We can provide the hope so desperately needed in many parts of the world. The authorities examined in his chapter suggest a model for working with the poor, designed not only to better their condition, but also their outlook. To successfully minister, we must resolve to identify, edify, integrate and model.

Identify

- Identify the cause of poverty

We must understand the cause of poverty and prepare a relevant strategy designed to address its particular issue. The mistake of assuming that all the poor are the same can drastically limit effectiveness. Instead the approach must be tailored to the needs of the person.

---

[307] C. Nabukeera, Poverty Reduction. Federo website (Federo.com)

• Identify the personal barriers

Emotional barriers stand in the way of a relationship with Christ. They must be stripped away. Hebrews 12:1, "Therefore, since we are surrounded by such a huge crowd of witnesses to the life of faith, let us strip off every weight that slows us down, especially the sin that so easily hinders our progress. And let us run with endurance the race that God has set before us."[308] Emotional burdens can be seen as a weight which restricts us for running our race for the Lord.

• Identify leadership

Identify people gifted in ministering in the areas of need in accordance with the barrier you have identified and strategy you have established, "As each one has received a special gift, employ it in serving one another as good stewards of the manifold grace of God."[309] In accordance with Acts 6:1, make sure the leaders are filled with the Holy Spirit and gifted with wisdom.

Edify

• Fight against fatalistic thinking

Both the culture and environment of the poor may lead them to think their life cannot be improved, that their course is fixed. Deprived of hope, they will unable to understand the changes the Lord may accomplish. They will not understand the power of the Lord to do "... infinitely more than we would ever dare to ask or hope."[310] We must guard against a return to fatalistic thinking and support the believer through encouragement. It is critical to offer this support and encouragement to stimulate development and provide strength in times of weakness. 1 Thessalonians 5:11,14:

---

[308] N.L.T
[309] 1 Peter 4:10
[310] Ephesians 3:20, N.L.T.

11Therefore encourage one another and build up one another, just as you also are doing.

***

14We urge you, brethren, admonish the unruly, encourage the fainthearted, help the weak, be patient with everyone.

Encouragement is a key element of development. We are specifically instructed to join together to support each other, "Not forsaking our own assembling together, as is the habit of some, but encouraging one anther; and all the more as you see the day drawing near."[311]

- Teach ministry to the poor

We have already examined the honorable condition of the poor in the view of the Lord. Nevertheless, the growing societal disparity between rich and poor will continue to marginalize them in the world's view. To combat this trend we must continually preach the Bible's teaching on the place of the poor as our brothers and sisters.

- Teach people to be givers

To effectively minister to the poor one must invest one's heart. God is most concerned with the status of our hearts. However, it is difficult for one's heart to be fully invested without giving. "Where your treasure is there will your heart be also." [312] The action of giving impacts the giver as much or more than the recipient. In Philippians 4:12-1, Paul writes:

> I know how to get along with humble means, and I also know how to live in prosperity; in any and every circumstance I have learned the secret of being filled and going hungry, both of having abundance and suffering need.I can do all things through Him who strengthens me. Nevertheless, you have done well to share with me in my affliction. And you yourselves also know,

[311] Hebrews 10:25
[312] Matthew 6:21

> Philippians, that at the first preaching of the gospel, after I departed from Macedonia, no church shared with me in the matter of giving and receiving but you alone; for even in Thessalonica you sent a gift more than once for my needs. **Not that I seek the gift itself, but I seek for the profit which increases to your account.**

Giving, like the compassion shown through ministering to the poor, serves as a proof of the principles of the gospel and encourages generosity in others. As a result we see numerous places in scripture where the gifts of others are used as a testimony to encourage us to give:

> Now I want to tell you, dear brothers and sisters, what God in his kindness has done for the churches in Macedonia. Though they have been going through much trouble and hard times, their wonderful joy and deep poverty have overflowed in rich generosity. For I can testify that they gave not only what they could afford but far more. And they did it of their own free will. They begged us again and again for the gracious privilege of sharing the gift for the Christians in Jerusalem. Best of all, they went beyond our highest hopes, for their first action was to dedicate themselves to the Lord and to us for whatever directions God might give them.[313]

Teaching about giving is an obligation of church leadership. In I Timothy 6:17-19, Paul tells Timothy as a young minister of the gospel to:

> Instruct those who are rich in this present world not to be conceited or to fix their hope on the uncertainty of riches, but on God, who richly supplies us with all things to enjoy. Instruct them to do good, to be rich in good works, to be generous and ready to share, storing up for themselves the treasure of a good foundation for the future, so that they may take hold of that which is life indeed.

---

[313] 2 Corinthians 8:1-5

Paul expected Timothy to take an active role in teaching generosity to those who were blessed with resources.[314]

Model

It is easy and emotionally satisfying to speak of the poor and occasionally shed a few tears on their behalf, but this will not lead to a radical change in ministry. Teaching must be reinforced with modeling, "Remember those who led you, who spoke the word of God to you; and considering the result of their conduct, imitate their faith."[315] Remember always that the new believers you reach out to are, "considering the result of your conduct" and "imitating your faith."

We must not only model care for the poor but also demonstrate that our care is an extension of our compassion and love for them, "If anyone has material possessions and sees his brother in need but has no pity on him, how can the love of God be in him? Dear children, let us not love with words or tongue but with actions and in truth."[316] The emphasis is on lack of compassion. If one sees the need but feels no pity, "how can the love of God be in him?" In other words how can one love God but not act as God requires? How can one love God and not love those who bear his image? To withhold help from a brother in need, to shut off compassionate action, is to deny the presence of God's love in one's own heart. As Dodd says, "If such a minimal response to the law of charity, called for by such an everyday situation, is absent, then it is idle to pretend that we are within the family of God, the realm in which love is operative as the principle and the token of eternal life." [317]

Attempting ministry to the poor without compassion leaves one vulnerable to many traps:

1. The power of money and the helplessness of the poor can give rise to arrogance.
2. The poor cannot pay back funds nor is their friendship beneficial.

---

[314] See also Chapter Ten, Giving
[315] Hebrews 13:7
[316] I John 3:17-18, NIV
[317] John Nine Epistles, p. 86

Without compassion even though you minister to their needs, they can be viewed as a nuisance.

3. The poor can be very demanding; their helplessness and their fallen nature can cause them to be very selfish and self-seeking.
4. Discouragement sets in easily as you work with the poor. Their worldview, lack of motivation to do work, their reactive attitude, and their general lethargy, can drain you.
5. The smells, lack of cleanliness and physical disabilities of the poor can be distressing.
6. The overwhelming needs of the poor and corresponding lack of resources to respond to them can be crippling.

Compassion, an honest caring for the poor, will be our protection in avoiding these traps. Serving without compassion can lead to a misunderstanding of the honorable position of the poor in God's kingdom and to treating them without the dignity they deserve. [318]

Integrate

The Bible teaches us to make the poor a part of a unified church:

And the congregation of those who believed were of one heart and soul; and not one of them claimed that anything belonging to him was his own, but all things were common property to them. And with great power the apostles were giving testimony to the resurrection of the Lord Jesus, and abundant grace was upon them all. For there was not a needy person among them, for all who were owners of land or houses would sell them and bring the proceeds of the sales and lay them at the apostles' feet, and they would be distributed to each as any had need.[319]

The expressions, "one heart" and "one soul" denote a "tender union." They felt similarly, or were attached to the same things, and this prevented dissension. It would be difficult to conceive of a better way to express unity than to say people had "one soul." The picture is one

[318] James 2:5-6, NASB
[319] Acts 4:32-35, NASB

of close friendship. The Hebrews spoke of friends being, "one man." It appears that the early church understood how want could divide them and affect their ministry by being a source of division. They had, "all things in common," that is, all their property or possessions.

The poor were helped so that they could be effective members of the church, not as a ministry separated form the church. The Biblical picture is not a distant handout but rather a warm embrace. Consider James 2:1-5:

> My brethren, do not hold your faith in our glorious Lord Jesus Christ with an attitude of personal favoritism. For if a man comes into your assembly with a gold ring and dressed in fine clothes, and there also comes in a poor man in dirty clothes, and you pay special attention to the one who is wearing the fine clothes, and say, "You sit here in a good place," and you say to the poor man, "You stand over there, or sit down by my footstool," have you not made distinctions among yourselves, and become judges with evil motives? Listen, my beloved brethren: did not God choose the poor of this world to be rich in faith and heirs of the kingdom which He promised to those who love Him? But you have dishonored the poor man. Is it not the rich who oppress you and personally drag you into court? Do they not blaspheme the fair name by which you have been called? [320]

No one in God's church would ask a poor person to stand aside as a result of his poverty. But how often do we tacitly communicate this by making our service to the poor the subject of short term projects and ministries which are outside the church. Just as the Bible commands us to integrate the teaching of the great commission with that of the greatest commandment, it asks us to treat the poor as an important asset of our church, not just the focus of our ministry. The New Testament picture is that of the wealthy and the poor fellowshipping together at a banquet, "But when you give a reception, invite the poor, the crippled, the lame, the blind, and you will be blessed, since they do not have the means to repay you; for you will be repaid at the resurrection of the righteous."[321]

Those in the Western world who are blessed with resources should

---

[320] NASB
[321] Luke 14:13-14, NASB

remember that the Biblical picture of sharing with the poor is a banquet, not a bread line.

CONCLUSION

The focus on progress in the sciences so prevalent in the western world should not distract us from the regression which is occurring is ministering to the disadvantaged. As Christians, our duty to care for the poor is mandatory. While management principles may force churches to designate specific ministry as "missions", "local outreach" or "poor and needy" ministries, the organizational conveniences should not distract us from the fact that care for the poor is meant to be integrated into every facet of a Christian's life. One cannot manifest the character of God without manifesting His concern for the poor, nor can this duty be delegated to para-church organizations or a separate portion of the church.

To effectively serve the poor, we must avoid the temptation to see them as a single group with a single cause. Rather we must examine the specific causes of the poverty that the person endures. We must also discover the personal emotional barriers that may prevent growth. Only then may we effectively begin our ministry to help transform them into fully devoted followers of Christ. The goal is to embrace the poor into the work of ministry, not to keep them the focus of our ministry.

CHAPTER 5

Cultural Relevance and the Church

CASE STUDY: SRI LANKA

W E begin by expressing deep appreciation for the work that was done by true missionaries who worked for the good of our people, missionaries who have a sincere motivation of saving the lost and building God's kingdom. Despite this appreciation, respect for improving the understanding of effective ministry compels an examination of their errors. This examination is done for the purpose of reaping a better harvest. The actions of the missionaries to Sri Lanka are instructive.

Early Western missionaries, based on their upbringing and world view, concluded Sri Lankan culture was evil and to be avoided. They considered the culture so dangerous that in 1711 they passed a law allowing punishment of any who participated, "Christians participating in the ceremonies of heathenism would be liable to a public whipping and imprisonment in irons for one year."[322]

This draconian measure forced a division between new indigenous converts and their culture and families. The converts, desiring modernization and identification with the colonial rulers, assimilated into the new culture. On the other hand, the Sinhala Buddhists resented the anglicized lifestyle of the Christians; their abandonment of the culture and the class opportunities gained as a result of conversion. As a

---

[322] Michael M. Ames, *Westernization or Modernization : the Case of the Sinhalese Buddhism.* Sage Journals online

result of the resentment the local community was fractured. This forced separation from indigenous culture was the result of three factors:

1. The missionaries steered Christians away from the local culture out of fear of creating a synchronistic religion; a religion that merged local culture at the expense of Biblical truth.
2. The missionaries were too indoctrinated by their own worldview to see any other models. Absent the ability to adapt, the missionaries concluded the local culture was evil rather then considering new approaches in keeping with local customs.
3. The modern scientific and technological advances of the west impressed the people in the third-world in the early nineteenth century. This prompted them to believe and ape an alien western culture.

As a result, evangelism in Sri Lanka was hindered by the division caused by the manner of its propagation. In addition, the attempt to evangelize by the whip left a lasting resentment, common it countries with a colonial history, that hinders the Christian church in Sri Lanka to this day. This resentment makes it imperative to incorporate local culture into current efforts.

PRESENT DAY BATTLES BETWEEN GOSPEL AND CULTURE

The attempt to use the local culture as a vehicle to communicate the Gospel to non-Christians has attracted two opposite reactions from the Christian community. One group has concluded that the attempt is a compromise and a betrayal of the trust that has been placed upon the church. They have further argued that this attempt would lead to syncretism. Hendricks Kraemer defines syncretism as "a systematic attempt to combine, blend and reconcile inharmonious, even often conflicting elements in a so-called synthesis."[323] The 1966 Wheaton Declaration defines syncretism as, "the attempt to unite or reconcile biblically revealed Christian truth with diverse or opposing tenets and

---

[323] 1966 Wheaton Declaration, pg 10, *Mission and Syncretism*

practices of non-Christian religions or other systems of thought that deny it." [324]

The other group has advocated the use of culture as an imperative for communicating the gospel. They conclude "truth cannot be communicated in a vacuum; it must be couched in a human culture if it is to be understood." When we avoid the use of local culture, it automatically results in using another cultural form to communicate. They conclude that we have avoided using the local culture because of the fear of syncretism, but have used a foreign culture and cultural forms to communicate truth. This camp argues that evangelism without cultural reference is incomprehensible. It is incomprehensible because truth has been couched in a cultural and thought form which is alien to the listener. In his book Discipling the Cities in Sri Lanka[325] Ranjith de Silva comments:

> The continual use of foreign forms of church services, evangelism, church architecture, and hymns 30 years after Sri Lanka received independence, has been a hindrance to the non-Christians from even considering the claims of Christ. The foreignness of the Christian message, its mode of presentation couched in the vernacular of western conceptual thought, has kept the non-Christian away from the church.[326]

To be relevant, argues the second group, we must contextualize. Contextualization is the effort to understand and take seriously the specific context of each human group on its own terms and in all its dimensions - cultural, religious, social, political, economic - and to discern what the Gospel says to people in that context. This requires a profound empirical analysis. Contextualization takes seriously the example of Jesus in the sensitive and careful way he offered each person a gospel tailored to his own context.[327] By adapting the message

---

[324] Charles H. Kraft, *Christianity in Culture* (Mary Knoll, NY; Orbis Books 1979), p.195.

[325] Ranjith de Silva, *Discipling the Cities of Sri Lanka* (Colombo, Sri Lanka, Calvary Church Media Department 1980)

[326] Ibid, at 88.

[327] Charles R. Tober, *Contextualization: indigenization and /or transformation in the Gospel and Islam*: a 1978 Compendium, ed. Don M. McCurry (Monrovia, CA: MARC, 1979), p.146.

to the cultural patterns and the worldview of the target audience, the communicator can effectively communicate the gospel.

Contextualisation is not the altering of the essential content of the Biblical message, but enclosing it in culturally relevant verbal and thought forms. We have no right to change the content of the Gospel - that would be a betrayal of our trust - but we have the obligation to fit the same content into culturally meaningful forms so that the message will be intelligible to the listeners. Milk can be delivered in a variety of containers. It may be in a tin can, a glass bottle, a cardboard carton, or a plastic bottle. The type of the container is not important, as long as the milk is pure. However, the purchaser may prefer one container over another. He may refuse to buy milk in a tin can, but be most willing to purchase it in a cardboard carton. In the same way, the Christian messenger has no right to water down the content of the gospel - it must be the truth - but we certainly must present it in such a form that will be meaningful to the listener.[328]

Since we are exploring how scripture interacts with culture we must define the word "culture". The Lausanne Committee for World Evangelization has offered the following definition.

> Culture is an integrated system of beliefs (about God or reality or the ultimate meaning); of values (about what is true, good, beautiful and normative); of customs (how to behave, relate to others, talk, pray, work, play, trade, farm, eat etc.) and institutions which express these beliefs, values and customs (government, law courts temples or churches, family, schools, hospitals, factories or churches, family, schools, hospitals, shops, unions, clubs etc.) which binds a society together and gives it a sense of identity dignity, security and continuity.[329]

In other words culture effects every aspect of human life. At the center of any culture is a world-view. Charles Kraft defines world-view as, "Perceptions of reality are patterned by societies into conceptualizations of what reality can or should be, and what is to be regarded as actual, probable, and impossible. The conceptualizations form what is termed

---

[328] J. T. Seamands. Tell it well: Communicating the Gospel across Cultures (Deacon Hill Press of Kansas City, 1981), p.130

[329] Lausanne Occasional Paper #2, The Willowbank Report: Consultation on Gospel and Culture.

the world-view of the culture."[330] The worldview, then, according to this model, is the central systematization of conceptions of reality to which the members of society assent and from which stems their value system. The world-view lies at the very heart of a culture, touching, interacting with and strongly influencing every other aspect of the culture. Each society looks at the world in its own way, and that way is encoded in its language and culture; no language is unbiased; no culture theologically neutral. To be successful we must understand and relate to the four main spiritual world views found in today's society: secular, animistic, pantheistic and theistic.

A *secular* worldview divides the world into natural and supernatural realms and focuses accepts only the natural realm. God either does not exist or does not care. To the secularist, a human is totally in control of his own future. An *animistic* person believes that distinct spiritual beings and bodiless spiritual forces have power over humans. They will seek to identify the particular spiritual force acting upon them to ward off its powers.

A *pantheistic* worldview maintains that some essence, sometimes called God, fills the universe. They may believe that essence can be reflected in many ways as representations of God. Pantheists believe that through meditation or other disciplines we can become one with that essence. A *theistic* world view holds that God created the universe and continues to care for His creation. Both Christians and Muslims would be considered theists. Each of these views affects how the gospel will be received.

In the process of ministry, we are involved directly or indirectly in human culture, but many still attempt to stay above the culture line and deal only with matters of the soul. This effort is hopeless, as is the effort of the social scientist who eliminates God from this world and tries to explain Christianity in cultural terms only.[331] The minister of the gospel cannot communicate without concerning himself with culture, because communication is inextricable from culture. Christ became flesh and dwelt among men. Propositional truth must have cultural incarnations to be meaningful.

---

[330] Charles H. Kraft, *Inter-cultural Communication and World-view Change* (Pasadena School of World Mission, 1976), p.1

[331] David J. Hesselgrave. Communicating Christ cross-culturally (Grand Rapid: Zondervan Publishing House. 1978), p. 80

BIBLICAL BASIS FOR CULTURE'S
IMPACT ON MINISTRY

No matter how sound our argument may be, it is still human thought, so it becomes imperative that we seek the scripture and let God's word guide our thinking. Let us review how God views His relationship with mankind and its culture. Genesis describes God as creating a mankind capable of governing the world.[332] We see God's tender care and love for the well-being of this masterpiece of his workmanship in creating the world before the creation of man, "He prepared everything for him, for his convenience, and pleasure, before he brought him into being; so that, comparing little with great things, the house was built; furnished, and amply stored, by the time the destined tenant was ready to occupy it." [333]

God created mankind, male and female, in his own likeness by giving them distinctive human faculties - rational, moral, social, creative and spiritual. He also told them to have children, to fill the earth and to subdue it.[334] These divine commands are the origin of human culture. Having established human culture, God revealed himself to Adam and Eve, to Cain and Abel, to Moses and Abraham. He used the common practices of the human world at that time to communicate. During early human civilization, agreement between two people or two groups was sealed with a covenant. God adopted this human culture to communicate his love for the people. By making a covenant with Abraham, God promised to bless His descendants and to make them His special people. Abraham, in return, was to remain faithful to God and to serve as a channel through which God's blessings could flow to the rest of the world.[335] Consider this verse, " Can a mother forget the baby at her breast and have no compassion on the child she has borne? Though she may forget, I will not forget you! See, I have engraved you on the palms of my hands; your walls are ever before me."[336]

---

[332] Genesis 1:26-31, NIV
[333] Adam Clarke Commentary
[334] Genesis 1:26-28
[335] Genesis 12:1-3
[336] Isaiah 49:15-16 (NIV)

Adam Clarke's Commentary describes the connection with culture at the time:

> This is certainly a reference to some practice common among the Jews at that time, of making marks on their hands or arms by punctures on the skin, with some sort of sign or representation of the city or temple, to show their affection and zeal for it. They had a method of making such punctures indelible by fire, or by staining. It is well known, that the pilgrims at the Holy Sepulcher get themselves marked in this manner with what are called the ensigns of Jerusalem, and this art is practiced by traveling Jews all over the world at this day.[337]

Later in the history of man, Jesus became a man to bear man's sins but also in order to relate to mankind. Philippians 2:5-8 states:

> Have this attitude in yourselves which was also in Christ Jesus who, although He existed in the form of God, did not regard equality with God a thing to be grasped, but emptied Himself, taking the form of a bond-servant, and being made in the likeness of men. Being found in appearance as a man, He humbled Himself by becoming obedient to the point of death, even death on a cross. [338]

When Jesus took on the form of a human being, He identified with mankind, entered human culture, and lived and ministered within human culture. Having lived among us, He commissioned us: Again Jesus said, "Peace be with you! As the Father has sent me, I am sending you."[339] This verse simply says: "as I was sent to proclaim the truth of the Most High, and to convert sinners to God, I send you for the very same purpose, clothed with the very same authority, and influenced by the very same Spirit."

Jesus ministered within the confines of a Jewish culture and worldview. A careful analysis of Jesus' ministry on earth reveals the depth of his willingness to identify with people, to understand their worldview and to communicate within a cultural context of his audience, "The disciples came to him and asked, "Why do you speak to the people in parables?" He replied, "The knowledge of the secrets of

---

[337] Adam Clarke Commentary
[338] NASB
[339] John 20:21(NIV)

the kingdom of heaven has been given to you, but not to them."[340] The range of Jesus' parables and teachings is a good guide to show how he carefully watched people and used his observations to make his teaching relevant. Jesus entered their frame of reference and communicated truth. Jesus used common and daily experiences of life to introduce them to the unknown love and grace of God. Tom Houston comments on the question about speaking in parables raised by the disciples in Matthew 13:10-11 and suggests that: "The disciples were learning that Jesus took different approaches to different audiences. His preaching was not an instrument with only one string."[341] If God did not enter the human culture and communicate within that context, conveying the message would have been nearly impossible.

The differences between the heavenly Kingdom and the earthy world are not subtle. Revelation chapter one verses nine through nineteen describes John on the island of Patmos. He has a vision of heaven, (this is outside human culture) and he tries to describe what he is seeing, so he employs the word "like" - it is like what we know, yet not the same. This would have been the level of communication possible, if God did not enter human culture and communicate truth within the human cultural context. John wrote:

> I, John, your brother and companion in the suffering and kingdom and patient endurance that are ours in Jesus, was on the island of Patmos because of the word of God and the testimony of Jesus. On the Lord's Day I was in the Spirit, and I heard behind me a loud voice like a trumpet, which said: "Write on a scroll what you see and send it to the seven churches: to Ephesus, Smyrna, Pergamum, Thyatira, Sardis, Philadelphia and Laodicea." I turned round to see the voice that was speaking to me. And when I turned I saw seven golden lamp stands, and among the lamp stands was someone "like a son of man", dressed in a robe reaching down to his feet and with a golden sash round his chest.

> His head and hair were white like wool, as white as snow, and his eyes were like blazing fire. His feet were like bronze glowing in a furnace, and his voice was like the sound of rushing waters. In his right hand

---

[340] Matthew 13:10-11 (NIV)
[341] Tom Houston, The Work Of An Evangelist, Ed. J. D. Douglas (Minnesota; Worldwide Publication, ed.), p.89.

he held seven stars, and out of his mouth came a sharp double-edged sword. His face was like the sun shining in all its brilliance. When I saw him, I fell at his feet as though dead. Then he placed his right hand on me and said: "Do not be afraid. I am the First and the Last. [342]

This language of heaven would be incomprehensible to a man unless put into a cultural context. The Apostle Paul took pains to identify with all people and meet them within their culture:

> For though I am free from all men, I have made myself a slave to all, so that I may win more. To the Jews I became as a Jew, so that I might win Jews; to those who are under the Law, as under the Law though not being myself under the Law, so that I might win those who are under the Law; to those who are without law, as without law, though not being without the law of God but under the law of Christ, so that I might win those who are without law. To the weak I became weak, that I might win the weak; I have become all things to all men, so that I may by all means save some. I do all things for the sake of the gospel, so that I may become a fellow partaker of it.[343]

The principle that Paul espoused was mobility in methods, not mobility in morals.[344] In discussing his self-sacrificing concern in verses nineteen through twenty-three, Paul mentions three groups of people; (1) to the Jews I became like a Jew, to win the Jews, (2) to the Gentiles, to those not having the law I became like one not having the law, (3) to the weak I became weak, to win the weak. The purpose of his identification with the people at this level is "so that by all possible means I might save some." In verses twenty-four through twenty-seven, Paul makes it clear he conducts himself in this manner to be effective:

> Do you not know that those who run in a race all run, but only one receives the prize? Run in such a way that you may win. Everyone who competes in the games exercises self-control in all things. They then do it to receive a perishable wreath, but we an imperishable. Therefore I run in such a way, as not without aim; I box in such a way, as not beating the air; but I discipline my body and make it my

---

[342] Revelation 1:9-19 (NIV)
[343] 1 Corinthians 9:19-22, NASB
[344] Wycliffe Commentary

slave, so that, after I have preached to others, I myself will not be disqualified.[345]

Paul identified with the culture of the people so that he could relate to them and communicate the gospel in understandable terms. There is more evidence of contextualization in the actions of the apostles; Peter's and Paul's sermons to the Jews and to the Gentiles, when carefully analyzed, highlight their sensitivity and willingness to work within the confines of the target audience.

Peter's Sermons to the Jews

Peter's sermon to the Jews [346] was addressed to an audience which had a strong understanding of God and the Old Testament. Peter, in his sermon, appeals to this knowledge and cites the Old Testament to reinforce his arguments:

> But Peter, taking his stand with the eleven, raised his voice and declared to them: "Men of Judea and all you who live in Jerusalem let this be known to you and give heed to my words. "For these men are not drunk, as you suppose, for it is only the third hour of the day; but this is what was spoken of through the prophet Joel: 'AND IT SHALL BE IN THE LAST DAYS,' God says, 'THAT I WILL POUR FORTH OF MY SPIRIT ON ALL MANKIND; AND YOUR SONS AND YOUR DAUGHTERS SHALL PROPHESY, AND YOUR YOUNG MEN SHALL SEE VISIONS, AND YOUR OLD MEN SHALL DREAM DREAMS; EVEN ON MY BONDSLAVES, BOTH MEN AND WOMEN, I WILL IN THOSE DAYS POUR FORTH OF MY SPIRIT And they shall prophesy. AND I WILL GRANT WONDERS IN THE SKY ABOVE AND SIGNS ON THE EARTH BELOW, BLOOD, AND FIRE, AND VAPOR OF SMOKE. 'The SUN WILL BE TURNED INTO DARKNESS AND THE MOON INTO BLOOD, BEFORE THE GREAT AND GLORIOUS DAY OF THE LORD SHALL COME. 'AND IT SHALL BE THAT EVERYONE WHO CALLS ON THE NAME OF THE LORD WILL BE SAVED.' [347]

[345] 1 Corinthians 9:24-27 NASB
[346] Acts 2:14-36
[347] Acts 2:14-21, NASB

Peter addresses the claims that the men were drunk by logical appeal to the customs and traditions of the Jews. On a festival day, such as Pentecost, a Jew would not break his fast until at least 10:00 a.m. So it was extremely unlikely that a group of men would be drunk at such an early hour. In verses six through twenty-one, Peter explains the phenomena taking place among the apostles as the fulfillment of Joel's prophecy. In Acts 2:28-32, Peter quotes from Psalms 16:8-11 and Psalms 110:1 in support of what he said about Jesus:

> Men of Israel, listen to these words: Jesus the Nazarene, a man attested to you by God with miracles and wonders and signs which God performed through Him in your midst, just as you yourselves know—this Man, delivered over by the predetermined plan and foreknowledge of God, you nailed to a cross by the hands of godless men and put Him to death. "But God raised Him up again, putting an end to the agony of death, since it was impossible for Him to be held in its power. For David says of Him, 'I SAW THE LORD ALWAYS IN MY PRESENCE; FOR HE IS AT MY RIGHT HAND, SO THAT I WILL NOT BE SHAKEN.' THEREFORE MY HEART WAS GLAD AND MY TONGUE EXULTED; MOREOVER MY FLESH ALSO WILL LIVE IN HOPE; BECAUSE YOU WILL NOT ABANDON MY SOUL TO HADES, NOR ALLOW YOUR HOLY ONE TO UNDERGO DECAY. You HAVE MADE KNOWN TO ME THE WAYS OF LIFE; YOU WILL MAKE ME FULL OF GLADNESS WITH YOUR PRESENCE.

> Brethren, I may confidently say to you regarding the patriarch David that he both died and was buried, and his tomb is with us to this day. "And so, because he was a prophet and knew that GOD HAD SWORN TO HIM WITH AN OATH TO SEAT one OF HIS DESCENDANTS ON HIS THRONE, he looked ahead and spoke of the resurrection of the Christ, that HE WAS NEITHER ABANDONED TO HADES, NOR DID His flesh SUFFER DECAY. "This Jesus God raised up again, to which we are all witnesses. Therefore having been exalted to the right hand of God, and having received from the Father the promise of the Holy Spirit, He has poured forth this which you both see and hear. "For it was not David who ascended into heaven, but he himself says: 'THE LORD SAID TO MY LORD, "SIT AT MY RIGHT HAND, Until I MAKE YOUR ENEMIES A FOOTSTOOL FOR YOUR FEET."' Therefore let all the house of Israel know for

certain that God has made Him both Lord and Christ—this Jesus whom you crucified.' [348]

Peter argues his point within the cultural context of the Jewish community and constantly refers to the Old Testament to support his arguments. The Jews were the chosen people who had God's revelation; hence, Peter uses that knowledge to communicate the gospel. He moves from the known to the unknown.

PETER'S SERMON TO THE GENTILES

In Acts chapter ten Peter addresses a different audience,[349] the Gentiles. This audience, even though knowing something about Jesus of Nazareth from living in Palestine, would require more details of Jesus' life and work than a Palestinian-Jewish audience would. To them Peter states:

Opening his mouth, Peter said: "I most certainly understand now that God is not one to show partiality, but in every nation the man who fears Him and does what is right is welcome to Him. "The word which He sent to the sons of Israel, preaching peace through Jesus Christ (He is Lord of all)—you yourselves know the thing which took place throughout all Judea, starting from Galilee, after the baptism which John proclaimed. "You know of Jesus of Nazareth, how God anointed Him with the Holy Spirit and with power, and how He went about doing good and healing all who were oppressed by the devil, for God was with Him. "We are witnesses of all the things He did both in the land of the Jews and in Jerusalem. They also put Him to death by hanging Him on a cross. "God raised Him up on the third day and granted that He become visible, not to all the people, but to witnesses who were chosen beforehand by God, that is, to us who ate and drank with Him after He arose from the dead. "And He ordered us to preach to the people, and solemnly to testify that this is the One who has been appointed by God as Judge of the living and the

---

[348] NASB
[349] Acts 10:34-48

dead. "Of Him all the prophets bear witness that through His name everyone who believes in Him receives forgiveness of sins."

While Peter was still speaking these words, the Holy Spirit fell upon all those who were listening to the message. All the circumcised believers who came with Peter were amazed, because the gift of the Holy Spirit had been poured out on the Gentiles also. For they were hearing them speaking with tongues and exalting God. Then Peter answered, "Surely no one can refuse the water for these to be baptized who have received the Holy Spirit just as we did, can he?" And he ordered them to be baptized in the name of Jesus Christ. Then they asked him to stay on for a few days.[350]

To this culture, Peter begins his sermon from John's baptism and continues to the resurrection of Jesus. Peter's more lengthy account of Jesus' ministry is appropriate to the Gentile audience and their more limited knowledge of Jesus' ministry.

PAUL'S MESSAGE TO THE JEWS

In Acts chapter thirteen,[351] Paul gives his message to the Jews:

Men of Israel, and you who fear God, listen: "The God of this people Israel chose our fathers and made the people great during their stay in the land of Egypt, and with an uplifted arm He led them out from it. "For a period of about forty years He put up with them in the wilderness. "When He had destroyed seven nations in the land of Canaan, He distributed their land as an inheritance—all of which took about four hundred and fifty years. "After these things He gave them judges until Samuel the prophet. "Then they asked for a king, and God gave them Saul the son of Kish, a man of the tribe of Benjamin, for forty years. "After He had removed him, He raised up David to be their king, concerning whom He also testified and said, 'I HAVE FOUND DAVID the son of Jesse, A MAN AFTER MY HEART, who will do all My will.' "From the descendants of this man, according to promise, God has brought to Israel a Savior, Jesus, after John had proclaimed before His coming a baptism of repentance to all the

---

[350] NASB
[351] Acts 13:16-27

people of Israel. "And while John was completing his course, he kept saying, 'What do you suppose that I am? I am not He. But behold, one is coming after me the sandals of whose feet I am not worthy to untie.'

Brethren, sons of Abraham's family, and those among you who fear God, to us the message of this salvation has been sent. "For those who live in Jerusalem, and their rulers, recognizing neither Him nor the utterances of the prophets which are read every Sabbath, fulfilled these by condemning Him. "And though they found no ground for putting Him to death, they asked Pilate that He be executed. "When they had carried out all that was written concerning Him, they took Him down from the cross and laid Him in a tomb. "But God raised Him from the dead; and for many days He appeared to those who came up with Him from Galilee to Jerusalem, the very ones who are now His witnesses to the people. "And we preach to you the good news of the promise made to the fathers, that God has fulfilled this promise to our children in that He raised up Jesus, as it is also written in the second Psalm, 'YOU ARE MY SON; TODAY I HAVE BEGOTTEN YOU.' "As for the fact that He raised Him up from the dead, no longer to return to decay, He has spoken in this way: 'I WILL GIVE YOU THE HOLY and SURE blessings OF DAVID.' "Therefore He also says in another Psalm, 'YOU WILL NOT ALLOW YOUR HOLY ONE TO UNDERGO DECAY.' "For David, after he had served the purpose of God in his own generation, fell asleep, and was laid among his fathers and underwent decay; but He whom God raised did not undergo decay. "Therefore let it be known to you, brethren, that through Him forgiveness of sins is proclaimed to you, and through Him everyone who believes is freed from all things, from which you could not be freed through the Law of Moses. "Therefore take heed, so that the thing spoken of in the Prophets may not come upon you.[352]

Paul's exhortation begins with a recitation of Israel's history that emphasizes the pattern of God's redemptive activity from Abraham to David. It is an approach in line with Jewish interests and practices. Highlighted in this recitation is a four-point confessional summary that, for the Jews, epitomized the essence of their faith: God is the God of the people of Israel, He chose the patriarchs for Himself, He redeemed

---

[352] Acts 13:16-41, NASB

His people from Egypt, leading them through the wilderness, and He gave them the land of Palestine as an inheritance. [353]

To such a confessional recital, Jews often added God's choice of David to be king and the promise made to him and his descendants. [354] Paul proclaims these great confessional truths of Israel's faith which speak of God's redemptive concern for his people and underline the Christian message.[355] Paul refers to the truths preciously held by the Jews and builds a bridge to communicate the gospel to the Jews. By anchoring Israel's *kerygma* (good news) in the Messianically relevant "Son" passage of 2 Samuel 7, Paul begins to build a textual bridge for the Christian *kerygma*; a *kerygma* which he will root in the Messianic "Son" passage of Psalms 2:7.[356] By drawing these two passages together, Israel's confession and the church's confession, he demonstrates both the continuity and the fulfillment of the passages. [357]

PAUL'S MESSAGE TO
THE GENTILES

Contrast the previous message with Paul's sermon to the Gentiles.[358] In his message in Athens, Paul begins, "… "Men of Athens, I observe that you are very religious in all respects. "For while I was passing through and examining the objects of your worship, I also found an altar with this inscription, 'TO AN UNKNOWN GOD.' Therefore what you worship in ignorance, this I proclaim to you."[359]

In verse twenty-two, Paul does not begin his address by referring to Jewish history or by quoting the Jewish scriptures as he did in the synagogue of Pisidian Antioch.[360] He knows that it would be futile to refer to a history no one knew or to argue from the fulfillment of a

---

[353] G.E. Wright, *God Who Acts* (London: SCM, 1952), p.76.
[354] Psalm 78:67-72; 89:3-4; 19:37
[355] Richard N. Longnecker, "Acts," The Expositor's Bible Commentary, ed. Frank E. Gaebelein (Grand Rapids, Michigan: Zondervan Corporation, 1981), p.425.
[356] "I will surely tell of the decree of the LORD: He said to Me, 'You are My Son, Today I have begotten You." NASB
[357] Longnecker, "Acts", Supra, p.475.
[358] Acts 17:21-31
[359] NASB
[360] Acts 13:16-41

prophecy no one was interested in. Neither would it help to quote from a book no one had read or accepted as authoritative. It would also be futile to develop his arguments about the God who gives rain and crops in their season and provides food for the stomach and joy for the heart, as he does in Acts 14:15-17. Instead, he looks for points of contact with the group he is addressing. After he sees the inscription, "To an unknown God" in the city, he uses these words to introduce his call to repentance. He continues:

> The God who made the world and all things in it, since He is Lord of heaven and earth, does not dwell in temples made with hands; nor is He served by human hands, as though He needed anything, since He Himself gives to all people life and breath and all things; and He made from one man every nation of mankind to live on all the face of the earth, having determined their appointed times and the boundaries of their habitation, that they would seek God, if perhaps they might grope for Him and find Him, though He is not far from each one of us; for in Him we live and move and exist, as even some of your own poets have said, 'For we also are His children. [361]

The substance of Paul's sermon concerns the nature of God and the responsibility of man to God. Contrary to all pantheistic and polytheistic notions, Paul says that God is the one who has created the world and everything in it and that He is also the Lord of heaven and earth. To put his message in context, Paul refers to Greek poets, borrowing from their works. Some of the words quoted by Paul are to be found verbatim in the works of Cleanthus, in whose "Hymn to Jupiter" the same words (Εκ σου γαρ γενος εσμεν) occur.[362] Furthermore, Paul, in verse twenty-eight, quoted from Epimenides' *Cretica* ("For in him we live and move and have our being") and Aratus' *Phaenomena* ("For we are also his offspring"). For the sake of establishing a connection, Paul used these pagan poets to make a point.[363] Paul finally reaches the climax of his argument by unfolding the divine message of redemption and calling for repentance. The present day church, like Paul, should custom the

---

[361] Acts 17:24-28
[362] Adam Clarke's, Commentary on the New Testament
[363] *Epimenides' Paradox: A Logical Discrepancy In Titus 1:12?*, From AP Press.org

truth of scripture to the culture being addressed, never diluting the word, but by making it more relevant, making it more vibrant.

CULTURE AND COMMUNICATION

The actions of Peter and Paul are fully in line with modern psychology and communication theory. Culture's effects on perception are well known to modern science. In their article *"Do cultural factors affect causal beliefs? Rational and magical thinking in Britain and Mexico,"* Eugene Subbotsky and Graciela Quintero[364] note the impact of culture in thinking:

> During recent decades, interest in the role that cultural factors play in determining the style of an individual's thinking has increased within cultural psychology and anthropology. One of the pioneering studies of the role of culture in the development of cognitive processes was conducted by Alexander Luria (Luria, 1931, 1971, 1976). In this study, cognitive processes of individuals living traditional ways of life in villages of Soviet Central Asia were examined and compared to similar cognitive processes in individuals incorporated in a more Western style of life and education, but living in the same cultural areas. These findings showed that the type of logical reasoning of the traditional people differed substantially from that of the individuals involved in the Western type of life. One specific feature that distinguished the 'traditional' type of thinking was that it was short on abstract reasoning and formal categorization. Instead, the traditional thinking was strongly embedded in concrete situations and realities of everyday life. [365]

In his book, Cross-Cultural Psychology, Paul Laugani[366] notes a few of the differences between the cognitive views of those in eastern culture contrasted with western culture. He describes differences in four core values: [367]

---

[364] British Journal of Psychology (2002), 93, 519–543
[365] Ibid.
[366] (Sage Publications, 2007)
[367] Ibid. pg 57

Western	Eastern
Individualism	Communalism (collectivism)
Cognitivism	Emotionalism
Free Will	Determinism
Materialism	

Laugani examines one of these core values in more detail in this table contrasting individualism with communalism[368]

Individualism	Communalism
Emphasis on personal responsibility and self achievement	Emphasis on collective responsibility and collective achievement
Identity achieved	Identity ascribed
Anxiety is related to the acquisition of identity	Anxiety may be related to the 'imposition' of a familial and caste-related identity.
Family life operates on a horizontal model	Family life runs on a hierarchical model
Emphasis on nuclear (and one-parent) families	Emphasis on extended families
Social behaviors "class related"	Social behaviors caste and religion-related
Pollution and purification seen in terms of hygiene	Pollution and purification seen in spiritual and caste-related terms.
Religion tends to be less important; secularism important	Religion plays a dominant role in everyday life.
Rituals, if any, tend to be secular	Religious rituals play a dominant role in day-to-day behaviors

This table illustrates *some* of the aspects of *one* of the core values.

---

[368] Ibid, pg 69

How can we claim to effectively share the gospel if we ignore these profound differences? They are not minor; they effect how a member of a culture perceives, how he measures information and opportunity. In short, these cultural factors determine their entire world view. This "worldview" is the essence of cultural influence:

> At [culture's] centre is a world-view, that is, a general understanding of the nature of the universe and of one's place in it. This may be "religious" (concerning God, or gods and spirits, and of our relation to them), or it may express a "secular" concept of reality, as in a Marxist society.
>
> From this basic world-view flow both standards of judgment or values (of what is good in the sense of desirable, of what is acceptable as in accordance with the general will of the community, and of the contraries) and standards of conduct (concerning relations between individuals, between the sexes and the generations, with the community and with those outside the community).[369]

Accepting Christ and living the life He requires involves the *transformation* of the inner person. That inner person, according to Viv Grigg

> :...is deeply molded by one's culture, a culture that may include values close to those of Christ, as well as others directly opposed to Him. The perception of which values need transformation, at which stage of Christian development, and how this can be accomplished requires a deep understanding of culture. [370]

Both the acceptance of Christ and the change that acceptance implies are deeply rooted in one's cultural and world view. To ignore these factors is a disservice to our ministry.

Communication theory also recognizes the importance of culture. The standard communication model recognizes four elements of communication; a source, a message, a channel and a receiver. However each of these elements has sub-elements which critically impact the

---

[369] Lausanne Occasional Paper #2, *The Willowbank Report: Consultation on Gospel and Culture*

[370] Grigg, Viv. 1990. *Companion to the Poor*. Monrovia, CA: MARC, pg. 63

success of the communication. Consider the following model from David Berlo:[371]

Berlo's Model of Communication

Source	Encodes →	Message	→	Channel	Decodes →	Receiver
communication skills		content		hearing		communication skills
attitudes		elements treatment structure		seeing		attitudes
knowledge		code		touching		knowledge
social system				smelling		social system
culture				tasting		culture

A Source encodes a message for a channel to a receiver who decodes the message: S-M-C-R Model.

Examine the source and receiver columns. Note how many of the factors listed are cultural or impacted by culture and social standing. One's attitude toward the source or receiver may be influenced by cultural standards. For example, a receiver may be disinclined to receive a message from a sender who he associates with past colonization, due to distrust. A sender may downgrade the information conveyed or the feedback received based on racial or ethnic stereotypes. One's culture and standing certainly affect one's knowledge, which is an encoding and decoding factor. These influences on the source and receiver are "noise" which degrades the message at both ends. These effects are compounded by the dynamic nature of communication.

---

[371] David K. Berlo, *The Process of Communication* (New York: Holt, Rinehart, and Winston, 1960)

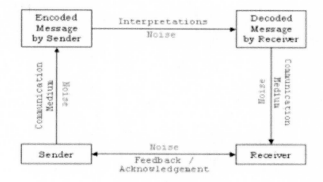

As this standard model shows, noise impacts both the original message and the feedback necessary to clarify it. As we can see, communication is a complex process. Truth does not travel in a vacuum but is impacted by the cultural encoding done by both the source and receiver, minds preprogrammed by their culture and world views. The table below illustrates this reality:

Culture A	Noise Factors	Culture B
	World View: Ways of perceiving the world	
Source	Cognitive Process: Ways of thinking	Message
Encoding	Linguistic Forms: Way of expressing ideas	Decoding
Message	Behavioral Patterns: Ways of acting	Response
Response	Social Structure: Ways of channeling the message	
	Motivational Resources: Ways of deciding	

When the source in Culture A encodes a message, that message passes through a cultural grid or screen, which largely determines the way in which that message will be decoded by the respondent in Culture

B. This grid or screen has several dimensions, which collectively influence the message and the way in which the respondent will decode the message[372] Communicating the gospel to the Buddhist community in Sri Lanka could be illustrated by the table below:

Culture A	Noise Factors	Culture B
	Buddhist Ascetic World View	
Christian	Sinhala Buddhist Culture	Message
Preaching	Sinhala Linguistic Forms	Decoded
Encodes	Sinhala Buddhist Behavioral Patterns	Buddhist
Message	Sinhala Buddhist Social Structure	Believe
	Media Motivational Resources	

The message communicated will be decoded from a perspective of the Buddhist worldview and culture. This is a major barrier in communicating the gospel to the Buddhist community. Let's consider just a few concrete examples. In Buddhism, the ultimate goal is *nirvana*, a state of enlightenment which can only be achieved by a human. Buddhists believe that upon death one is reborn into any of six realms. These include rebirth as a *deva*, an *asura*, a human being, an animal, a hungry ghost, or a being in *Naraka* (hell) according to the individual's karma. The hungry ghost (or *petra* realm), the *asura* realm and the *naraka* realm are supernatural realms

Those born into these worlds must be freed and return to human form to achieve *nirvana*. How could one preach the sovereignty and power of God to one who believes a god is lower than a man without taking this fact into consideration? What does the phrase "born again" convey to one who believes in reincarnation? Consider the Buddhist view of god:

> The Buddhist view is that gods may lead more comfortable lives and be addicted to all the sense pleasures, but in terms of wisdom might be inferior to humans. They are even represented as coming to

[372] Hesselgrave, pp. 98-100

receive instruction from monks and even lay persons. Later on with the Hindu revival and proliferation of God-cults the Buddhists were increasingly vocal against the pretensions of God and his retinue of lesser gods. Nargarjuna the Indian Buddhist philosopher of the 2nd century CE expressed a commonly shared Buddhist view when he wrote:

The gods are all eternal scoundrels Incapable of dissolving the suffering of impermanence.

Those who serve them and venerate them May even in this world sink into a sea of sorrow.

We know the gods are false and have no concrete being; Therefore the wise man believes them not The fate of the world depends on causes and conditions Therefore the wise man many not rely on gods.
373

Indeed, Buddhism has no place for God in the sense Christians use the word:

Buddhism is unique amongst the religions of the world because it does not have any place for God in its soteriology. Indeed most Asian religions (with the possible exception of some extremely devotional forms of Hinduism) are essentially non-theistic, in that God does not occupy the central place that is accorded to him in monotheistic religious traditions. But Buddhism goes beyond most of these other religions in that it is positively anti-theistic because the very notion of God conflicts with some principles which are fundamental to the Buddhist view of the world and the role of humans in it.[374]

Do we honestly feel we can ignore these world views and represent the gospel effectively? If communication is so complicated, how can we communicate effectively without taking the culture of our people into consideration? To effectively communicate consider culture and the following influences: the society's worldview, their understanding of the scriptures or their prejudice against them, their cognitive

[373] *The Buddhist Attitude to God*, By Dr V. A. Gunasekara
[374] Ibid.

knowledge, (Am I speaking the language they understand?), and their felt needs (Do I know their real needs?).

CONCLUSION

Most Asian countries which were colonized by foreign rulers have spent their post-independence years striving for a national identity. An integral part of the national identity is perceived as being anti-Christian. In Sri Lanka, for example, the Buddhist clergy is developing a term called the "Sinhala Buddhist" referring to the fact that if you are a Sinhalese, you also have to be a Buddhist. To become a Christian is to become a traitor, turning one's back on one's family, community and country. We cannot effectively increase our ministries unless we take culture into account. Indeed, the derivation of the word "culture" itself suggests a close relationship with growth. Etymologically, it comes from the Latin verb *colere*, which refers literally to *agriculture*, tilling the ground in order to grow things. Ralph Winter and Bruce Koch's comment confirm this etymological relationship:

> The church does not really grow within peoples where relevant churches do not exist. While there are tens of millions who have never heard the name of Jesus at all there are hundreds of millions who may have heard of Jesus and may even have high regard for him, but who cannot see a way of becoming his disciples. Standing before them are barriers ranging from the relatively trivial to the seemingly insurmountable, many of them beyond the demands of the gospel. [375]

There is no magic formula that will universally make the church relevant to the local culture. Paul G. Hiebert in his book, Anthropological Insights for Missions[376,] provides a guideline for responsible contextualization:

1. The Bible is the final and definite authority for Christian belief

---

[375] *Mission Frontiers Magazine*, June 2000
[376] Paul A. Hiebert, *Anthropological Insights for Missionaries* (Michigan : Baker Book House, 1985)

and practices. Everyone therefore must begin at the same place.

2. The priesthood of all believers is accepted as scriptural teaching. The priesthood of believers assumes that all the faithful have the Holy Spirit to guide them in the understanding and application of the scripture to their own lives.

3. The contextualization of the Gospel is ultimately not the task of individuals or individual leaders, but of the church as a discerning community; "within that community, individuals contribute with their gifts and abilities".[377]

Within these reasonable confines are several areas that should be considered. To become relevant, we should rethink our worship, ceremonies and Christian celebrations. In this effort we should consider using more indigenous forms of music, develop culturally relevant forms of worship, and rethink and develop culturally relevant forms of celebrating Christmas, Easter and other important occasions. We should also develop architectural models in keeping with the local culture and take advantage of the community life and use it as a means for evangelism. We need to discover and develop indigenous public preaching styles and incorporate local art forms of communication. We need to become involved in community life, adopting an incarnational approach to ministry and a holistic approach to ministry[378] to relate better in poorer areas.

Our teaching methods must be tailored, and our life style must fit in with those of the community. In consultation with others, we should develop a relevant national and local theology and develop relevant models to train leaders and leadership styles. In summary, we must embrace and celebrate healthy, wholesome cultural practices within the local community that are not in conflict with biblical teaching.

Culturally dislocated models or western models might work in cosmopolitan areas where there are western influences, but if the church is to impact a country, culturally relevant models are essential. There are, of course, truths that are central to the Gospel, which may not be altered in any manner. These "super-cultural' core truths must be preserved. Despite this imperative, in all other matters, we must strive

---

[377] Ibid, pg. 53.
[378] See Chapter 2

to be effective. To be effective we must, following the examples of Peter and Paul, become relevant to the community.

CHAPTER 6

Partnership

THE CALL TO PARTNERSHIP

But speaking the truth in love, we are to grow up in all aspects into
Him who is the head, even Christ, from whom the whole body, being
fitted and held together by what every joint supplies, according to the
proper working of each individual part, causes the growth of the body
for the building up of itself in love.[379]

IN Ephesians, Paul writes that Christ gave gifts to the church "to
prepare God's people for works of service so that the body of
Christ may be build up, until we all reach unity in the faith and in
the knowledge of the Son of God and become mature, attaining to the
whole measure of the fullness of Christ."[380] We are gifted specifically
to improve each other to accomplish God's plan, "From him the whole
body, joined and held together by every supporting ligament, grows and
builds itself up in love, as each part does its work."[381] Any barrier that
prevents the combination of God's gifts and resources is a barrier to the
accomplishment of God's plan. In short, we are called to partner.

As followers of God, we are His partners in the accomplishment
of His mission. We are to heal the sick, feed the hungry, set the
captives free, make disciples of all nations and in doing so, proclaim
the Kingdom's presence.[382] Jesus did not abandon us to the effort. He

---

[379] Ephesians 4:15-16, NASD
[380] Ephesians 4:12-13
[381] Ephesians 4:16
[382] Isaiah 61:1-3, Luke 4:18-19, Matthew 28:19-20

provided His Spirit[383] to guide us, comfort us and provided us with the tools necessary for the job. He has also provided millions of potential collaborators; the unreached people of the earth. We are to find them and empower them to join us in the work.

Missionary Frampton Fox reminds us that "the greatest scriptural precedent for formal partnership in ministry is God's own model of how he did ministry throughout biblical history."[384] God partnered with Adam in the care of the created world.[385] To end its evil deviation from His purposes he partnered with Noah.[386] Moses was His partner in freeing His people from Pharaoh's hand.[387] He spoke to Israel through His prophets and built His church through common fishermen and workers. God needed no help from mankind but still, "in His wisdom chooses to somehow limit himself to work in, through, and in spite of men as agents tainted by the fall." [388]

Paul reminds us over and over again throughout scripture that we, the Church of Jesus Christ, as the body of Christ, are like a human body with its varying parts each with its own responsibility to help the whole body carry out its function. The parts are interdependent of one another, each given a specific task "for the common good"[389] of whole body. If a part of the body fails, the body is diminished. In fact, the story of Paul's ministry is a story of Christian partnership. Paul entered into several different partnerships: the mutual agreement reached at the Jerusalem Conference; the special relationship with Philemon and Onesimus, transcending the slave-master barrier, and the partnership with the church at Philippi by which they agreed to contribute financially and share otherwise in Paul's evangelistic and church-building efforts.[390]

In Gethsemane Jesus prayed for the unity of his disciples and for the unity of those who would believe their testimony, "that all of them may be one, Father, just as you are in me and I am in you. May they

---

[383] Matthew 28:21, Acts 1:8, John 14:12

[384] 2001, Fox "Partnership: More than a Buzzword." Evangelical Missions Quarterly. 294-304

[385] Genesis 2

[386] Genesis 7

[387] Exodus 4-14

[388] Fox, Ibid, at 300

[389] 1 Corinthians 12:7, 1 Corinthians 12:12

390 See Sampley, Paul: Pauline Partnership in Christ: Christian Community and Commitment in Light of Roman Law, Philadelphia, Fortress, 1980.

also be in us so that the world may believe that you have sent me?"[391] There is perfect clarity in the Bible's instruction for believers to cooperate to achieve God's mission, in another words to partner. Let us review a few of the many verses in support of this principle, "Only conduct yourselves in a manner worthy of the gospel of Christ, so that whether I come and see you or remain absent, I will hear of you that you are standing firm in one spirit, with one mind striving together for the faith of the gospel"[392]

John expresses the same thought:

I do not ask on behalf of these alone, but for those also who believe in Me through their word; that they may all be one; even as You, Father, are in Me and I in You, that they also may be in Us, so that the world may believe that You sent Me. "The glory which You have given Me I have given to them, that they may be one, just as We are one; I in them and You in Me, that they may be perfected in unity, so that the world may know that You sent Me, and loved them, even as You have loved Me [393]

Not only are we called to be unified in our actions and purpose, we are required to be diligent in guarding our unity:

Therefore I, the prisoner of the Lord, implore you to walk in a manner worthy of the calling with which you have been called, with all humility and gentleness, with patience, showing tolerance for one another in love, being diligent to preserve the unity of the Spirit in the bond of peace. There is one body and one Spirit, just as also you were called in one hope of your calling; one Lord, one faith, one baptism, one God and Father of all who is over all and through all and in all.[394]

We are called to this unity to show the love of Christ,[395] to share

---

[391] John 17:20-21
[392] Philippians 1:27, NASB
[393] John 17:21-23, NASB
[394] Ephesians 4:1-5 NASB
[395] John 13:35 NASB

of various gifts,[396] for protection against evil[397] and to encourage each other.[398] Our unity is for a purpose as Paul made clear when he exhorted the Philippians to "contend as one person for the faith of the gospel." [399] By doing this we share the rich harvest of the gifts God dispersed among His followers.

In addition to the Bible's support for partnership there is an equally compelling practical rationale. World globalization has created an awareness of the needs of our brothers and sisters in the third world and a realization of the effort needed to meet those needs. The International Monetary Fund defines globalization as "the growing economic interdependence of countries worldwide through increasing volume and variety of cross-border transactions in goods and services, free international capital flows, and more rapid and widespread diffusion of technology." This interdependence crosses cultural barriers as, "Cultures, economies, and politics appear to merge across the globe through the rapid exchange of information, ideas, and knowledge, and the investment strategies of global corporations."[400]

We see corporations working worldwide, not allowing artificial borders to inhibit their business objectives. We witness companies gain advantage through association with companies in other markets. Should we be less concerned about meeting our objectives than business? Failure to partner leads to poor service and as a result, a poor witness. Stan Guthrie gives this example:

> Not long ago at a city pack in a Central American nation, missionary Patrick McDonald spotted a group of 30 street children. He was heartened to see a group of Christians begin ministering to the kids. Then, as he watched, another group of Christians arrived, then another, all within half an hour. All were targeting the same 30 kids.
>
> Another time McDonald discovered that five soup kitchens in one city in South America were providing food to poor children. However, all

---

[396] Ephesians 4:11-13, NASB
[397] John 17:11-32
[398] Hebrews 10:24
[399] Philippians 1:27
[400] David Held, et al., in A Globalizing World? Culture, Economics, and Politics

five ministries offered food only on Mondays. None was available for the rest of the week. [401]

This lack of efficiency exposes our witness to ridicule. We need to ask our selves, where is God working in the world and then look for ways to be effective in serving Him in those areas. Just as corporations form cooperatives in pursuit of higher gain, each believer is part of the Church body, each association of believers, or church, is also a part of the body. When the churches fail to work together, the body is again diminished. Paul again, "the eye cannot say to the hand, 'I don't need you!' And the head cannot say to the feet, 'I don't need you!'"[402] How then can we, through failing to act, contend that we don't need the churches across the world from us? How can we assume a dominant position is our dealing with them? God created us in partnership and for partnership. We must always strive to work together.

DEFINING PARTNERSHIP

George Peters states that partnership among churches means equals are bound together in mutual confidence, unified purpose, and united effort. They accept equal responsibilities, authority, praise, and blame; they share burdens, joys, sorrows, victories, and defeats. Partnership means joint planning, joint legislation, and joint programming.[403] Peters continues, "Partnership is a relationship rooted in the mission's identification with the churches on the deepest levels of fellowship in the Spirit, and in mutual burdens, interests, purposes, and goals."[404]

One example of partnership is shown in the relationship between Paul and the believers in Philippi. The church in Philippi had been started by Paul who then moved on to spread the word of the Lord. Later he was imprisoned in Rome, but despite his absence, his friends in Philippi did not forsake him. They provided for him in his journeys and, learning of his imprisonment sent an additional gift brought by

---

[401] Guthrie, Stan, Missions in the Third Millennium, pg. 117
[402] 1 Corinthians 12:21
[403] Peters 1997:51
[404] Ibid, at 52

Epaphroditus. Paul was touched and sustained by their partnership with him:

> Paul and Timothy, bond-servants of Christ Jesus, To all the saints in Christ Jesus who are in Philippi, including the overseers and deacons: Grace to you and peace from God our Father and the Lord Jesus Christ. I thank my God in all my remembrance of you, always offering prayer with joy in my every prayer for you all, in view of your participation in the gospel from the first day until now. For I am confident of this very thing, that He who began a good work in you will perfect it until the day of Christ Jesus. For it is only right for me to feel this way about you all, because I have you in my heart, since both in my imprisonment and in the defense and confirmation of the gospel, you all are partakers of grace with me. For God is my witness, how I long for you all with the affection of Christ Jesus. And this I pray, that your love may abound still more and more in real knowledge and all discernment, so that you may approve the things that are excellent, in order to be sincere and blameless until the day of Christ; having been filled with the fruit of righteousness which comes through Jesus Christ, to the glory and praise of God.[405]

The essence of partnership is mutual support and sacrifice. We provide support in many ways. We are to love one another,[406] pray for one another,[407] share in each other's troubles,[408] provide for each other's needs,[409] provide hospitality,[410] fellowship and learn together,[411] and encourage one another.[412] In the early church, new converts were immediately brought into the church "partnership." In Acts 2:37-42, the word translated "fellowship" in verse forty-two may also be translated as "partnership". In short, we are to cooperate in every way that might strengthen each other and advance the Kingdom. Ecclesiastes 4:9-12 describes it in this way:

---

[405] Philippians 1:1-11
[406] John 13:34
[407] Acts 12:5
[408] Philippians 4:14-19
[409] Ibid
[410] Acts 16:13-15
[411] Acts 2:42-47
[412] Acts 11:23

Two are better than one because they have a good return for their labor. For if either of them falls, the one will lift up his companion. But woe to the one who falls when there is not another to lift him up. Furthermore, if two lie down together they keep warm, but how can one be warm alone? And if one can overpower him who is alone, two can resist him. A cord of three strands is not quickly torn apart.[413]

Often we will not even realize the manner in which we may aide each other until God reveals it to us. Elijah, a prophet of God, confronts Ahad, the king of Israel, who provoked the anger of the Lord more than all the kings of Israel before him.[414] Ahad's wife Jezebel worshipped Baal. Although a prophet, Elijah needed support. Elijah needed to be affirmed, empowered and encouraged. The apparent power was with the king but spiritually Ahad was lacking, God was angry with him.

Due to the lack of rain, Elijah was in a desperate situation. He lived by the Wadi Cher'ith, until it dried up. God then sent him to Sidon where the Lord had the widow of Zarephath provide for him. She had little to offer, some water, a handful of meal and a jug of oil that was almost empty. In fact, when Elijah arrived, the widow and her son were helpless and almost starving to death. [415] Two desperate people but God used them together. Elijah knew the Lord was with him and empowered the widow, asking her to trust him and serve him the little food remaining. He assured her God would provide:

> Then Elijah said to her, "Do not fear; go, do as you have said, but make me a little bread cake from it first and bring it out to me, and afterward you may make one for yourself and for your son. 'For thus says the Lord God of Israel, 'The bowl of flour shall not be exhausted, nor shall the jar of oil be empty, until the day that the Lord sends rain on the face of the earth.'[416]

Supported by her faith in Elijah's word and her trust in him the widow gave her remaining pittance to him. Her faith was rewarded, "So she went and did according to the word of Elijah, and she and he and

---

[413] NASB
[414] 1 Kings 16.33
[415] 1 Kings 17:8-12
[416] 1 Kings 17:13-14

her household ate for many days. The bowl of flour was not exhausted nor did the jar of oil become empty, according to the word of the Lord which He spoke through Elijah."[417] Elijah now had been sustained through the faith of the widow. When her son died, empowered by her hospitality, Elijah prayed that the son's life be restored:

> So she said to Elijah, "What do I have to do with you, O man of God? You have come to me to bring my iniquity to remembrance and to put my son to death!"He said to her, "Give me your son." Then he took him from her bosom and carried him up to the upper room where he was living, and laid him on his own bed. He called to the Lord and said, "O Lord my God, have You also brought calamity to the widow with whom I am staying, by causing her son to die?" Then he stretched himself upon the child three times, and called to the Lord and said, "O Lord my God, I pray You, let this child's life return to him." The Lord heard the voice of Elijah, and the life of the child returned to him and he revived. Elijah took the child and brought him down from the upper room into the house and gave him to his mother; and Elijah said, "See, your son is alive." Then the woman said to Elijah, "Now I know that you are a man of God and that the word of the LORD in your mouth is truth."[418]

Two persons, without apparent means, were in fact, by the grace of God, exactly what each other needed. Each provided a lesson in faith for the other. This experience helped prepare Elijah for his confrontation with the king. Ahad had been searching for Elijah for years, but the prophet now readily revealed himself. He had the King bring four hundred and fifty prophets of Baal. Elijah and the prophets of Baal each built an alter for a burnt offering of a slaughtered oxen. Each prayed to their God to provide the fire. After a full day of entreating by those of Baal, nothing happened. Elijah had the offering on his alter soaked with water several times, yet when he prayed to God, He provided the fire needed. Elijah had been fortified by his experience of witnessing how God supported his children by having each empower the other.

Although we do not know how God will call us to partner and what gifts he will ask us to use, we know he calls us to partner. We should seek opportunities to do so. After the 2004 Tsunami, I was at the site of

---

[417] 1 Kings 17:15-16
[418] 1 Kings 17:18-24

the destruction of the Semandra Devi, a train swept away by the waters, killing thirteen hundred Sri Lankans aboard. A makeshift hospital had been erected nearby. There I met a wonderful woman from Canada. She was teaching English in the shade of a tattered cloth roof. I asked her how long she had been in Sri Lanka. She said she came as soon as she heard of the disaster. I asked what made her come and why she had decided to teach English. She answered, "When I heard, I knew I wanted to help. Teaching English was all I knew that could help. It was the only gift I had to give." How noble and Godly a thought. She did not worry about the impact of her talents; she offered them to the Lord in partnership with others and trusted Him for the results.

BARRIERS TO PARTNERSHIP

Culture and Communication

I once arranged a meeting between a pastor from across the world and the mission leaders of a church with whom he worked. I anticipated how much the church could learn to benefit their staff, volunteers and to effectively coordinate the ministry. I was shocked to find that the meeting lasted fifty minutes during which time the pastor accepted a series of calls on his cell phone. Because of this, a key opportunity to learn from each other and promote the partnership was lost, due to the failure to take the time to listen.

In addition to learning to listen, we must learn to listen well. As detailed in our chapter on cultural relevance, the worldview and culture of each participant in a conversation has a dramatic impact on perception. If a partnership is to work, each member must take the time to learn what is culturally appropriate in the other member's context. We may have to alter our manner of dress or speaking or our methods of evangelizing so as not to create artificial barriers that prevent full understanding. What is appropriate or effective in one culture may not be in another culture.

We have all heard stories about a language or cultural mistake having unintended consequences. We will review a few to keep the danger in mind. In John F. Kennedy's June 26, 1963 speech in West Berlin, he chose to show his support by saying, "*Ich bin ein Berliner,*" which he thought meant, "I am a Berliner." Unfortunately, Germans do not use an article (ein) before a statement of residence or citizenship. What Kennedy really said was, "I am a jelly donut." The gracious German crowd forgave the error, took the intent and applauded wildly. The rest of us, however, should not expect the grace given to world leaders.

Problems with language are common in the business world as well. Pepsico advertised Pepsi in Taiwan with the advertisement, "Come Alive with Pepsi." It was translated into Chinese as "Pepsi brings your ancestors back from the dead." Pepsi, though an aggressive marketer, was not prepared to stand behind that claim. One last language story because it is my favorite. A woman, who traveled to Japan for a ministry opportunity, valiantly learned some Japanese to honor the culture. After checking into her room, she noticed that the bureau of drawers provided to store her clothes had a terrible odor. She went down to the front desk to see if the hotel could fix the problem. Unfortunately the word in Japanese for "bureau" is similar to the Japanese word for "bottom" meaning the rear end of a person. She thought she told the clerk that her bureau smelled, but used the other word. The deeply embarrassed clerk blushingly gave her directions to a nearby pharmacist.

Other problems are caused by misunderstanding the culture rather than the language. An American manager in Hong Kong tried to control employees' promptness at work. He insisted they come to work on time instead of fifteen minutes late, as was the custom. They complied, but then left exactly on time instead of working into the evening, as was their previous practice. The workload of the office dropped dramatically. Culture and language differences create a gulf that we must cross to partner effectively.

Remember God sent His Son to earth so that He could reach through the gulf that separated God and man.[419] Philippians 2:5-11 says:

> Have this attitude in yourselves which was also in Christ Jesus, who, although He existed in the form of God, did not regard equality with God a thing to be grasped, but emptied Himself, taking the form of a bond-servant, and being made in the likeness of men. Being found in appearance as a man, He humbled Himself by becoming obedient

---

[419] John 1:14

to the point of death, even death on a cross. For this reason also, God highly exalted Him, and bestowed on Him the name which is above every name, so that at the name of Jesus EVERY KNEE WILL BOW, of those who are in heaven and on earth and under the earth, and that every tongue will confess that Jesus Christ is Lord, to the glory of God the Father"[420]

We must accustom ourselves to effectively serve. This obligation includes taking the time to understand the culture of the Christian brothers and sisters with whom we serve and taking the time to communicate effectively.

According to Dr. Charles Kraft of Fuller Theological Seminary's School of World Mission, the scriptures provide us with an outline of God's communication goals and strategy. According to Kraft, God seeks a relationship with us, He wants us to respond to Him, and He wants us to understand him.[421] God follows three principles. First, He models love by taking whatever action is necessary so that we understand Him. Second, He forms a personal relationship with those He wants to listen. The most compelling instance God's desire to form a relationship came through the incarnation of his Son, Jesus Christ, in the form of a man, in order to relate to mankind. Third, God communicates His message with impact. God creates the impact by (1) developing credibility with His audience, (2) living His message, (3) specifically dealing with people's needs, (4) leading His listeners to discover the message, and (5) trusting His listener to respond appropriately.[422] Our own communication should use this approach.

The more involved we are with our partners, the more known, the more trusted, the less "noise" there is in our message. Think of how easily we grasp nuances from family members. Moreover our ability to communicate effectively is not solely defined by the spoken word, but rather depends on past history and expectations of the future. The more there is mutual understanding between the parties, the better the communication. Each person holds his own meaning of a word or phrase used by the other. Often we assume others hear things precisely

---

[420] NASB

[421] Kraft, Charles H., 1991, *Communication Theory for Christian Witness*. 2nd ed. Maryknoll, NY: Orbis Books.

[422] Ibid at 15-18

how we meant them to be heard. We must guard against this dangerous and false assumption.

We must also understand that what we say almost never stops with the person spoken to; instead it may be passed to others and altered with each such additional telling. Do we take this into account when speaking? Also, how we say things is effected by those who have influence over us. A thought may be communicated in one manner when alone, another in the presence of one's boss. Finally, our non verbal signals effect how our message is received, and in some cases the same physical appearance may have a different message in two cultures. The circled finger and thumb that means "OK" in the west is an obscene gesture in much of the world. Body language, gestures and facial expressions may also have different meanings in different parts of the world. These complexities are mediated by time, relationship and by keeping then in mind when setting a communication strategy.

Christian partnership is not a catch phrase; it is a necessary component of succeeding in the accomplishment of God's mission for his church. It involves time and effort. It involves making the goals of your partner as important as your own and taking the time to communicate in an effective and culturally appropriate manner.

Self Focus

In working together to achieve that mission we are warned not to let our own fallen nature or worldly measurements interfere, "Do nothing from selfishness or empty conceit, but with humility of mind regard one another as more important than yourselves; do not merely look out for your own personal interests, but also for the interests of others."[423] Christ is well aware of our human capacity to insert our failings into His mission. He knows we will take pride in the size of our church, its "relevance", its "truer beliefs" and other creations of human pride to separate us from others.[424] These human failings interfere with the peace of the cross and God's desires for His believers.[425]

We must avoid this trap in order to accomplish the many duties

---

[423] Philippians 2:3-4, NASB
[424] See e.g. Romans 14:1-15:2
[425] Ephesians 2:14-16

assigned to us. As Christians we are called to advance the gospel through evangelism,[426] defend it,[427] and if need be, suffer for it.[428] We are called to do these things together in partnership with other believers.[429] We not only serve together but are called to motivate each other for good works. We are even asked to think about how to stimulate the work of others, "And let us consider how to stimulate one another to love and good deeds, not forsaking our own assembling together, as is the habit of some, but encouraging one another; and all the more as you see the day drawing near."[430]

We, as Christians, are given great license to celebrate our individual gifts and apply our distinct resources for the Lord's work. We are not free however, to let these differences separate us from each other as we strive to accomplish His mission.[431] Often these differences come from a poor understanding of the local and universal church.

Our modern denominations may lead us to apply distinctions in a way that separate us. This separation may be done in the name of preserving and glorifying the "local church." We should examine the Biblical concept of a "church."[432] The word translated as church in the New Testament is from the Greek *ekklsia* meaning assembly. It is used in two senses, the universal church and the local church. The universal church is described in Mark 16:18-19:

> I also say to you that you are Peter, and upon this rock I will build My church; and the gates of Hades will not overpower it. "I will give you the keys of the kingdom of heaven; and whatever you bind on earth shall have been bound in heaven, and whatever you loose on earth shall have been loosed in heaven." [433]

And in Hebrews 12:22-24:

> But you have come to Mount Zion and to the city of the living God, the heavenly Jerusalem, and to myriads of angels, to the general assembly

---

[426] Philippians 1:4,12
[427] Philippians 1:7,16
[428] Philippians 1:28-30; cf. 2 Timothy 1:8, 2:9
[429] Philippians 1:5
[430] Hebrews 10:24-25
[431] 1 Corinthians 12:14-26
[432] For further discussion see Chapter Eleven
[433] NASB

and church of the firstborn who are enrolled in heaven, and to God, the Judge of all, and to the spirits of the righteous made perfect, and to Jesus, the mediator of a new covenant, and to the sprinkled blood, which speaks better than the blood of Abel.[434]

The local church refers to the body of believers in one geographical area such as the church at Corinth[435] or the church of the Thessalonians.[436] Paul was speaking of the local church in Romans 16:16, "Greet one another with a holy kiss. All the churches of Christ greet you..." and in Galatians 1:2. Failure to understand the nature of the universal and local church can have profound consequences for ministry. Let us quickly review some basic concepts. First and most important, there is but one church, "There is one body and one Spirit, just as also you were called in one hope of your calling; one Lord, one faith, one baptism, one God and Father of all who is over all and through all and in all." [437]

The membership of the universal church is the saved, living and dead:

But you have come to Mount Zion and to the city of the living God, the heavenly Jerusalem, and to myriads of angels, to the general assembly and church of the firstborn who are enrolled in heaven, and to God, the Judge of all, and to the spirits of the righteous made perfect, and to Jesus, the mediator of a new covenant, and to the sprinkled blood, which speaks better than the blood of Abel. [438]

The universal church was born with the resurrection and ascension of Christ.[439] Peter later refers to this time described in Acts as "the beginning".[440] Only the Lord keeps the membership of the universal church[441] and since there is only "one body",[442] the universal church

---

[434] NASB
[435] 1 Corinthians 1:2
[436] 1 Thessalonians 1:1
[437] Ephesians 4:4-6
[438] Hebrews 12:22-24
[439] Acts 2:1-47
[440] Acts 11:15
[441] 2 Timothy 2:19
[442] Ephesians 4:4

cannot be divided. Although the universal church has structure, that structure is not temporal:

> So then you are no longer strangers and aliens, but you are fellow citizens with the saints, and are of God's household, having been built on the foundation of the apostles and prophets, Christ Jesus Himself being the corner stone, in whom the whole building, being fitted together, is growing into a holy temple in the Lord, in whom you also are being built together into a dwelling of God in the Spirit. [443]

Not even death effects one's membership in the universal church.[444]

The local church is a natural reflection of the universal church in a particular area. As people respond to the Word, people respond and gather to share their gifts, to support and encourage each other. A local church is formed by the agreement of believers to work together. Local churches are formed at different times and in different ways as described in Acts 11:19-26:

> So then those who were scattered because of the persecution that occurred in connection with Stephen made their way to Phoenicia and Cyprus and Antioch, speaking the word to no one except to Jews alone. But there were some of them, men of Cyprus and Cyrene, who came to Antioch and began speaking to the Greeks also, preaching the Lord Jesus. And the hand of the Lord was with them, and a large number who believed turned to the Lord. The news about them reached the ears of the church at Jerusalem, and they sent Barnabas off to Antioch. Then when he arrived and witnessed the grace of God, he rejoiced and began to encourage them all with resolute heart to remain true to the Lord; for he was a good man, and full of the Holy Spirit and of faith. And considerable numbers were brought to the Lord. And he left for Tarsus to look for Saul; and when he had found him, he brought him to Antioch. And for an entire year they met with the church and taught considerable numbers; and the disciples were first called Christians in Antioch.[445]

---

[443] Ephesians 2:19-22, NASB see also I Peter 2:5
[444] Philippians 1:21-23, 1 Thessalonians 5:10
[445] NASB

Membership is within the purview of the local church leadership[446] and sometimes the decision to admit someone as a member is not made wisely.[447] A local church, unlike the universal church, could have nominal or unsaved members.[448] There are other distinctions but there is no need to belabor them. The key point to remember is that there is no Biblical identification of or support for a particular denomination. Confusing a particular denomination with the local church can lead to division within the one body of the universal church. Such was the case with the church in Corinth:

> Now I exhort you, brethren, by the name of our Lord Jesus Christ, that you all agree and that there be no divisions among you, but that you be made complete in the same mind and in the same judgment. For I have been informed concerning you, my brethren, by Chloe's people, that there are quarrels among you. Now I mean this, that each one of you is saying, "I am of Paul," and "I of Apollos," and "I of Cephas," and "I of Christ." Has Christ been divided? [449]

Thinking of the Church as an Institution

The failure to distinguish between the local church and a local denomination was recently driven home. A pastor I met at a missions conference recently stated he did not respect para-church organizations because they did not bring glory to "the local church." The organization under discussion was formed and maintained by local Christians and supported local churches in the third world. Upon examination, it became clear that his concern was this organization did not bring glory to *his* church. This is a misunderstanding of scripture. In 1 Corinthians, Paul wrote, "Is not the cup of blessing which we bless a sharing in the blood of Christ? Is not the bread which we break a sharing in the body of Christ? Since there is one bread, we who are many are one body; for we all partake of the one bread." [450]

---

[446] Acts 9:26-28

[447] 3 John 5-9

[448] Revelations 3:1-4

[449] 1 Corinthians 1:10-13, NASB

[450] 1 Corinthians 10:16-17, NASB

The sort of error described above will limit the effectiveness of partnership within the universal church and division among the local churches. There is one Lord, one church with many local manifestations. The local church has one commission, one Holy Scripture. Whatever divides us keeps us from our God mandated duties, and may not be embraced. It was this concern that prompted paragraph seven of the Lausanne Covenant:

> We affirm that the church's visible unity in truth is God's purpose. Evangelism also summons us to unity, because our oneness strengthens our witness, just as our disunity undermines our gospel of reconciliation. We recognize, however, that organizational unity may take many forms and does not necessarily forward evangelism. Yet we who share the same biblical faith should be closely united in fellowship, work and witness. We confess that our testimony has sometimes been marred by sinful individualism and needless duplication. We pledge ourselves to seek a deeper unity in truth, worship, holiness and mission. We urge the development of regional and functional co-operation for the furtherance of the church's mission, for strategic planning, for mutual encouragement, and for the sharing of resources and experience.[451]

The example of my discussion at the missions conference deserves some exploration. Those who take this view will argue that Christian para-chruch organizations do not fit the New Testament model of the local church. They will point out that they do not have Biblical leadership models,[452] nor a Biblical method of oversight.[453] These statements are true but not relevant to the issue of partnering with a para-church organization. The structure of the local church was instituted by God to enhance God's mission. While church membership is a necessary component for a believer who wishes to mature, there is nothing in the Bible that suggests that the church cannot ally itself with others to be more effective. It is interesting to note that the same churches which disdain relations with para-church organizations will bring in non-Christian management consultants and sponsor outside recovery

---

[451] Lausanne Conference for World Evangelism, *Lausanne Covenant*, par. 7.
[452] Philippians 1:1
[453] Acts 14:23; Acts 20:17,28

groups on their campuses to be more effective. Often these arguments cover subconscious reasons for avoiding such alliances.

In many cases churches are focusing on maintaining their institution rather than advancing the Kingdom. Partnership can engender fears of loss of power and prestige, loss of control, fears of losing members and resources. To some, unless the victory can be attributed to "my church" they are not interested in the battle. It is the measurable advancement of "my church" that is the concern; its size, its prestige, its influence.

None of these goals is improper in itself, but when sought only for the glory of the single institution, they run afoul of Galatians 5:26, "Let us not become boastful, challenging one another, envying one another."[454]

Once again we return to the Lausanne for counsel:

The summons to fellowship and co-operation must not be interpreted as a warrant to impose a stereotype and to stifle initiatives. The same New Testament which calls us to unity of mind and spirit recognizes and encourages diversity of service. The classic passage is Ephesians 4:3ff, in which, after strongly emphasizing that there is "one God and Father of us all," "one Lord," "one Spirit," and therefore "one faith," "one hope," "one baptism" and "one body," the apostle immediately goes on to the diversity of the charismata which equip God's people for a diversity of tasks.

We have, therefore, to avoid two opposite mistakes. On the one hand, we must not emphasize our unity in Christ in such a way as to suppress or even hinder the diverse ministries to which God calls his people and for which he gifts them. On the other hand, we must not so revel in the diversity of our gifts and ministries that we make them an excuse to break the unity of Christ's body. Paul envisages this possibility in 1 Cor. 12:14-26, where he condemns both false modesty and false confidence in relation to our gifts. We are neither to denigrate our own gifts and envy others', nor despise others' and exaggerate our own, but rather to recognize and respect each other's gifts, and rejoice in this God-given diversity.[455]

We should be seeking partnership wherever its use will advance the

---

[454] NASB
[455] Lausanne Occasional Paper #24

Kingdom, without regard to the ambitions of the particular institution we serve. We should evaluate the partnership in terms of impact on the universal church and stewardship of the local church rather than its perceived impact on a particular institution. Consider this example: A large church in California had two church campuses within a few miles of each other. The strain of running multiple services was impacting its ability to function. But the church had a problem, either campus, by itself, did not have the facilities to serve its membership. The larger campus was adjoined by the property of another Christian church of a different denomination. The leadership went to that church and offered to trade campuses in order to obtain the adjoining property. However, the property that would be traded to obtain the adjoining property was worth more than one million dollars more than would be received in exchange, and the other church had no ability to pay the difference. How should the church react?

In the secular world, it would be an easy decision. The trade would not go through. If one looked only at the institution, the trade would "cost" over one million dollars. However the decision is different if one considers the roles of the universal and local church. The leadership of the local church had a duty to provide for its members. It could not accomplish that without making the trade. They realized there was no "loss" because the smaller church was also a member of the universal church. The leadership properly decided to go through with the trade. It received the land it needed to provide for its members, and the smaller church received greatly enhanced facilities to provide for its members. As a result, the Kingdom of God was advanced despite the "loss" on the balance sheet. This same approach should be used when deciding whether to accept a partner. The relevant question is, will the Kingdom be advanced?

Creating Dependency

Another barrier to true partnership occurs when we create a "one up" or dependent relationship. Often we assume a "charity mentality." We travel to our partner's side, we bring some items, we do some work, and we board our airplane to leave. This creates an unequal relationship where our "partner" is really just a recipient of our gifts. To truly partner we need to have long term commitments to ministries that serve the Kingdom after we board our flight home. Moreover, we need to assure our third world partners are also building into our ministries.

While many of our missions partners lack the resources we need they often possess critical knowledge. How to work with the poor, dealing with grief, celebrating God in the midst of hard living, are some of the subjects that third world leaders regularly deal with. We cannot afford to lose the opportunity of benefiting from the knowledge they have accumulated. Instead we often think of our "partnerships" as one way relationships where we funnel the resources and call the shots.

It is vogue in the mission ministries of Western churches to claim partnership with churches in other lands. However, many times this partnership consists of sending team after team, without regard to how the makeup of the team will impact the "partner's" ministry. When the time comes to pick leadership for the western churches, the foreign leader is not consulted. In one church a team had worked on another continent with a local pastor for years. After some acrimony between mission leadership and the volunteer team, the new mission leadership consulted the foreign pastor. They were amazed to learn that the area they had been working in for years was not a priority of their "partner". It was simply an area popular with the volunteer team; the prior church leadership had never thought to ask.

On another occasion, I asked the leader of a team what the goals of her next trip would be. She replied that she had not seen who had "signed up" for the trip yet. She would determine the trip goals when she saw what those who had signed up "wanted to do." The concept of cooperating with the pastor abroad, setting goals and recruiting a team to meet those goals was completely foreign to her. No doubt western churches have a need to expose their people to conditions of the third world so that they can witness both the need and how powerfully God works in these areas. However these needs must be balanced with the needs of the partner abroad.

In the West, there is a tendency to believe that since we supply the resources, we should be the dominant partner in the relationship. When this view is taken, God's kingdom is severely damaged. Not only are resources not used effectively, but the western church loses it ability to gain from the third world church. We arrange trips and bring things without understanding how to truly help. In his story, *When Two Bikes Split a Church,*[456] Christopher Little recounts how he once gave two church members bicycles in return for their work and kindness to him. Days later the local pastor met with him and explained how all resources must be allocated through leadership to prevent problems. Little apologized and thought the matter closed. Later he learned that the pastor had demanded the surrender of the bikes. One of the men refused. He was shunned by his fellow church members and, with others uncomfortable with the disharmony, formed another church.

Little was stunned by the effect of his gift. Later he received an explanation from a local friend:

> One day Bolacha explained to me that there are two kinds of gospels in this world. The first one, the Gospel of Christ, provides for forgiveness of sin, eternal life, and sets people free from the power of the devil. This Gospel involves suffering since Christ commanded us to take up our cross and follow Him (Matt. 16:24). The second gospel, the gospel of goods ("o evangelho dosbens" in Portuguese), is the counterfeit gospel which offers material wealth alongside the true Gospel, enticing people to become Christians. In his opinion, the fundamental problem with the gospel of goods is that when the goods run out the people run away. He said he had seen denomination after denomination import shipping containers of food, clothes, etc., during times of drought and famine, attracting thousands of people. But when the shipping containers stopped coming the people were nowhere to be found. He felt our church was presenting the true Gospel of Christ so that people would not be confused about the way of salvation and what it means to be a committed disciple of Christ.[457]

Little realized that Christ himself had experienced this effect. Little wrote:

I didn't recognize it at the time but Bolacha's experience was similar

---

[456] Little, Christopher, "When Two Bikes Split a Church: The Powerful Effect of An Act of Generosity." Into All the World: 2002 Annual Great Commission Opportunities. Pp. 20,22,53

[457] Ibid

to what Jesus encountered in His ministry. After feeding the 5,000 in Tiberias (John 6:1ff), the multitude began to follow Him. Jesus warned them, "You seek Me not because you saw signs, but because you ate of the loaves, and were filled" (John 6:26). Hence, the people were interested in the goods of the Kingdom without submitting to the King. Jesus would have none of it--and many of His "would be" disciples left Him (John 6:66).[458]

This is not to suggest that providing resources is not key to following scripture. It does suggest that resources themselves are not the answer. As partners we need to trust our overseas partners as to what is needed and how it should be applied. Often, western churches fail this test simply because we don't take the time to listen.

John Perkins of the Christian Community Development Association, urges the church to abandon its "charity mentality," which, because it is done impersonally, often does not meet the required needs, and tends to create a dependent attitude.[459] "Overcoming an attitude of charity is a difficult task", says Perkins, "because it requires givers to demand more of themselves than good will." The task is made more difficult by some Western mission ministries that focus exclusively on the need to build into their own people by creating missions experiences for them with little regard for the impact on the partner. Perkins continues by saying our partners need self-confidence, skills, and an opportunity, not hand-outs.[460]

CONCLUSION

Christian partnership is not created by calling someone a "partner". True partnership cannot be created without effort, careful relationship building, cultural study and an effective communication strategy. In addition, we must put aside our institutional bias and truly work to enhance God's universal church. God, in His dealing with mankind, has modeled not only partnership but effective communication between partners. If we follow these guides and treat our partner's needs as

---

[458] Ibid

[459] Perkins, John M, 1993 Beyond Charity: The Call to Christian Community Development. Grand Rapids, MI: Baker Books.

[460] Ibid

important as our own, we can develop the effective partnerships needed to accomplish God's mission.

CHAPTER 7

Worship

INTRODUCTION

A S believers we often struggle to understand the significance and necessity of worship. We see others enjoy worshipping the Lord, but we wonder whether it is required of us. Many times we would rather be active doing something for the Lord rather than be at His feet. We take pride in our actions unaware that we are merely using them to cover our insecurities.

We may ask "why does God need my worship?" or even believe that God is egocentric to demand worship. Unless we examine scripture, we may conclude that worship was something that man created on his own to fill a need in his own heart or that it is optional. Experience, study and prayer will resolve these false concerns. However, the church faces real dangers in its definition of worship. We have acknowledged the need to be relevant to culture, but there is a trap here; in seeking relevance we cannot abandon the true meaning of worship for the sake of entertainment.

MODERN DAY WORSHIP

There is a false idea today that the main reason we attend worship is to sefishly "get something out of the service." Instead we should attend to give our worship to God and to serve others who attend. For those who adopt a selfish view, the Biblical model of worship may be of little consequence as long as they are happy and feel good. We must be concerned with what God says on how He is to be worshipped, instead of what we might want to offer Him or receive in a Sunday service.

Much of worship today has digressed from its true purpose to be no more than entertainment. We have become the show's spectators. This is not this worship. It is disrespectful and demeaning toward God to reduce our worship to an afternoon's entertainment. Worship is not a spectator event. This would be a reversal of roles. In worship, it is God who is the spectator. Today, as in the time of the Judges, we expect the divine to conform to what seems right in our own eyes.[461] The sacredness of true worship must not be sacrificed on altars of entertainment. As Hebrews reminds us, "Through Jesus, therefore, let us continually offer to God a sacrifice of praise—the fruit of lips that confess his name. And do not forget to do good and to share with others, for with such sacrifices God is pleased." [462]

In worship we must be the participants, not the observers. Worship is God centered, not man centered. When our worship is to please God instead of ourselves, then and only then, will our worship be meaningful and spiritually uplifting to us and acceptable to God.

When people seek an "emotional high" from worship and don't get it, they are disappointed and blame the song, the service, or the preacher. In these cases one might hear that "the spirit did not move." In reality, what is meant is that the service was not sufficiently emotionally charged. Many believers want the worship service to be "more entertaining" and "emotionally gratifying," and therefore feel they are failing to worship God in spirit and in truth if these needs are not satisfied. But where in scripture is there support for the view that worship is designed to please the worshipper?

Asian religions and Asian cultures are very god-centered, with a heavy use of symbolism and outward piety. Buddhists, when they attend the temple to worship, dress in white and take their footwear off before entering the temple. They behave as if they were in the presence of an all powerful god. They sit on the floor whether young or old, rich or poor. Contrast this worship with our modern day Christian worship

---

[461] See Judges 21:25
[462] Hebrews 13:15-16

177

service. Our services look like music shows, the main actors are the worship team and the worshipers. God sits on the sidelines.

It is vital that we develop a healthy biblical understanding of worship and make it relevant to the culture in which we live. If our worship is a stumbling block to others in our culture, we need to revise our methods. As Corinthians teaches:

> Be careful, however, that the exercise of your freedom does not become a stumbling block to the weak. For if anyone with a weak conscience sees you who have this knowledge eating in an idol's temple, won't he be emboldened to eat what has been sacrificed to idols? So this weak brother, for whom Christ died, is destroyed by your knowledge. When you sin against your brothers in this way and wound their weak conscience, you sin against Christ. Therefore, if what I eat causes my brother to fall into sin, I will never eat meat again, so that I will not cause him to fall. [463]

Our worship culture is engrained; changing our approach is no small matter. We will carefully and look at and invite you to join in studying worship in the Old Testament, the New Testament and the worship practices of other religions. We then conclude by suggesting areas that need our attention.

BIBLICAL WORSHIP

The understanding of Biblical worship is the act of paying honor to a deity; i.e. religious reverence and homage. The most common example of worship in the Old Testament is exemplified by the word *shaha* (to "bow down"), to prostate oneself before another in order to do him honor and reverence.[464] This word is used ninety-four places in the Old Testament. This mode of salutation consisted of falling upon the knees and then touching the forehead to the ground[465] and is often translated as "bowed". This word specifically means to bow down before God; either the true God or false gods.[466] The word worship in

---

[463] 1 Corinthians 8:9-13 (NIV)
[464] Genesis .22:5
[465] Genesis 19:1; Genesis 42:6; Genesis 48:12; 1 Samuel 25:41
[466] Genesis 22:5; Exodus 24:1; 33:10; Judges 7:15; Job 1:20; Psalms 22:27; 86:9.

the Old Testament is the reverential attitude of mind or body, combined with the more generic notions of religions adoration, obedience, and service.

The principal New Testament word for worship is *proskuneo*, meaning "kiss (the hand or the ground) toward." It is used fifty-nine times in the New Testament. Think of the Asian fashion of bowing prostrate upon the ground. In the New Testament, it is to render homage to men, angels, demons, the Devil, the "beast," idols, or to God. It is rendered sixteen times to Jesus as a beneficent superior; and at least twenty-four times to God or to Jesus as God. The root idea of bodily prostration is much less prominent than in the Old Testament. It is always translated "worship."[467]

Worship in this context suggests man acknowledging the greatness of God, while realizing his own inadequacy and falling before him and acknowledging him as Lord. Churches may have different styles of worship, but the heart of worship is acknowledging God as Lord and giving him the due glory and honour. We have access to God through Jesus.[468] Despite our loving relationship through Christ, God is still holy and desires our awe and reverence. The fear of God is the beginning of wisdom.[469] Our worship must properly express the awesome nature of God, "Therefore, since we are receiving a kingdom that cannot be shaken, let us give thanks, by which we offer to God an acceptable worship with reverence and awe; for indeed our God is a consuming fire."[470]

The English word "worship" comes from the Old English word 'worth-ship', a word that denotes the worthiness of the one receiving the special honor or devotion. Certainly nothing could be truer than that God is worthy of our worship. He deserves our worship because of who He is, because of the perfection of His character, and because of His sovereignty as Creator.

---

[467] International Standard Bible Encyclopaedia, Electronic Database Copyright (C) 1996 by Biblesoft
[468] Ephesians 3:12
[469] Proverbs 9:10
[470] Hebrews 12:28-29

Worship in the Old Testament

Worship in the Temple

The general public worship, as developed in the Temple services, consisted of many elaborate elements. There were sacrificial acts on extraordinary occasions, such as at the dedication of the Temple, when the blood of the offerings flowed in profusion,[471] in the regular morning and evening sacrifices, or on the great annual days, like the Day of Atonement. The worship included ceremonial acts performed with reverence or adoration. These symbolized the seeking and receiving of the divine favor, as when the high priest returned from presenting incense offerings in the holy place, and the people received his benediction with bowed heads reverently standing.[472] Often the worshippers prostrated themselves as the priests sounded the silver trumpets at the conclusion of each section of the Levites' chant.

Praise was offered by the official ministrants of the people or both together. This service of praise was either instrumental, such as silver "trumpets and cymbals and instruments of music," in song, or by the chant of the Levites (very likely the congregation took part in some of the antiphonal psalms). It might also be both vocal and instrumental, as in the magnificent dedicatory service of Solomon,[473] when "the trumpeters and singers were as one, to make one sound to be heard in praising and thanking Yahweh." The praise might also be simply spoken: "And all the people said, Amen, and praised Yahweh."[474] The books of Psalms and Chronicles bear witness to how fully and splendidly this musical element of worship was developed among the Hebrews.[475] It is a pity that our actual knowledge of Hebrew music is so limited.

We recognize the death of Christ as a replacement for the Old Testament sacrificial system and therefore no longer perform animal sacrifices. That does not mean however, that this Old Testament practice has nothing to teach us. Just as the Old Testament Jews offered

[471] 2 Chronicles 7
[472] 2 Chronicles 7:6
[473] 2 Chronicles 5:13
[474] 1 Chronicles 16:36
[475] See e.g.,1 Chronicles 15-16,25; 2 Chr.5,29-30

sacrifices every morning and every evening, so we too could remember Christ's atonement for our sins on the cross at least every morning and every evening and offer a sacrifice of *praise* to Him. In addition, we are instructed in Romans 12:1 to offer our own bodies as a "living sacrifice" to God.

The Old Testament practice of animal sacrifice fell prey to a human weakness that still plagues us today: the outward ritual was preserved, but people's hearts ceased to be involved with the worship. The prophets, like Isaiah and Amos[476] and Malachi [477] called attention to this problem. We would do well to heed their warnings. Worship must never be the outward performance of rituals, but should come from the heart. How often do we let our minds slip out of gear when we are singing in church--just singing the words without meaning them? How often do we repeat the Creeds or the Lord's Prayer mechanically without contemplating their meaning? How often are we like the Pharisee in Luke 18 who disdained the uncouth, yet sincere worship of the publican? Consider Jesus' reaction to this:

> And He also told this parable to some people who trusted in themselves that they were righteous, and viewed others with contempt: "Two men went up into the temple to pray, one a Pharisee and the other a tax collector. "The Pharisee stood and was praying this to himself: 'God, I thank You that I am not like other people: swindlers, unjust, adulterers, or even like this tax collector. 'I fast twice a week; I pay tithes of all that I get.' "But the tax collector, standing some distance away, was even unwilling to lift up his eyes to heaven, but was beating his breast, saying, 'God, be merciful to me, the sinner!' "I tell you, this man went to his house justified rather than the other; for everyone who exalts himself will be humbled, but he who humbles himself will be exalted. [478]

---

[476] Amos 4:4
[477] Malachi 1:13
[478] Luke 18:9-15, NASB

We must love the Lord our God with all our heart, mind, and strength, and we must worship actively.

Worship through Singing

Chronicles and Nehemiah illustrate the importance of singing in worship.[479] Singing and singers are often noted in the Old Testament:

> The Levites who were the singers, all of them, even Asaph, Heman, Jeduthun, and their sons and their brethren, arrayed in fine linen, with cymbals and psalteries and harps, stood at the east end of the altar, and with them a hundred and twenty priests sounding with trumpets; it came to pass, when the trumpeters and singers were as one, to make one sound to be heard in praising and thanking Jehovah; and when they lifted up their voice with the trumpets and cymbals and instruments of music, and praised Jehovah, saying, For he is good; for his loving-kindness endureth forever[480]

> ***

> And the children of Israel that were present at Jerusalem kept the feast of unleavened bread seven days with great gladness; and the Levites and the priests praised Jehovah day by day, singing with loud instruments unto Jehovah.[481]

> ***

> And at the dedication of the wall of Jerusalem they sought the Levites out of all their places, to bring them to Jerusalem, to keep the dedication with gladness, both with thanksgivings, and with singing, with cymbals, psalteries, and with harps.[482]

Singing was a significant part of the Temple worship. A whole company of priests were dedicated to the specific purpose of singing praise to God. Singers also led the army on occasions. Although other

---

[479] See e.g., 1 Chronicles 9: 33-34
[480] 2 Chronicles 5:12-13 NIV
[481] 2 Chronicles 30:21, NIV
[482] Nehemiah 12:27

people are recorded as singing in other circumstances, it appears that the Levites were the only ones who sang in Temple worship. There are many Psalms which make it clear that King David (who was not one of the appointed Levitical singers) sang praise to God and that he calls all the people--and even the trees--to sing praise to God. It is therefore apparent that there is a place for public singing, albeit not in the Temple. Only male priests led in the singing until after the exile. Women are first mentioned as being part of the choir in Ezra 2:65 (although the Temple hadn't been rebuilt yet when they are mentioned). There are passages that speak of the priests singing and the people responding with worship. Because there are two different verbs here ("singing" and "worshiping") it's possible that the Bible is making a distinction between the two acts, one done by the ordained Levites, and one done by the larger group of people.

Our tradition of choirs probably comes from this history. Although only certain people were allowed to sing in the Old Testament, since all believers are priests there is no longer a need for this division.[483] Where only a certain tribe could sing before the Lord in worship in the Old Testament, now all believers are qualified to sing. The Temple is now our own body and not a building in Jerusalem.[484] The end of this distinction between singing inside and outside the temple should encourage us to sing praise to God not only in church worship, but everywhere.

Private Worship

It appears that regular worship ceased when the Temple was destroyed and the Israelites were taken captive to Babylon. During this time, we mostly have records of people's private worship.[485] Daniel's habit of praying three times a day is a famous example of this form of worship.[486] Private worship was not new; it has plenty of precedents in the Psalms and elsewhere (note all the "I's" and "me's" in Psalm 16, for instance). The devout exiles were merely carrying on a tradition of private worship without the accompanying form of corporate worship.

---

[483] Peter 2:5
[484] 1 Corinthians 6:19
[485] Hosea 2:11; Ps.137:1-5
[486] Daniel 6:10

Often their prayers look forward to the restoration of the Jews to their land, addressing God as "the God who keeps His covenant..." and confessing the sins that brought about the Babylonian captivity.[487]

If calamity were to come to our nation and our churches were destroyed, would we continue to worship God as Daniel did? Of course. Yet, while we are free, we must recognize the importance both of corporate worship (church meetings, services) and of private worship (devotional life, "quiet times"). We must be diligent in maintaining both aspects of worship; we cannot neglect gathering together with other believers and we cannot neglect private worship, prayer and Bible study.

Confession

Solomon's prayer in Second Chronicles makes it clear that confession of sin was a significant aspect of prayer and worship.[488] We find Nehemiah and Ezra both privately confessing sin at the beginning of their books, and we have a beautiful prayer of confession recorded in Daniel:

> I prayed to the LORD my God and confessed and said, "Alas, O Lord, the great and awesome God, who keeps His covenant and loving kindness for those who love Him and keep His commandments, we have sinned, committed iniquity, acted wickedly and rebelled, even turning aside from Your commandments and ordinances. "Moreover, we have not listened to Your servants the prophets, who spoke in Your name to our kings, our princes, our fathers and all the people of the land. [489]

***

> Now while I was speaking and praying, and confessing my sin and the sin of my people Israel, and presenting my supplication before the LORD my God in behalf of the holy mountain of my God [490]

---

[487] Nehemiah 1, Ezra 10, Daniel 9
[488] 2 Chronicles 6:37
[489] Daniel 9:4-6, NASB
[490] Daniel 9:20, NASB

Later on, when Ezra and Nehemiah are dealing with a particular problem of the Jews marrying pagan wives, there is a time of public confession of sin[491] where the people redeemed themselves with God, "Now on the twenty-fourth day of this month the sons of Israel assembled with fasting, in sackcloth and with dirt upon them. The descendants of Israel separated themselves from all foreigners, and stood and confessed their sins and the iniquities of their fathers."[492] In gatherings such as this, the confession of sin wasn't private, it was embarrassingly public. The names of all the people who sinned in taking foreign wives are recorded right there for the entire world to see throughout the rest of history! This was very humiliating, but God loves it when His people humble themselves before Him and publicly confess their sin.

Public confession has been a part of revivals throughout history. It takes humility and courage to do it, and maturity on the part of other believers to respond appropriately when a brother confesses sin, but it is right and good. It is the way God's attitude toward His people is turned from wrath to favor. Notice also that the prayers of confession in the Bible are not merely for the sins of the individual but also for the sins of the fathers and even the nation as a whole. If we are to follow this Biblical pattern, we must confess the sins of our people. The prayer of Daniel chapter nine would be a good one to pray regularly in church.

Reading the Law

Reading God's law has always been a part of obedience to the Lord:

> Then the king sent, and they gathered to him all the elders of Judah and of Jerusalem. The king went up to the house of the LORD and all the men of Judah and all the inhabitants of Jerusalem with him, and the priests and the prophets and all the people, both small and great; and he read in their hearing all the words of the book of the covenant which was found in the house of the LORD. The king stood by the pillar and made a covenant before the LORD, to walk after the LORD, and to keep His commandments and His testimonies and His

---

[491] cf. Ezra 9-10, NASB
[492] Nehemiah 9:1-2, NASB

statutes with all his heart and all his soul, to carry out the words of this covenant that were written in this book. And all the people entered into the covenant.[493]

Again this is exemplified in Nehemiah:

And Ezra opened the book in the sight of all the people; (for he was above all the people;) and when he opened it, all the people stood up: and Ezra blessed Jehovah, the great God. And all the people answered, Amen, Amen, with the lifting up of their hands: and they bowed their heads, and worshipped Jehovah with their faces to the ground. Also Jeshua, and Bani, and Sherebiah, Jamin, Akkub, Shabbethai, Hodiah, Maaseiah, Kelita, Azariah, Jozabad, Hanan, Pelaiah, and the Levites, caused the people to understand the law: and the people stood in their place. And they read in the book, in the law of God, distinctly; and they gave the sense, so that they understood the reading.[494]

In an age when books required the skins of several animals and the painstaking handwriting of a scribe, not many people had their own copy of God's Word. Yet every man needed to know God's word because it was the foundation of worship and life. Therefore, the reading of the Scriptures was an important part of corporate worship. Moses commanded that the entirety of the law be read to every man woman and child in Israel every seven years.[495] The reading of the Scriptures was a regular part of synagogue worship in New Testament times.[496] Through these readings, the people became familiar with God's Word. There were times when this element of worship was neglected, as in the days of Manasseh and Amon (kings of Judah). The book of the law had been lost and forgotten even by the priests when Josiah ascended the throne, until the Scriptures were rediscovered and read to all the people under Josiah's reformation.[497]

Tradition has it that the Targums were developed later on as the readings of the scriptures were carried on during the exile. The Targums

---

[493] 2 Kings 23:1-3
[494] Nehemiah 8:5-8
[495] Deuteronomy 31:9-12
[496] Luke 4:16*ff*
[497] 2 Kings 23

were loose translations of the Hebrew Scriptures into Aramaic, the language of the common people in Semitic regions of the world from the time of the Babylonian empire to the time of the Roman Empire. It is believed that this is what Nehemiah meant when he describes the worship service held by the returned exiles in which they read the Scriptures. "And they read in the book, in the law of God, distinctly; and they gave the sense, so that they understood the reading."[498]

We should learn from the tradition of scripture reading that *God's word is quite able to speak for itself* without us concocting long sermons about it. Certainly there is a place for sermons--that's basically what the Prophetic books are--but we must be careful to value God's words over our own. We should not muddle our church worship services with too many of our own words. Reading of scripture must be a very important aspect of our worship.

Public Prayer

Public prayer is a prevalent part of Old Testament worship. An example is Solomon's prayer at the dedication of the Temple:

> Now Solomon had made a bronze platform, five cubits long, five cubits wide and three cubits high, and had set it in the midst of the court; and he stood on it, knelt on his knees in the presence of all the assembly of Israel and spread out his hands toward heaven. He said, "O LORD, the God of Israel, there is no god like You in heaven or on earth, keeping covenant and showing lovingkindness to Your servants who walk before You with all their heart; who has kept with Your servant David, my father, that which You have promised him; indeed You have spoken with Your mouth and have fulfilled it with Your hand, as it is this day. "Now therefore, O LORD, the God of Israel, keep with Your servant David, my father, that which You have promised him, saying, 'You shall not lack a man to sit on the throne of Israel, if only your sons take heed to their way, to walk in My law as you have walked before Me.' "Now therefore, O LORD, the God of Israel, let Your word be confirmed which You have spoken to Your servant David....[499]

---

[498] Nehemiah 8:8
[499] 2 Chronicles 6:13-17

Examples may also be found in Deuteronomy 26 or in Psalms 60, 79 and 80.

Prostration

According to 2 Chronicles 20:18, "Jehoshaphat bowed his head with his face to the ground, and all Judah and the inhabitants of Jerusalem fell down before the LORD, worshiping the LORD." [500]

Whenever the Bible describes what people are doing when they worship, three things are consistent: 1) they are near the thing they are worshipping; "before God," "in God's holy mountain," or in front of an idol; 2) they are offering sacrifices of some sort, and 3) they are bowing. In the church today, we have a pretty good understanding of the first two principles, but prostration in worship bowing down to the ground out of respect, is not a common practice. Perhaps it should be.

Meditation

Meditation may be defined as, "A private devotional act, consisting in deliberate reflection upon some spiritual truth or mystery, accompanied by mental prayer and by acts of the affection and of the will, especially formation of resolutions as to future conduct." [501]

Meditation is presented in the Bible as beneficial to spiritual interests. It should be deliberate, close, and continuous. The Bible instructs, "But his delight is in the law of the LORD, And in His law he meditates day and night" [502] and says, "O how I love Your law! It is my meditation all the day." [503] We are most frequently instructed to meditate on the works of creation; [504] the perfections of God; [505] the character, office, and work of Christ; [506] the office and operations of the Holy

---

[500] 2 Chronicles 20:18, NASB
[501] The Century Dictionary: An Encyclopedic Lexicon of the English Language
[502] Psalms 1:2
[503] Psalms 119:97
[504] Psalms 19:1-6
[505] Deuteronomy 32:4
[506] Hebrews 12:2-3

Spirit;[507] the dispensations of Providence;[508] the precepts and promises of God's words;[509] the value, powers, and immortality of the soul;[510] the depravity of our nature, and the grace of God in our salvation.

Worship in the New Testament

The first uses of 'worship' and 'worshiped' in the New Testament are in Matthew 2:2, and in verses 2:8, and 2:11. In verse two, the wise men are looking for the one born King of the Jews in order to worship Him. In verse eight Herod states he wants to worship Him also. In verse eleven the wise men worship Jesus after discovering Him the manger. The King James Version, New King James Version, and Revised Standard translated the verse as "they fell down and worshipped" while the New International Version translates it as "they bowed down and worshipped him." The words used are [*proskunhsai*]; "to worship" in verse 2; [*proskunhsw*]; "may worship" in verse 8, and [*prosekunhsan*]; "they worshipped" in verse eleven. The root for all of these is [*proskunew*]: to do reverence or homage by prostration. Also, verse eleven contains [*pesontes*] which is from the root [*piptw*] meaning: to fall, to fall prostrate, to fall down. (There are other meanings for [*piptw*], depending on use.)

The next occurrence of worship in the New Testament is in Mathew 4:8-9, "Again, the devil took Him to a very high mountain and showed* Him all the kingdoms of the world and their glory; and he said to Him, "All these things I will give You, if You fall down and worship me." [511]

In verse nine, the Devil offers Jesus all the kingdoms of the world and their glories if Jesus will bow down and worship him. The word "fall" is used in the King James, New King James and Revised Standard Versions, while it is translated "bow" in the New International Version. Here again, the physical act of showing reverence is shown.

Jesus answers the Devil in verse ten, saying only God is to be worshiped, and only He is to be served. Again, the King James Version,

---

[507] John15-16
[508] Psalms 97:1-2
[509] Psalms 119
[510] Mark 8:36
[511] NASB

New King James Version, New International Version, and Revised Standard Version quote Jesus respectively as follows: "Thou shalt worship the Lord thy God and Him only shalt thou serve," "You shall worship the Lord your God and Him only you shall serve," "Worship the Lord your God, and serve him only.

In verse ten, the NGT employs [proskunhseis], "thou shalt worship," which also has [proskunew] as its root. Also included in Jesus' statement is the element of serving. The Greek word translated as "thou shalt serve" [latreuseis] which has the root [latreuw], which the Analytical Greek Lexicon[512] defines as: "to be a servant, to serve; to render religious service and homage, worship." "Servant" here is used in the sense a household servant, not a worship service. Clearly, proper worship that which is acceptable to God, requires the element of serving Him, that is, being submissive to Him.

John 4:7-26, depicts an encounter between Jesus and a woman at a well in Samaria:

> There came a woman of Samaria to draw water. Jesus said to her, "Give Me a drink." For His disciples had gone away into the city to buy food. Therefore the Samaritan woman said to Him, "How is it that You, being a Jew, ask me for a drink since I am a Samaritan woman?" (For Jews have no dealings with Samaritans.) Jesus answered and said to her, "If you knew the gift of God, and who it is who says to you, 'Give Me a drink,' you would have asked Him, and He would have given you living water." She said to Him, "Sir, You have nothing to draw with and the well is deep; where then do You get that living water? "You are not greater than our father Jacob, are You, who gave us the well, and drank of it himself and his sons and his cattle?" Jesus answered and said to her, "Everyone who drinks of this water will thirst again; but whoever drinks of the water that I will give him shall never thirst; but the water that I will give him will become in him a well of water springing up to eternal life."

> The woman said to Him, "Sir, give me this water, so I will not be thirsty nor come all the way here to draw." He said to her, "Go, call your husband and come here." The woman answered and said, "I have no husband." Jesus said* to her, "You have correctly said, 'I have no husband'; for you have had five husbands, and the one whom you

---

512 Harold K. Moulton Editor (1978)

now have is not your husband; this you have said truly." The woman said to Him, "Sir, I perceive that You are a prophet. "Our fathers worshiped in this mountain, and you people say that in Jerusalem is the place where men ought to worship." Jesus said to her, "Woman, believe Me, an hour is coming when neither in this mountain nor in Jerusalem will you worship the Father. "You worship what you do not know; we worship what we know, for salvation is from the Jews. "But an hour is coming, and now is, when the true worshipers will worship the Father in spirit and truth; for such people the Father seeks to be His worshipers. "God is spirit, and those who worship Him must worship in spirit and truth." The woman said to Him, "I know that Messiah is coming (He who is called Christ); when that One comes, He will declare all things to us." Jesus said to her, "I who speak to you am He" [513]

Jesus initiates the discussion in verse seven. The woman knows Jesus is a Jew, and that Jews do not associate with Samaritans. The woman concludes Jesus is a prophet and in verse twenty points out the conflict between Samaritans and Jews regarding worshiping. Their discussion continues through verse twenty-four. Prophetically, Jesus tells the woman of a change that is going to take place in the whole arena of worshiping God.

Jesus tells her true worshipers will worship the Father in "spirit and in truth." What is He telling her? What does He mean? What is the change that is to take place? The seat of worshiping God for the Jews was Jerusalem at the Temple. Worshiping was physical: physical sacrifices, physical offerings, physical rites performed by the priests. Worshiping was physically limited. The limitation for the Jews was the Temple. The synagogues were seats of teaching, not worshiping. In the New Testament there is not a single mention of acts of worship taking place in a synagogue. For the Jews, worshiping God was restricted to the Temple.

Jesus was referring to the change that would take place with the birth of the Church that commenced with Christ's resurrection. With the indwelling of the Holy Spirit His presence is no longer restricted to the Temple. The physical elements of worshiping are no longer required. Each believer is a priest. Worshiping is no longer confined to a specific event or activity.

---

[513] John 4:7-26, NASB

Worship in Revelation

Revelation pictures worship as it takes place in heaven. In its vivid images, elders fall down on their faces before God. Homage is unceasingly given God the Father as angels sing. We see a multitude of people and creatures paying homage to God day and night without ceasing:

> And the four living creatures, each one of them having six wings, are full of eyes around and within; and day and night they do not cease to say, "HOLY, HOLY, HOLY IS THE LORD GOD, THE ALMIGHTY, WHO WAS AND WHO IS AND WHO IS TO COME."

> And when the living creatures give glory and honor and thanks to Him who sits on the throne, to Him who lives forever and ever, the twenty-four elders will fall down before Him who sits on the throne, and will worship Him who lives forever and ever, and will cast their crowns before the throne, saying, "Worthy are You, our Lord and our God, to receive glory and honor and power; for You created all things, and because of Your will they existed, and were created. [514]

Our worship must represent this understanding of the nature of God. Revelation contains the word "worship" more times than any other New Testament book. Each occurrence has the root [*proskunew*]. Further understanding of worship can be found from studying these verses:

Revelation Reference	Description of Worship
Revelation 3:9	Jesus is addressing the church at Philadelphia - He is saying He will make those who are from the synagogue of Satan but who say they are Jews, worship before the feet of the church (at Philadelphia)

---

[514] Revelation 4:8-10

Revelation 4:10	The twenty-four elders fall before the One on the Throne and worship Him
Revelation 5:14	The twenty-four elders fell down and worshiped
Revelation 7:11	All the angels.... fell before the Throne on their faces, and worshiped God
Revelation 9:20	And the rest of the men ... who did not repent ... they should not worship devils (demons)
Revelation 11:1	John is told to measure the Temple of God and the altar and them that worship therein
Revelation 11:16	The twenty-four elders ... fell on their faces and worshiped God
Revelation 13:4	They (All the world - See v.3) worshiped the dragon (See 12:3) and they worshiped the beast (See 13:1)
Revelation 13:8	All who dwell on earth and whose names are not written in the Book of Life shall worship him (probably the beast - See verses 5-7)
Revelation 13:12	A second beast (See verse eleven) causes all (Those of verse eight) to worship the first beast
Revelation 13:15	The second beast causes those who would not worship the image of the first beast to be killed (See verses11-18 for continuity.)
Revelation 14:7	One of the angels in heaven (see v.6) has a role to say to all on earth with a loud voice: "Fear God ... and worship Him that made heaven, and earth, and the sea, and the fountains of water." The word here is in the imperative mood, hence is a command.

Revelation 14:9	A third angel in heaven (see verses 7-8) has a role to say to all (on earth) with a loud voice the wrath of God (See verses 10-11) that will be dispensed upon any man if he worship(s) the beast.
Revelation 14:11	A confirmation of those subject to the wrath of God, those of verse 9. They have no rest day nor night, those worshiping the beast, and his image. This is in the present tense indicating they are continuing to worship the beast.
Revelation 15:4	John sees a scene of those who had victory over the beast (see verse 2) singing the song of ... the Lamb (see verses 3-4) including the phrase: all nations shall come and worship before thee.
Revelation 16:2	A bad and evil sore inflicts men having the mark of the beast and worshiping its image. This is in the present tense indicating they are continuing to worship the beast.
Revelation 19:4	The scene is in heaven again and there are people saying: Halleluiah (spelling of MNGT), salvation, and glory, and honor, and power, unto the Lord our God (see verses 1-3) and the twenty-four elders and four beasts fell down and worshiped God that sat on the throne.
Revelation 19:10	John falls to worship the one whose voice came out of the throne (see verse 5) but is told not to since he, the voice, is also a fellow servant having the same witness of Jesus, and to worship God. The second worship here is the imperative mood, hence a command to John.

Revelation 19:20	The beast and the kings of the earth and their armies are gathered for the final battle of the seven year period (see verse 19). The beast and the false prophet who deceived.... the ones worshiping the image of the beast are taken alive and cast into the lake of fire. There is yet to be another deception and battle at the end of the thousand years (see verse 20:1-3)
Revelation 20:4	John sees the souls of those who had been beheaded for the witness of Jesus and for the Word of God and who did not worship the beast.
Revelation 22:8	John falls before the feet of the angel (who had shown him what he had seen) to worship him.
Revelation 22:9	The angel (of verse 8) tells John not to worship him,.... , but worship God.

Conclusions from New Testament Study

After studying the New Testament passages related to worshiping, I am forced to conclude:

1. The New Testament does not contain any passage that allows us to define what constitutes worshiping for the church on earth. From the Greek words, we see the specific act involved bowing down or falling in prostration, as being worship, whether directed to Jesus, God, idols, or the beast. Note the same word root is used regardless of the object of worship.

2. With respect to the Jews worshiping in the Temple in Jerusalem, we only know that worshiping took place. The New Testament does not provide any detail of their worshiping, other than bowing or rendering homage.

3. References to worshiping God and Jesus taking place

in Heaven refer only to bowing or prostration and confession as the consummation of worshiping.

4. No instruction of how to worship is given to the church. Also, there is no instruction regarding worshiping the Holy Spirit, or recording of anyone worshiping Him.

Therefore, what we may have believed to be worshiping, and what we may have prescribed as worshiping, may not have any scriptural substantiation as being acceptable worship. Furthermore, if we insist on a formula or particular mode or content as the format for our worshiping, then we are establishing standards of spirituality, and are deceiving ourselves. But since worshiping and having worship services is universal throughout the church, there must be some scriptural enjoinment for its existence. What is the basis for what we do when we gather together? What should we do? What should we not do?

SERVING IN OUR DAILY LIVES AS WORSHIP

Paul, in his letter to the believers in Rome, presents the arguments and rationale for the superiority of faith in Christ as the deliverance over the previous deliverance Israel obtained through the Law of Moses. Under the Law, righteousness was obtained by obeying the Law and offering sacrifices. But the sacrifice of Christ has removed the sacrifices required under the Law, and the righteousness of Christ is now imparted to the believer; not because of his obedience to the Law, but because of his faith in Christ.[515]

In verse 12:1 Paul says that because of all of this, (meaning all that he discussed in chapters one through eleven,) the believer should present his own body as a living sacrifice, holy and acceptable to God. According to Paul, doing so is nothing less than being reasonable in serving God. Although this is not a requirement for our salvation, it does direct us to making our bodies a living sacrifice. Paul implicitly asks: If we do not worship through service in our daily lives, how can we worship Him on Sundays?

---

[515] See Romans Chapters 1-11.

He goes on in verse 12:2 to tell us how to affect daily worship: by not being conformed to the behavior and conduct of the world, but by being transformed by the renewing of our minds. The word for "transformed" is in the passive voice, which means the subject receives the action, he does not cause it to happen. Perhaps a more accurate translation would be: "allow yourselves to be transformed." The transformation, although it does not require action, requires submission on the part of the one undergoing it. It has the root [*metamorfow*] which means: "to change one's form", "be transfigured." The same root occurs in Matthew 17:2 and in Mark 9:2, in which Christ is transfigured. We can conclude this transformation is accomplished by God through the Holy Spirit and our submission to His transformation is through our spiritual nature.

Our submission to God's transformation and resulting service and sacrifice is the essence of worship. Our weekly meetings provide a foundation for understanding the nature of God and for submission to His will.

INDWELLING OF THE HOLY SPIRIT AND WORSHIP

The unique characteristic that makes the church different from all other bodies of believers is that her members are indwelt by the Holy Spirit, fully and permanently. In First Corinthians Paul teaches that the body of the believer is a temple of God.[516] Also, our bodies are members of Christ; a believer must not ever join his body with that of a prostitute, or be sexually immoral, because his body is the temple of the Holy Spirit.[517]

When we consider this indwelling, a number of questions are suggested. Since our bodies are the temple of God, can we gather for worshiping in any building or place that is a more appropriate "temple"? Since our bodies are continuously temples of the Holy Spirit, can we ask Him to meet with us when we gather to worship? Since our bodies are continuously temples of God, can we leave Him at the church when worshiping ends and we go our way? Since our bodies are continuously temples of the Holy Spirit, are we not "temple keepers"?

[516] 1 Corinthians 3:16
[517] 1 Corinthians 6:15-19

Because Christ dwells within us, Paul gives us three imperatives regarding our relationship with the Holy Spirit; we are to walk by means of the Spirit and not gratify our sinful desires,[518] we are not to grieve the Holy Spirit of God,[519] and we are not to quench the Spirit. [520] In this manner, we may live in submission. If our living is not in submission to the Holy Spirit and is grieving or quenching Him, our worship is mockery.

Offer God your Praise

> Through Christ then, let us continually offer up a sacrifice of praise to God, that is, the fruit of the lips that give thanks to his name. Through Jesus, therefore, let us continually offer to God a sacrifice of praise—the fruit of lips that confess his name. And do not forget to do good and to share with others, for with such sacrifices God is pleased. [521]

The verse has two clear themes; we must constantly offer the sacrifice of praise to the Lord and we must also offer the sacrifice of doing good and sharing with others. The practice of thankfulness to God is stressed over and over again in the New Testament.[522] Why is this? Does God need our gratitude so that he can feel good? Such a view obviously does not befit the God of the Bible; He is the only being in the universe who is completely self-existent and therefore needs nothing. We add nothing to God by praising and thanking him. God is indeed pleased by our gratitude, but we are the ones who benefit from this practice. As we choose, often against our present feelings and circumstances, to recall God's blessings and then to thank him for these, we are keeping ourselves properly aligned with reality. Rather than buying into the lie that we are mistreated and unfortunate, we are by faith asserting the truth; that we are fantastically blessed beyond anything that we could ever deserve. In spite of our rebellion against God, which deserves His wrath, He has forgiven us, adopted us into his family, guaranteed us

---

[518] Galatians 5:16
[519] Ephesians 4:30
[520] 1 Thessalonians 5:19
[521] Hebrews 13:15-16
[522] See 1 Thessalonians 5:16-18; Colossians 3:15-17

eternal life, given us a significant role in his purpose, indwelt us with his Spirit, and provided us with Christian friends.

The author's emphasis is that we should worship God in this way "continually." The idea that Christian worship takes place only, or even especially, in a corporate worship meeting is utterly foreign to this verse. Because of Christ's payment for our sins, we have the privilege to draw near to God and communicate with him in this way at any time: in the morning when we wake up, on the way to work, during the busy day, when we are together with other Christians, alone in our room, "continually." It is wonderful to praise God with other Christians in song,[523] but this should be only the "tip of the iceberg" of our thanks to God.

Offer God your Material Resources and Service

Hebrews 13:16 reminds us, "And do not forget to do good and to *share* with others, for with such sacrifices God is pleased." [524]

The author touches on two more ways in which we can worship God: doing good and sharing. "Sharing" refers to the generous giving of our material resources to God's people and God's work. This is explicitly identified by Paul as a sacrifice which pleases God, "But I have received (your money gift) in full, and have an abundance; I am amply supplied, having received from Epaphroditus what you have sent, a fragrant aroma, an acceptable sacrifice, well-pleasing to God." [525]

Many Christians regard giving financially to God in the same way that they pay their taxes to the government, they have to do it, and they look for ways to give as little as possible.[526] Paul's view is very different from this. He says that giving is a privilege[527] and something that we should do generously[528] as an expression of our commitment to God. [529]

[523] Ephesians 5:19
[524] Hebrews 13:16, NIV
[525] Philippians 4:18
[526] See also Chapter ten, *Giving*
[527] 2 Corinthians 8:4
[528] 2 Corinthians 9:6
[529] 2 Corinthians 8:5

When we give our money to God in this way, by supporting our local church, by supporting other Christian workers and ministries, and by helping the needy, God regards this as an expression of worship fully as spiritual as praising him. Giving of our money represents giving of ourselves, since money represents the time, effort and creativity that we have invested in order to gain it. Such giving is also an expression of our trust in God's faithfulness to continue to meet our material needs, which Paul tells us God will fully supply. [530]

The other sacrifice mentioned in this verse is "doing good." This phrase refers to ministry; performing deeds of loving service to other people as representatives of Christ. When we relate to the people God brings into our lives with Christ-like, sacrificial love, God regards this as an expression of our worship to him, " . . . walk in love, just as Christ loved you, and gave himself up for us, an offering and a sacrifice as a fragrant aroma."[531]

God is pleased by this kind of lifestyle not only because He wants to love people through us, but also because this demonstrates that we are living with an attitude of trust in his love for us. We are motivated to love others because we understand and believe in the love that God has for us. [532] Everyday, God gives us dozens of creative opportunities to say "thank you!" to him in this way; serving our spouses, caring for our children, performing deeds of service for those in need, showing and sharing the love of Christ to our neighbors, those at work or school; the examples are endless.

We also have the special privilege of worshiping God through the exercise of our spiritual gifts. Paul speaks of his own apostolic ministry in this way, ". . . because of the grace that was given to me from God, to be a minister of Christ Jesus to the Gentiles, ministering as a priest the gospel of God, that my offering of the Gentiles might become acceptable, sanctified by the Holy Spirit."[533]

In Romans 12:1, after urging us to present our lives to God as an act of worship, Paul also urges us to express that worship through the use of our spiritual gifts.[534] As we discover our spiritual gifts and exercise them regularly in the service of others, and give God praise for

---

[530] Philippians 4:19

[531] Philippians 4:18

[532] 1 John 4:16-19

[533] Romans 15:15, 16

[534] Romans 12:6-8

the fruit of this ministry, we discover a form of worship that is uniquely satisfying! It should be clear from this study that worship in the New Testament is a lifestyle made up of many kinds of activity, not only a corporate meeting.

ESSENTIAL ELEMENTS
FOR TRUE WORSHIP

Justice

> Hear the word of the LORD, you rulers of Sodom; listen to the law of our God, you people of Gomorrah! "The multitude of your sacrifices—what are they to me?" says the LORD."I have more than enough of burnt offerings, of rams and the fat of fattened animals; I have no pleasure in the blood of bulls and lambs and goats. When you come to appear before me, who has asked this of you, this trampling of my courts? Stop bringing meaningless offerings! Your incense is detestable to me. New Moons, Sabbaths and convocations—I cannot bear your evil assemblies. Your New Moon festivals and your appointed feasts my soul hates. They have become a burden to me; I am weary of bearing them. When you spread out your hands in prayer, I will hide my eyes from you; even if you offer many prayers, I will not listen. Your hands are full of blood; wash and make yourselves clean. Take your evil deeds out of my sight! Stop doing wrong, [17] learn to do right! Seek justice, encourage the oppressed. Defend the cause of the fatherless, plead the case of the widow.[535]

"You rulers of Sodom": The destruction Sodom provides powerful imagery for this spirited address. The leaders' character and destiny were almost like those of Sodom, and the prophet therefore openly addresses the rulers as governing a people like those in Sodom. There could have been no more severe or cutting reproof of their wickedness than to address them as resembling the people whom God overthrew for their enormous crimes.[536] Because of the wickedness, in verses eleven

---

[535] Isaiah 1:10-17 (NIV)
[536] Barnes' Notes

through fifteen, God rejects their worship. Even though God rejects the worship of the people of Israel He offers them hope, by highlighting their failures to allow change. He says, "Your hands are full of blood"; you need to "learn to do right", and you must "seek justice", "encourage the oppressed", "defend the cause of the fatherless" and "plead the case of the widow."

"Your hands"- this is given as a reason why he would not hear them. The expression "full of blood" denotes crime and guilt of a high order; as in murder, the hands would be dripping in blood, and the stain on the hands would be proof of guilt. It is probably a figurative expression, not meaning literally that they were murderers, but that they were given to injustice; to the oppression of the poor and the widow. The sentiment is, that because they indulged in sin, and came, even in their prayers, with a determination still to indulge it, God would not hear them. The same sentiment is expressed elsewhere in the Bible; "If I regard iniquity in my heart, the Lord will not hear me,"[537] "He that turneth away his ear from hearing the law, even his prayer shall be abomination."[538] This is the reason why the prayers of sinners are not heard. A proper relationship with God, accompanied with God honouring acts is a prerequisite for worship.

Forgiving Others and Living in Harmony

Matthew 5:23-24 states, "Therefore, if you are offering your gift at the altar and there remember that your brother has something against you, leave your gift there in front of the altar. First go and be reconciled to your brother; then come and offer your gift." [539]

The Pharisees were intent only on the external acts in worship. They did not consider the internal state of the mind. If a man conformed to the external rites of religion, however much envy, and malice, and secret hatred he might have, they thought he was doing well. Our Saviour taught a different doctrine. Under His doctrine it was of more consequence to have the heart right than to perform the right acts. So

[537] Psalms 66:18
[538] Proverbs 28:9
[539] Matthew. 5:23-24 (NIV)

even if a man has brought his gift to the alter, if his heart is not right, he must leave and be reconciled before offering his gift. He must resolve the dispute with his brother before the gift is acceptable. The worship of God will not be acceptable, however well performed externally, until we are at peace with those that we have injured because, "To obey is better than sacrifice," [540] One who comes to worship his Maker filled with malice, hatred, envy, and at war with his brethren, is a hypocritical worshipper and must meet with God's displeasure. God is not deceived, and He will not be mocked.[541]

The modern day church must pay attention. We have neglected the heart in our corporate services. Let me suggest that all worship services must begin with a time of confession. This would give an opportunity for believers to cleanse their hearts before offering praise to God.

CONCLUSION

When Christians correctly view worship as the most important priority but have a incomplete view of what worship is, the result is often a superficial and dichotomized Christian life. Such Christians are faithfully committed to attending the Sunday worship service, but because they view that as the essence of worship, fail to develop a lifestyle of wholehearted commitment to God. God is more pleased, and we are more fulfilled when we develop lifestyles characterized by the worship described in the New Testament.

To completely worship God we must combine both Old and New Testament concepts of worship. The focus of our worship services must be worship of God and not entertainment of the crowd. We must design our services to allow maximum participation by the believers so that worshipers do not become spectators. We need to create an appropriate environment to help people prepare for worship. To do so we may have to evaluate our songs and consider their theological content. We should also ask if the music used enhances or distracts from worship.

We have to model and teach people how they must behave in the house of God. We must emphasize a lifestyle of worship rather than an hour of corporate meeting. We will have to pay close attention to the

[540] 1 Samuel 15:22
[541] Barnes' Notes

local culture and work at developing culturally relevant, but biblically sound, models of worship. Finally, we must pay attention to the example we set to the non Christians as we worship the only, living, Holy God.

CHAPTER 8

Christian Community

I battled for a couple of days about the title of this chapter. My options were to name it "small groups", "cell groups", or "Christian communities." The battle raged within me because I am unhappy with the strategies that are used in small groups. My struggle began with the realization that in Asia we enjoy a deep community life, but the church, in its quest to seek strategies that the West has adopted, has replaced our understanding of community life with a shallow strategy of cell groups within the church.

The cell groups will meet for a maximum of two hours a week and express some care for its members. However, the focus is the spiritual growth of the individual and their training for ministry. This is not community life, but an effective strategy to teach new converts. While this is important, we need to create Christian communities which deeply care for and protect one another. Effective community living influences those outside the faith to bring about transformation in their communities. Consider the following:

His Magazine, November 1968, reported an in-depth study done by Inter-Varsity Christian Fellowship staff in North America on the rate of growth of their various University groups compared to the size of their gatherings. They described the problems found by any group as it grows and how the growth rate invariably slows as size increases. Problems included a drop in personalness, sense of mission and evangelistic work achieved, and an immense rise in demands on leaders. From this they devised an effective strategy which included the following: "The big meeting should serve the small group rather than vica versa."[542]

---

[542] Quoted from *Exploring Christianity-the Church*. (web article www.christianity. co.nz/church6.htm)

By forming Christian communities we assure the proper role of smaller gatherings of believers, and assure they are not transformed to serve the church institution.

THE NEW TESTAMENT CHURCH

The early church met in the temple and Jewish synagogues as well as private homes of believers.[543] Meeting in the synagogues was short lived due to opposition from the Jewish community compelling believers to seek alternative meeting places, the homes of believers. This was carried out in absolute secrecy because of the two-pronged persecutions they encountered from the Roman government and the Jewish leadership. The importance of community and especially the home in the early church can hardly be exaggerated. Jason's house in Thessalonica was used for evangelism to the point it was subject to attack by the Jewish leaders.[544] Titius Justus worked for the Lord from his house adjacent to the synagogue.[545] Phillip's house was also used for this purpose.[546] Lydia, a new believer, made one of her first acts the offer of her house for service to the Lord,[547] as did Paul's jailer:

> They said, "Believe in the Lord Jesus, and you will be saved, you and your household." And they spoke the word of the Lord to him together with all who were in his house. And he took them that very hour of the night and washed their wounds, and immediately he was baptized, he and all his household. And he brought them into his house and set food before them, and rejoiced greatly, having believed in God with his whole household.[548]

Later we learn that the jailer's household remained faithful in His service.[549] The upper room of John Mark's house served as a gathering place for the early Christians:

> Then they returned to Jerusalem from the mount called Olivet, which

---

[543] Acts 5:42
[544] Acts 17:5
[545] Acts 18:7
[546] Acts 21:8
[547] Acts 16:15
[548] Acts 16:32-34
[549] 1 Corinthians 16:14

is near Jerusalem, a Sabbath day's journey away. When they had entered the city, they went up to the upper room where they were staying; that is, Peter and John and James and Andrew, Philip and Thomas, Bartholomew and Matthew, James the son of Alphaeus, and Simon the Zealot, and Judas the son of James. These all with one mind were continually devoting themselves to prayer, along with the women, and Mary the mother of Jesus, and with His brothers.

At this time Peter stood up in the midst of the brethren (a gathering of about one hundred and twenty persons was there together), and said, "Brethren, the Scripture had to be fulfilled, which the Holy Spirit foretold by the mouth of David concerning Judas, who became a guide to those who arrested Jesus. "For he was counted among us and received his share in this ministry. [550]

The house of the believer was the church of the believer's community, "Greet Prisca and Aquila, my fellow workers in Christ Jesus, who for my life risked their own necks, to whom not only do I give thanks, but also all the churches of the Gentiles; also greet the church that is in their house." [551] As L. Michael White, Professor of Classics and Director of the Religious Studies Program University of Texas at Austin notes:

The worship of an early Christian house church probably centered around the dinner table. The term communion actually comes from this experience of the dining fellowship. We also know that all other aspects of worship that we think of as going with early Christian practice probably happened around the dinner table as well. Paul refers to one person having a song and another person bringing a prayer. Everyone is contributing to the banquet whether it's in the form of food or in the form of their piety and worship.[552]

The Christian communities that were established by the New Testament church stand out as the best example of community living:

Those who accepted his message were baptized, and about three thousand were added to their number that day. They devoted themselves to the apostles' teaching and to the fellowship, to the

---

[550] Acts 1:13-17, NASD, See also Acts 12:12
[551] Romans 16:3, See also 1 Corinthians 16;19, Philemon 1:2
[552] Audio excerpt from, *"From Jesus to Christ.'*

breaking of bread and to prayer. Everyone was filled with awe, and many wonders and miraculous signs were done by the apostles. All the believers were together and had everything In common. Selling their possessions and goods, they gave to anyone as he had need. Every day they continued to meet together in the temple courts. They broke bread in their homes and ate together with glad and sincere hearts, praising God and enjoying the favor of all the people. And the Lord added to their number daily those who were being saved.[553]

Lacking both the modern structure characteristic of the modern church and the professional pastors associated with it, the early church thrived by following Biblical guides. They devoted themselves to the apostles' teaching, to fellowship, to the breaking of bread, to prayer, to providing for each others needs, to spending time together, to Christian communion.

The aspect of this community is further detailed in Acts 4:32-37:

All the believers were one in heart and mind. No one claimed that any of his possessions was his own, but they shared everything they had. With great power the apostles continued to testify to the resurrection of the Lord Jesus, and much grace was upon them all. There were no needy persons among them. For from time to time those who owned lands or houses sold them, brought the money from the sale sand put it at the apostles' feet and it was distributed to anyone as he had need. Joseph, a Levite from Cyprus, whom the apostles called Barnabas (which means Son of Encouragement),sold a field he owned and brought the money and put it at the apostles' feet. [554]

Note the power achieved: all the believers were one in heart and mind; no one claimed that any of his possessions was his own; they shared everything they had; there were no needy persons among them. From time to time those who owned lands or houses sold them, brought the money from the sales and put it at the apostles' feet, which was then distributed to the needy. Scripture is careful to note the impact and dedication to Christian community, "And every day, in the temple and from house to house, they kept right on teaching and preaching Jesus as

---

[553] Acts 2:41-47 (NIV)
[554] NIV

the Christ."[555] No wonder the early Church was able to stand against the cruel persecution of the Roman Empire and still show vibrant growth.

THE CHURCH IN THE BIBLE

Say the word, "church" and the mind's eye conjures a beautiful building. However, though the buildings are important, the church is not a building. Contrast this with the Biblical image of "church". God's people are a building, "not built by human hands" [556] which God is constructing. The Old Testament temple is replaced with those who know Christ who now house his Spirit:

> For no man can lay a foundation other than the one which is laid, which is Jesus Christ. Now if any man builds on the foundation with gold, silver, precious stones, wood, hay, straw, each man's work will become evident; for the day will show it because it is to be revealed with fire, and the fire itself will test the quality of each man's work. If any man's work which he has built on it remains, he will receive a reward. If any man's work is burned up, he will suffer loss; but he himself will be saved, yet so as through fire.

> Do you not know that you are a temple of God and that the Spirit of God dwells in you? [17]If any man destroys the temple of God, God will destroy him, for the temple of God is holy, and that is what you are."[557]

As believers we are the individual stones built into this temple, ""And coming to Him as to a living stone which has been rejected by men, but is choice and precious in the sight of God, [5]you also, as living stones, are being built up as a spiritual house for a holy priesthood, to offer up spiritual sacrifices acceptable to God through Jesus Christ.'"[558]

The Greek word for church is *ekklesia*. This word is used 115 times in the New Testament, most frequently in Acts but also in the writings of the apostle Paul and the general epistles. At least ninety-two times in its

---

[555] Acts 5:42 NASD, see also Acts 12:12

[556] 2 Corinthians 5:1

[557] 1 Corinthians 3:11-17, see also Ephesians 2:20-22

[558] 1 Peter 2:4,5

usage, this word refers to local members of a Christian community. The other references are to the church universal or all believers everywhere for all ages.

When the church universal is implied, "church" refers to all who follow Christ, without respect to locality or time, whether living or dead. The most general reference to the church universal occurs in Ephesians 1:22; and 5:23-32. Since the church universal refers to all believers of all ages, it will not be complete until after the judgment; and the assembly of the entire redeemed in one place. This will become a reality only after the return of Christ.[559] Because the church universal will not become a tangible reality until after Christ' return, the greatest emphasis in the New Testament is placed upon the idea of the local church. The local church is the visible operation of the universal church in a given time and place.

After His resurrection, Jesus commissioned the church to make disciples and teach them what He had taught.[560] The entire book of Acts is the story of the early church's struggle to be loyal to this commission. As one reads this book, one is impressed by the reality that Christ, through the presence of the Holy Spirit, continues to direct His church as it carries out its commission.

TRANSFORMATION OF THE NEW TESTAMENT CHURCH

The New Testament church was based on small groups, but the conversion of Constantine caused changes. In 313 Licinius and Constantine joined forces and issued the Edict of Milan which allowed all religions to practice freely under their governance. As a result, Christians returned to their confiscated lands, clergy became exempted from imperial taxes, and Sundays were recognized as the official day of rest. However the consequences were not all beneficial. As the church was given political recognition and sanction it lost some of its vibrancy. Christians who formerly professed their faith with the

---

[559] (See Hebrews. 12:23, "to the general assembly and church of the firstborn who are enrolled in heaven, and to God, the Judge of all, and to the spirits of the righteous made perfect", *NASD)*; see also Rev.21-22).
[560] Matthew 28:16

possibility of execution upon discovery, were now welcome as part of the governmental establishment. The model of good news to the poor was replaced with one of seeing wealth and societal success as a sign of God's blessing.

As churches were built with government funds, the small home communities lost importance and were removed from the wineskin. The secret power of the church was in the small groups, nurturing, witnessing and training. When the emphasis was taken away from this dynamic life giving strategy, it was replaced by the "cathedral model." Much of the vitality of the church evaporated. In her book Jerusalem to Irian Jaya, Ruth A Tucker comments:

> Few decades later with the conversion of the Roman Emperor Constantine, Christianity became a state religion, and as a result the churches were flooded with nominal Christians who has less concern for spiritual things. Christianity became the fashion. Elaborate structures replaced the simple house churches, and creeds replaced the spontaneous testimonies and prayers. The need for aggressive evangelism seemed superfluous - at least within the civilized Roman world.[561]

The impact of the Edict of Milan lingers. Compare the New Testament church with the church of today:

Area	New Testament Church	Reference	Today's Church
Location	Moved From house to house	Acts 2:46 Rom 16:5	Meet in church buildings
Size of Groups	Small intimate groups & large celebration	Acts 2:46 Acts 5:42	Large, impersonal groups
Activities	Daily fellowship	Acts 5:42	Weekly worship service

---

[561] Tucker, Ruth, Zondervan (2004), pg. 25

Support Systems	Building up one another	1 Theses 5:11	Problem? See the pastor
Relationships	Intimate; helping one another	Acts 2:44, 45 James 5:16	Remote: little transparency
Discipline	Modeling, personal values shaped	I John 1:1-3 1 Thess 1:5-7	Classes, little modeling values not shaped
Primary Tasks of Leaders	Every believer equipped to do the work of the ministry	Eph 4:11-12	Directing the program, and base design
Prayer Life	Hours spent, daily, heavy emphasis	Acts 3:11 Thess 5:17	Individual choice, limited
Expectations of members	Ministering to others; total servanthood and stewardship	Eph. 4:7-12 Mark 16:17,18	Attendance; tithing; working in the programs
Challenge	Go and make disciples	Matt 28:19	Come and grow with us
Teachings	Apply the scriptures to needs and relationships	Acts 20:32	Subscribe to the distinctive beliefs of the church
Spiritual Gifts	Regularly exercised by all believers to build up others in the cell group gatherings	1 Cor. 12:7 1 Peter 4:10	Either downplayed or often, used as a "crowd pleaser" in public services
Commitment	To increase the kingdom; unity, body life	1 Cor. 3:4-9	To enlarge the institution; uniformity

Evaluation	How you serve	1 Cor. 8:1	What you know
Source of Staff	Servant workers developed; Tested before they are set apart for ministry.	Eph. 4:12	Professional clergy, friends and relations

As we can see, the departure from the early church is substantial.

APPLICATION: THE CHURCH IN SRI LANKA

Background

The social structure of Sri Lanka is community based. Our emphasis is not on the nuclear family, but on an extended family. It is not unusual for parents and children to live together even after they are married. If they live separately, links are very close, parents demand regular visits from the children, and failure to do so will be met with great disapproval.

Decision-making in Sri Lanka is a complex process. Individuals can make decisions that will affect their lives, but implementation depends on the blessing of the family and community. The best example is in the area of marriage. Young people today tend to find their own life partner. However, this must be approved by the parents and in some families the extended family also plays a vital role. If the parents disapprove, the child will either have to buckle under the pressure or proceed and accept rejection from family and community. If the decision is upheld by the community, there is great rejoicing. The community will rally around the couple, people will pool their resources, and the wedding will be celebrated by the community. It is the whole community's event.

Case Study

On Monday June 19th 2006, I received a call from one of the leaders of the Tamil Language Church informing me that a child in the church had passed away. I rushed to the hospital; I was of course surprised to see the entire leadership of the Tamil church and large number of believers on the hospital premises. Doctors confirmed that the child passed away in the early hours of the morning. Because it was a sudden death, they would not release the body without a post-mortem. The entire community decided to stay with the grieving parents until the body was released.

After the body was released that evening, the community took over the planning of the funeral service; they visited me and confirmed the time of the service. The church leadership decided to pay part of the funeral expenses, people pooled their resources, and the young couple was released from the financial responsibility. The community flocked to the home of the grieving couple, they stayed with them. The neighbours provided food. The entire community was grieving, and few went to work the next day. They gathered at church for the service, and accompanied the parents to the cemetery. At the conclusion of the sad burial, the community returned to the home of grieving couple. A few left but a large number of people stayed, not only for that night but for seven days.

Within this culture the community will protect and safeguard their members and share resources. In times of sickness or grief, the community will offer support, even at great sacrifice to its individual members. Long hours spent visiting and enjoying conversation are normal. Weddings, when endorsed by the community, are celebrated as a community event. Often the community will pay for the celebration. However, when one fails to meet the expectation of the community, all this support is lost, and isolation is the consequence.

These same forces come into play when someone is converted. An individual or a family will make the decision to follow Christ due to an inner need or because they witnessed a kind act of our sovereign God. Even though this is a private decision, the larger community will respond to it, either endorsing the decision or opposing it. If they oppose the decision they will cut off the family from the community. This is one of the most difficult forms of persecution for those who have been raised in countries where community life is strong.

In this rich context of community life, the church must create small communities so that conversion does not deprive the new converts of their community life. I am strongly opposed to creating small groups for the sake of having small groups or because it is the program of the church. The church must intentionally create Christian communities, they are essential; they are the life blood of our society.

Our Approach

When we recognized this need we divided the church into six geographical zones. The zone leader is empowered to establish genuine Christian communities that care for one another and support each other in times of need. These Christian communities meet once a week for prayer, but visit each other as often as they can. We have encouraged each zone to meet regularly for meals. The community responds to and cares for each other. We train our Christian communities to look outside their walls and respond to the needs of the larger community. They are taught that we are called to be the light of the world and salt of the earth. Evangelism must take place in the places we live; it must be genuine and natural. These new communities replace what they have lost in the process of joining the church.

These communities are effective because we have tapped into the culture of the Sri Lankan community. The essence of community is a sense of belonging. There is a powerful Christian comradeship established when people belong to each other. Moreover, if the new communities are guided with proper training and encouraged to adopt incarnational living, they influence the larger community for Christ through their example. These Christian enclaves penetrate deeply into the structures of the larger community reaching people in a personal way. The genuine community life among the Christians will also encourage others who may have been intimidated by the possibility of ostracism from considering the claims of Christ. In addition, the gifts of the members are used in natural settings and not isolated within the church.

Small Christian communities provide an ideal environment to grow without attracting the attention of the larger community. The New Testament proved the reality of this truth, as does our own experience. Establishment of these communities is an effective and inexpensive method to reach our country for Christ. Its form provides protection in a hostile environment. It also maximizes the effect of leadership, by providing manageable groups to mentor. It also promotes community prayer and care for the sick and needy, just as the New Testament church did. Since all the gifts of the community are evident it is also conducive to promoting leadership values.

In the processes of building many small Christian communities, it is possible that we may sacrifice our leadership standards in order to achieve our goal. With this in mind we have incorporated the qualification of a leader based on the first Timothy passages into our training program and introduced what we call the ten commandments of leaders of small communities. We require each leader to be mature men and women exhibiting qualities as presented in first Timothy:

> Here is a trustworthy saying: if anyone sets his heart on being an overseer, he desires a noble task. now the overseer must be above reproach, the husband of but one wife, temperate, self-controlled, respectable, hospitable, able to teach, not given to drunkenness, not violent but gentle, not quarrelsome, not a lover of money. he must manage his own family well and see that his children obey him with proper respect. (if anyone does not know how to manage his own family, how can he take care of god's church?) he must not be a recent convert, or he may become conceited and fall under the same judgment as the devil. he must also have a good reputation with outsiders, so that he will not fall into disgrace and into the devil's trap. [562]

We require our leaders to commit themselves to key principles outlined below:

---

[562] 1 Timothy 3:1-7 (NIV)

Commitment	Reference
I commit myself to wait upon the Lord daily	"…but those who hope in the LORD will renew their strength. They will soar on wings like eagles; they will run and not grow weary, they will walk and not be faint."[1]
I commit myself to pray for my church, the leaders of Kithu Sevana, other Churches in Sri Lanka and for world missions	"In the morning, O LORD, you hear my voice; in the morning I lay my requests before you and wait in expectation."[2]
I commit myself to study the word of God on a daily basis	"I have hidden your word in my heart that I might not sin against you."[3]
I commit myself to walk in the light with God and man.	"If we claim to have fellowship with him yet walk in the darkness, we lie and do not live by the truth. But if we walk in the light, as he is in the light, we have fellowship with one another, and the blood of Jesus, his Son, purifies us from all sin."[4]
I commit myself to make Jesus known to all human beings	"Then Jesus came to them and said, "All authority in heaven and on earth has been given to me.Therefore go and make disciples of all nations, baptizing them in the name of the Father and of the Son and of the Holy Spirit, and teaching them to obey everything I have commanded you. And surely I am with you always, to the very end of the age."[5]

I commit myself to teach, encourage, rebuke and take care of the sheep God has entrusted to my care	"All Scripture is God-breathed and is useful for teaching, rebuking, correcting and training in righteousness" [1]
I commit myself to be accountable to the body, taking responsibility for my behavior	"so that there should be no division in the body, but that its parts should have equal concern for each other. If one part suffers, every part suffers with it; if one part is honored, every part rejoices with it. Now you are the body of Christ and each one of you is a part of it."[2]

---

[1] Isaiah 40:31 (NIV)
[2] Psalms 5:3 (NIV)
[3] Psalm 119:11 (NIV)
[4] I John 1:6-7 (NIV)
[5] Matthew 28:18-20 (NIV)

I commit myself to be a loving and a responsible spouse and a good parent to my children	"Wives, submit to your husbands as to the Lord. For the husband is the head of the wife as Christ is the head of the church, his body, of which he is the Savior. Now as the church submits to Christ, so also wives should submit to their husbands in everything. Husbands, love your wives, just as Christ loved the church and gave himself up for herto make her holy, cleansing her by the washing with water through the word, and to present her to himself as a radiant church, without stain or wrinkle or any other blemish, but holy and blameless. In this same way, husbands ought to love their wives as their own bodies. He who loves his wife loves himself."
	"After all, no one ever hated his own body, but he feeds and cares for it, just as Christ does the church--for we are members of his body. "For this reason a man will leave his father and mother and be united to his wife, and the two will become one flesh. "This is a profound mystery-- but I am talking about Christ and the church. However, each one of you also must love his wife as he loves himself, and the wife must respect her husband." [1]
	"Fathers, do not exasperate your children; instead, bring them up in the training and instruction of the Lord." [2]

[1] 2Timothy 3:16 (NIV)
[2] 1 Corinthians 12:25-27 (NIV)

I commit myself to take care of my health	"Don't you know that you yourselves are God's temple and that God's Spirit lives in you?"[1]
I commit myself to give my tithes, and raise money to support the ministry of Kithu Sevana	"Will a man rob God? Yet you rob me. "But you ask, 'How do we rob you?' "In tithes and offerings. You are under a curse-- the whole nation of you-- because you are robbing me. Bring the whole tithe into the storehouse, that there may be food in my house. Test me in this," says the LORD Almighty, "and see if I will not throw open the floodgates of heaven and pour out so much blessing that you will not have room enough for it. I will prevent pests from devouring your crops, and the vines in your fields will not cast their fruit," says the LORD Almighty. "Then all the nations will call you blessed, for yours will be a delightful land," says the LORD Almighty."[2]

In addition to being qualified the leader must be effectively trained. This subject is discussed in the next chapter.

Conclusion

Although small groups may be effective training grounds for believers, they cannot substitute for true Christian communities. Only in these communities can there be adequate modeling, support and relationships. Separating Christian growth from society by isolating it to within a church robs it of much of its vitality. Churches must develop methods to take discipleship from the classroom to the sitting room.

---

[1] Ephesians 5:22-33 (NIV)
[2] Ephesians 6:4 (NIV)

CHAPTER 9

Leadership Foundation

THE IMPORTANCE OF LEADERSHIP

A successful businessman friend told me that in his opinion the chances of succeeding in any enterprise depends on the size of the problems confronting you divided by the quality of the solution and methods you are using to overcome those problems multiplied by the quality of your leadership to the third power. It could be mathematically expressed like this; where P stands for problem, S stands for solution, L stands for leadership and CS stands for chance of success; $CS=P/(S \times L^3)$. If true, it would mean the leadership is exponentially more important than any other factor in success. I tend to agree with this opinion. God, in His universal Church has given use a multitude of gifts to accomplish His mission. Identifying and harnessing those gifts is the job of leadership.

THE NATURE OF LEADERSHIP

People view leadership from many different angles. For some it is a position to be aspired to because it is connected with power, honor and

---

[1] 1 Corinthians 3:16 (NIV)
[2] Malachi 3:8-12 (NIV)

prestige. For others it is the gateway for an easy and comfortable life. The scriptures have a different emphasis. Several years ago, I was asked to join a training team headed to the Ukraine. Mikhail Gorbachev's *glasnost* policy had opened the former Soviet block to religion. I was asked to teach the new leaders on the office of church elder. To prepare myself, I studied all the Bible verses that discussed elders, bishops, and pastors which I then broke down into subjects. I expected and found verses on qualifications and duties, but I was surprised to find that the vast majority of the verses dealt with the attitude of an elder, not his duties. Typically, as I sought a handbook on rules and responsibilities, my study sent me back to where God always focuses-the heart. Examine how the Bible treats leadership:

> To the elders among you, I appeal as a fellow elder, a witness of Christ's sufferings and one who also will share in the glory to be revealed: Be shepherds of God's flock that is under your care, serving as overseers—not because you must, but because you are willing, as God wants you to be; not greedy for money, but eager to serve; not lording it over those entrusted to you, but being examples to the flock. And when the Chief Shepherd appears, you will receive the crown of glory that will never fade away.[563]

Let us review the elements expressed in this verse. "Be shepherds of God's flock that is under your care, serving as overseers-not because you must, but because you are willing, as God wants you to be; not greedy for money, but eager to serve, not lording it over those entrusted to you, but being examples to the flock." Peter's command is to "shepherd" (*poimanate*) God's "flock" (*poimnion*). The comparison of God's people to a flock of sheep and the Lord to a shepherd is prominent in Scripture. (See, for example, Jacob's words: "The God who has been my Shepherd all my life";[564] David's Shepherd Psalm;[565] (Psalm 100:3: "We are his people, the sheep of his pasture".)[566]

The verb *poimaino* ("shepherd") occurs in Christ's command

---

[563] 1 Peter 5:1-4 (NIV)
[564] Genesis 48:1
[565] Psalms 23
[566] See also Isaiah 53:6-7; Luke 15:3-7, the parable of the lost sheep, and John 10:1-16.

to Peter[567] and Paul's charge to the Ephesian elders.[568] Its meaning embraces protecting, leading, guiding, feeding and caring. This is the role God calls us to. Peter's exhortation to the elders "Be shepherds of God's flock" is followed by three contrasting statements that tell how this responsibility is and is not to be handled, "Serving as overseers ... because you are willing ... eager to serve." [569]

Biblical leadership is not a burden; we are to cheerfully approach our work. The labors of the ministry are arduous but there is no work on earth for which a man can and should labor more cheerfully, [570]"not because you must, but because you are willing."[571] Since the responsibilities of the office of elder are great and since elders will be required to give account of their work,[572] no one should be forced into this position. God will work in men's lives and make them willing to do his will. One's attitude should be, "not greedy for money, but eager to serve;" [573]

The motivation of leaders must be divine, not human. Although elders were paid in the early church and handled the finances of the congregations,[574] financial interest is excluded as a reason for service. Enthusiasm and zeal for God and His work should be the motivation for elders. They are not to be "lords" over "those entrusted to"[575] (kleroi, "allotted to") them. Probably in each congregation, individual elders had portions of the congregation for which they were particularly responsible. The elders were to serve the people eagerly,"...being examples to the flock. " [576] The phrase means in humility, self-abasement self-renunciation, and heavenly-mindedness, they are to be examples to the flock, molds of a heavenly form, into which the spirits and lives of the flock may be cast, that they may come out in a perfect pattern.[577]

Leadership positions are often sought because to the prestige and

---

[567] John 21:16
[568] Acts 20:28
[569] 1 Peter 5:2
[570] Barnes' Notes, Electronic Database Copyright 1997, 2003 by Biblesoft, Inc.
[571] 1 Peter 5:2
[572] Hebrews 13:17
[573] 1 Peter 5:2
[574] cf. 1 Corinthians 9:7-11; 1 Timothy 5:17
[575] 1 Peter 5:3
[576] 1 Peter 5:3-4 (NIV)
[577] Adam Clarke Commentary

power that accompany the position. Biblical leadership is based on service to the needs of others, and the leader's reward is not obtained in this lifetime, *"And when the Chief Shepherd appears, you will receive the crown of glory that will never fade away."* [578]As leaders of God's mission we "…. shall receive a crown of glory." Unlike the rewards of the earth this crown of reward will "not fade away". The phrase "not fade away" is the same usage found in 1 Peter 1:4 and translated as "can never perish":

> Praise be to the God and Father of our Lord Jesus Christ! In his great mercy he has given us new birth into a living hope through the resurrection of Jesus Christ from the dead, and into an inheritance that can never perish, spoil or fade—kept in heaven for you. [579]

The phrase occurs nowhere else in the New Testament. It will not vanish, as that which we inherit in this world does. The meaning here is that the inheritance will be imperishable, or will endure forever. Our reward will be entirely as eternal as our salvation. This should be our goal. If we desire temporal goals they will fade and disappoint.

I would define Christian leadership as the ability to influence others to follow his or her lead toward a goal established by God. J. Robert Clinton puts it this way:

> A Christian leader is a person with a God-given capacity and the God-given responsibility to influence a specific group of God's people towards God's purpose for the group. This definition draws attention to the initiative of God in calling forth leadership, a point that is strongly emphasized throughout Scripture.

We have only to think of the call of Abram, Joseph, Moses, Gideon, David, Isaiah, the twelve Apostles and Paul, many of whom were not obvious choices in terms of their innate abilities and experience, but in each case, having been called, they were equipped by God in order to fulfill their calling. Their role was to "influence" their attendant group. How this influence exerts itself depends on the leader and the effected group. Some individuals exercise leadership behind the scenes by

---

[578] 1 Peter 5:4 (NIV)
[579] 1 Peter 1:3-4 (NIV)

advising and mentoring, other leaders have a more public and general sphere of influence.

Biblical leadership is quite different from the leadership theories of the 1980's that focused on high powered, entrepreneurial leadership, exercised by larger-than life "charismatic" personalities. James Kouzes and Barry Posner emphasize that 'leadership is not the private reserve of a few charismatic men and women. It is a process ordinary people use when they are bringing forth the best from themselves and others. Leadership is your capacity to guide others to places they (and you) have never been before.' In fact, although charisma is undoubtedly an asset for a leader, being charismatic is not the same as being a leader.

The Western world often mistakes charisma for leadership. Many organizations have persons they tout as "Leaders" who are nothing of the sort. These charismatic imposters are often larger than life. They invest heavily in relationships and are impressively affirming, generating intense loyalty from their followers. These are all good traits. How then are they not effective leaders? The problem lies with what they accomplish and what they recruit to. They will generate loyalty, not to any mission, vision for ministry or to their organization, but to themselves. Often their followers are more concerned about advancement and opportunities for their "leader" than they are about their mission.

There is a popular phrase, "You can judge the leader by his followers." This is partially true. However, when charisma and personal loyalty are substituted for leadership toward a goal, the saying loses its vigor. This type or leader may be distinguished by his lack of real accomplishment. There will always be statements of accomplishment, of great impact, of successes for the Lord. But like the Wizard of Oz, when one looks behind the curtain there is only disappointment. Charisma and human charm are admired in the world, but in God's kingdom, if not properly applied, they are only diverting.

Leadership is now understood to imply collective action, orchestrated in such a way as to bring about significant change while raising the competencies and motivation of all those involved. Robert Banks and Bernice M. Ledbetter, in offering their definition of leadership, embrace this border concept. For them, "Leadership involves a person, group, or organization who shows the way in an area of life, whether in the short or the long term, and in doing so influences and empowers enough people to bring about change in that area."

As Christians we must not clamor for positions of leadership but instead concentrate on how to effectively influence others towards God's mission. This emphasis should compel churches to refrain from appointing people to positions of leadership if they are not effective in influencing others in the right direction. As the great military leader Bernard Montgomery said, "Leadership is the capacity and will to rally men and women to a common purpose". United States President Harry S. Truman said "a leader is a person who has the ability to get others to do what they don't want to do, and like it."[580]

If by "leader" we mean one who holds a position of authority and responsibility, then every Christian is not a leader. Some are and some are not. But if by a "leader" we mean a person who enters into a relationship with another person to influence their behavior, values or attitudes, then all Christians should be leaders influencing the lives of those around them. The extent of one's influence may vary. Think of a television station. One may be a small local station reaching only a nearby city. Another may be a network station reaching an entire country. A third may be like satellite television influencing the entire world. A title may give one more scope, but that does not necessarily mean more influence.

I have two goods friends at church, a husband and wife. They are certainly capable of leading ministries, but they rarely accept such offers. Instead they live an exemplary life in the community. As a result, they have brought couple after couple to the church. Another person I know was given a leadership position without necessary experience and preparation. The position was offered based on the person's "passion" for the leadership position. Despite a dismal performance, the 'leader' fought to hold on to the title though any means necessary. The result was a ministry very nearly destroyed.

If we define leadership as influence, then our ability to influence or inability to influence will determine whether we are leading well. John Maxwell commented, "If you think you are leading and no one is following you, you have just taken a walk". Simply having followers is not the criteria. Christian leaders have followers moving toward a goal of the Kingdom.

---

[580] Spiritual Leadership. J. Oswald Sanders pp.27-28

DEVELOPING LEADERS

As the company of followers around Jesus increased in His second year of ministry He began to narrow the company to a more manageable number. Accordingly, from the disciples, He chose twelve, whom He named "apostles".[581] Regardless of the symbolical meaning one prefers to put upon the number twelve, it is clear that Jesus intended these men to have unique privileges and responsibilities in kingdom work. This does not mean that Jesus' decision to have twelve excluded others from following Him, for as we know, many more were numbered among His associates, and some of them became very effective workers in the church. Nevertheless, there was less time and training given to those outside the twelve.

The same rule could be applied in reverse, for within the select apostolic group Peter, James and John seem to enjoy a more special relationship to the Master than the other nine. Only these privileged few are invited to the sick room of Jairus' daughter[582] they alone go up with the Master and behold His glory on the Mount of Transfiguration;[583] and amid the olive trees of Gethsemane casting their ominous shadows in the light of the full Passover moon, these members of the inner circle waited near to their Lord while He prayed. [584]

Jesus lived with those he led, allowed them to watch Him, taught them in the context of daily living and involved them in the ministry. When the time was right He empowered them to carry on the ministry. Leaders build leaders, and Jesus took personal responsibility for each of the leaders He built. He did not delegate this to a "leadership development department" within His ministry. If leadership merely consisted of knowing a bunch of facts and mastering a few competencies, then the great task of building new leaders could be delegated to someone else. But leadership primarily consists of knowing God. It also critically consists of issues such as proper relationships with others, accountability, support and servanthood. Moreover, it involves deep issues of character and personal calling. These are matters that cannot and must not be delegated to others. Only a leader who first

---

[581] Luke:6
[582] Mark 5: 37; Luke 8:51
[583] Mark 9:2; Matthew17:1, Luke 9:28
[584] Mark 14:33; Matthew 26:37

has come to some level of personal maturity in these areas himself can lead another new leader into experiential maturity. These traits do not come from books and seminars; they are only imparted by a leader who possesses them. They cannot properly be taught in a classroom; they can only be shared in the context of life.

This does not mean Jesus' disciples were always physically present with Him. There were times when He sent them away, giving them tasks that He knew would help them grow and mature.[585] However, Jesus still personally designed the various transformational experiences He gave His disciples. Jesus built His new leaders "with Him." This was what they became known for, "When they saw the courage of Peter and John and realized that they were unschooled, ordinary men, they were astonished and they took note that these men had been with Jesus."[586] They lived with Jesus, walked with Him, talked with Him, ate with Him, rested with Him and they watched Him in every situation. They saw how He lived, how He reacted, how He dealt with good people, how He dealt with bad people. They watched how He prayed to His Father, how He lived and ministered entirely out of the indwelling life of His Father. They watched Him heal the sick, cast out demons, miraculously feed the multitudes and raise the dead. They watched Him in victory; they watched Him in the apparent defeat of His rejection and death on the cross. They watched Him cry over Jerusalem; they watched Him agonize over the hypocrisy of His people; they watched Him wrestle with the shortage of true laborers for the harvest. They saw how He exposed the false religious traditions of self-righteous men; they watched Him affirm the genuine purity and faith of the broken. They watched Him talk to God when things were going well, and they watched Him pour out His heart to His Father as He struggled and "learned obedience." [587]

Having invested time, He prayed with them, and for them and He empowered them for ministry:

> Then Jesus came to them and said, "All authority in heaven and on earth has been given to me. Therefore go and make disciples of all nations, baptizing them in the name of the Father and of the Son

---

[585] See e.g., Luke10:1
[586] Acts 4:13
[587] Hebrews5:8

and of the Holy Spirit, and teaching them to obey everything I have commanded you. And surely I am with you always, to the very end of the age."[588]

The word "authority" (*exousia* [ex-oo-see'-ah]) can be translated as "authority", "jurisdiction", "liberty", "power", "right, and strength". In other words, all authority, jurisdiction, liberty, power and strength have been given to Jesus. The ensuing commission is backed up by authority of God with power extending to every realm.

Jesus, who defeated the powers of darkness by his death and resurrection, and who is now seated at the right hand of the Father, empowers the apostles to gather and to baptise in his name while giving the promise to be with the apostles forever. This is empowering. Empowering is not using people to achieve your personal objectives, but rather equipping, supporting, motivating, and mentoring individuals to become all that God wants them to be and to achieve all that God has intended them to achieve.

PRAYER AND LEADERSHIP

In the process of leadership development, much emphasis is placed on techniques and principles to be observed. I do not dismiss them for they are essential, but I am deeply concerned that not enough emphasis is placed on prayer, especially the leader praying for those whom he is grooming for the future. A failure to support leadership in prayer is in sharp contradiction with what Jesus modeled. Turning to scripture, we find many examples of the power of prayer in supporting leadership.

Prayer for Protection

Christian leaders, as influencers of others, are prime targets for spiritual warfare. Our first duty must be to pray for their protection:

I pray for them. I am not praying for the world, but for those you have given me, for they are yours. "I pray for them" in view of their

---

[588] Matthew 28:18-20 (NIV)

dangers and trials, he sought the protection and blessing of God on them. All I have is yours, and all you have is mine. And glory has come to me through them.

I will remain in the world no longer, but they are still in the world, and I am coming to you. Holy Father, protect them by the power of your name -- the name you gave me -- so that they may be one as we are one. While I was with them, I protected them and kept them safe by that name you gave me. None has been lost except the one doomed to destruction so that Scripture would be fulfilled.[589]

"I am no more in the world," Jesus had finished His work among men and was about to leave the world and rejoin His Father.[590] His followers were still "… in the world." Jesus is aware they will be among wicked men and malignant foes. They will be subject to trials and persecutions. They will need the same protection which Jesus could give them if He were still with them.

Jesus asks God to protect them, "by the power of your name." Translators understood this expression to mean "keep by thy power," but this probably is not its meaning. It literally means "keep in thy name." And if the term "name" be taken to denote God Himself, it means, "keep in the knowledge of thyself. Preserve them in obedience to thee and to thy cause. Suffer them not to fall away from thee and to become apostates."

Prayer for Joy

Jesus prayed that His leaders experience the joy of service, "I am coming to you now, but I say these things while I am still in the world, so that they may have the full measure of my joy within them." [591]

"That you have the full measure of joy"; the usage here means completely (*pleeroothee*, grk 4137) filled up: a metaphor taken from a vessel into which water or any other thing is poured until it is full to the brim. Jesus is committed to the Apostles, He longs to see them happy, and towards this end He is praying for them. This is *agape* love

[589] John 17: 9-12
[590] See John 17:4
[591] John 17:13

in action; this is real leadership. Good leaders are committed to ensure that those who follow them are well-loved and cared for.

Prayer for Separation from Worldly Influences

Jesus knows that to effectively serve His followers must be immersed in the world, but He prays that they keep the perspective of heaven. He prays to assure that the Christian influencers are not themselves subject to the world's influences, "I have given them your word and the world has hated them, for they are not of the world any more than I am of the world. My prayer is not that you take them out of the world but that you protect them from the evil one."[592]

Jesus intercedes for the Apostles; He is aware that the evil one will do all that he can do undermine their faith, discourage them in the ministry, bring about interpersonal conflicts and destroy their potential. Aware of the schemes of the evil one, Jesus prays and asks the Father to protect them:

> They are not of the world, even as I am not of it. Sanctify them by the truth; your word is truth. As you sent me into the world, I have sent them into the world. For them I sanctify myself, that they too may be truly sanctified. "My prayer is not for them alone. I pray also for those who will believe in me through their message."[593]

This is fascinating; He prays for the Apostles and also for those who will put their trust in Him because of their ministry. He is fully aware that if the influencers fall, they will take others with them.

Prayer for Unity

Aware that unity is vital for both effectiveness and protection, Jesus next turns to pray for that virtue in His leaders:

> ...that all of them may be one, Father, just as you are in me and I am

[592] John 17 14-15
[593] John 16-20

in you. May they also be in us so that the world may believe that you have sent me. I have given them the glory that you gave me, that they may be one as we are one: I in them and you in me. May they be brought to complete unity to let the world know that you sent me and have loved them even as you have loved me.[594]

It is through this unity that the power of His followers is achieved. Jesus is concerned about the unity of the team as all Christian leaders should be. Jesus closes with a touching requests that God love His followers as He has loved His Son:

Father, I want those you have given me to be with me where I am, and to see my glory, the glory you have given me because you loved me before the creation of the world. "Righteous Father, though the world does not know you, I know you, and they know that you have sent me. I have made you known to them, and will continue to make you known in order that the love you have for me may be in them and that I myself may be in them."[595]

Based of Jesus' model of prayer for leaders, it is surprising to see a failure to emphasize prayer in modern Christian leadership books and manuals. The primary function of a leader in developing leaders begins when the leader gets on his knees on behalf of the people he is grooming for leadership.

MODELING

Jesus' actions show that he was more concerned in modeling a life of Godliness for the Apostles than expounding abstract information on leadership. Jesus lived with the Apostles, He taught them in the context of ministry, He ate with them, and He prayed with them and for them. The Apostles watched Him perform miracles, they saw His dependence on the Father, they saw how He related to the poor and the weak, they saw how He reacted to the Pharisees and they saw teaching took place must often in a form of modeling.

According to noted medical missionary Albert Schweitzer, "Example

---

[594] John 17: 21-23
[595] John 17: 24-26

is not the main thing in influencing others ... it is the only thing."[596] Part of creating an appealing climate is modeling leadership. People emulate what they see modeled. Positive model; positive response. Negative model; negative response. What leaders do, potential leaders around them do. What they value, their people value. The leaders' goals become their goals. Leaders set the tone. As Lee Iacocca suggests, "The speed of the boss is the speed of the team." A leader cannot demand of others what he does not demand of himself. In Shakespeare's Henry V, King Henry tries to convince Kathryn his fiancée to give him a kiss. Kathryn replies that it is not the custom in France to kiss before marriage. The King in response says, "We are the makers of manners." Leaders, for good or ill, are the makers of manners for their followers. Timothy writes, "Let no one look down on your youthfulness, but rather in speech, conduct, love, faith and purity, show yourself an example of those who believe."[597] The Greek for "example" is to stamp, as the image of a king is stamped on a coin. A leader through modeling stamps his life on the life of another.

As we improve as leaders, so will those we lead. We need to remember that when people follow us, they can only go as far as we go. If our growth stops, our ability to lead will stop along with it. Neither personality nor methodology can substitute for personal growth. We cannot model what we do not possess. Begin learning and growing today, and watch those around you begin to grow. As leaders, we are primarily followers of great principles and other great leaders.

About ten percent of leaders become leaders because of natural gifts, about five percent through the trauma of crises and a full eighty-five percent due to the influence of others.[598] We learn to lead by following. Paul said simply, "Follow my example, as I follow the example of Christ."[599] Paul's statement may at first seem arrogant. On the contrary he put himself squarely on the line by making this statement. Paul knew that if his followers were going to see Jesus at all, it had to be through him, not apart from him.

---

[596] Simpson's Contemporary Quotations, compiled by James B. Simpson
[597] NASB
[598] John Maxwell
[599] 1 Corinthians.11:1 (NIV)

Jesus Modeled Prayer

We have already noted that leaders must engage in prayer for their followers. In addition, they must also model prayer for their followers. It is fascinating to note that Jesus never called the disciples and said I am going to teach you to pray. Instead he slipped out in the mornings or late in the night and spent the whole night in prayer.

Luke noted the Savior's praying often. Thus, at His baptism,[600] in the wilderness,[601] before the appointment of the Apostles, He continued all night in prayer,[602] He was often alone praying,[603] His transfiguration also took place when He went up to pray.[604] He was modeling a life of prayer and dependence. Deeply impressed by the example, one of the disciples asked Him to teach them to pray.[605] He modeled prayer to the father acknowledging on His own He could do nothing, "Therefore Jesus answered and was saying to them, "Truly, truly, I say to you, the Son can do nothing of Himself, unless {it is} something He sees the Father doing; for whatever the Father does, these things the Son also does in like manner." [606] Seeking the will of the Father through prayer must be modeled by every Christian leader.

Jesus Modeled Compassion

Compassion was always on Jesus' heart, "When Jesus landed and saw a large crowd, he had compassion on them and healed their sick." [607] "Had compassion on them"; that is, He pitied them. In Mark it says he was moved with compassion because they were as sheep having no shepherd.[608] A shepherd is one who takes care of a flock. It was his duty to feed it; to defend it from wolves and other wild beasts;

---

[600] Luke 3:21
[601] Luke 5:16
[602] Luke 6:12
[603] Luke 9:18
[604] Luke 9:28-29
[605] Luke 11:1 (NIV)
[606] John 5:19 (NAU)
[607] Matthew 14:14 (NIV)
[608] Mark 6:34

to take care of the young and feeble; to lead it by green pastures and still waters.[609] In Eastern countries this was a principal employment of the inhabitants. When Christ says the people were as sheep without a shepherd, He means that they had no teachers and guides who cared for them and took pains to instruct them. The scribes and Pharisees were haughty and proud and cared little for the common people; and when they did attempt to teach them, they led them astray. They therefore came in great multitudes to Him who preached the gospel to the poor,[610] because He was the good shepherd.[611]

This verse is challenging to any Christian worker, because it reveals the depth of compassion that Jesus had for people. It becomes more challenging and fascinating when we study the context in which He responded to the needs of the people. Consider Jesus after the death of John the Baptist, "John's disciples came and took his body and buried it. Then they went and told Jesus. When Jesus heard what had happened, he withdrew by boat privately to a solitary place. Hearing of this, the crowds followed him on foot from the towns."[612]

When Jesus learned of John's death, He withdrew. Some have suggested that He moved away fearing that Herod might harm Him too, but his life and ministry contradict this position. Jesus moved away because He was sad that his friend and cousin, the one who baptized Him and the one who was appointed by God to prepare the way for His ministry was killed. Jesus as a man modeled the deep love and caring necessary to minister for the Lord, complete with its personal cost of sadness, "Have this mind in you, which was also in Christ Jesus: who, existing in the form of God, counted not the being on equality with God a thing to be grasped? but emptied himself, taking the form of a servant, being made in the likeness of men"[613]

The one who existed as God took on the form of a servant. The word "taking" (*labon*) does not imply an exchange, but rather an addition. The "form of God" could not be relinquished, for God cannot cease to be God; but our Lord could and did take on the form of a lowly servant when He entered human life by the incarnation.

---

[609] See e.g. Psalms 23
[610] Matthew 11:5
[611] See Barnes' Notes on John 10:14
[612] Matthew 14:12-13 (NIV)
[613] Philippians 2:5-7 (ASV)

Jesus Christ made Himself of no reputation; that is, He emptied Himself. The word "emptied" (*ekenosen*) means to completely empty. It is the picture of "pouring water out of a glass until it is empty" or of "dumping something until it is all removed."[614] The very picture of being completely empty stirs a feeling of just how far Christ went in humbling Himself for us. It is a picture of how much Christ gave up so He could relate to man, model for man and die in man's place. What was it that was poured out or emptied out of Jesus Christ when He left heaven and came to earth?

Christ did not lay aside His deity when He came to earth. He could not cease to be who He was; God. No person can ever cease to be who he is. A person may take on different traits and behave differently; a person may change his behavior and looks, but he is the same person in being, nature, and essence. Jesus Christ is God; therefore, He is always God; He always possesses the nature of God.

Christ "emptied himself" of some of His rights as God: He laid aside His right to experience the glory, majesty, honor and worship of heaven. In coming to earth as a man, He experienced anything but glory and majesty, honor and worship. Men would treat Him far differently than a heavenly being. Matthew Henry notes, "He emptied Himself, divested Himself of the honors and glories of the upper world and of His former appearance, to clothe Himself with the rags of human nature." [615]

He emptied Himself of the right to act as God and confined himself to being a mere human, humbling Himself even to die on the cross. Because He confined Himself to act as man on earth, He experienced all of the pain and suffering we humans experience. In this context, one could imagine what happened. He was sad and grieving because of John's death, but when He saw the needs of others He abandoned his sorrow so that He could minister to others in need. He was moved by compassion and modeled compassion. I am sure the Apostles took note of this attitude.

As evening approached, the disciples came to Him and said, "This is a remote place, and it's already getting late. Send the crowds away, so they can go to the villages and buy themselves some food."[616] The Apostles were getting desperate, finally they came to Him, "It is high

---

[614] Barclay The Letters to the Philippians, Colossians, and Thessalonians, p.44
[615] *Matthew Henry's Commentary, Vol.6, p.732f*
[616] Matthew 14:15, (NIV)

time you stopped, you are tired and these people need to go and buy some food." Jesus responds, "They do not need to go away. You give them something to eat." Tired and saddened, Jesus was still concerned for the crowd's spiritual welfare and physical needs.

JESUS MODELED
SERVANT LEADERSHIP

The leadership model that exists in most of the world is linear-from the top down. It is based on authority. The leadership model for the church is circular and based on the effective use of gifts and the sacrifice of the leader to serve the follower. Our primary example is Christ. He gave the example of a leader being a shepherd; He said, "I am the good shepherd. The good shepherd lays down his life for the sheep."[617]

Once again we must think of the life of a shepherd. Sheep are stupid and easily fall into all manner of hazards. They will become confused and frightened even when still close to the herd. They will stray away; they have no defense against predators, they will wonder into water and drown. The life of the shepherd is one of constant attention. He must see that they are fed, protected from wolves and led on safe paths. They must tend to an injured member of the flock and nurse the weaker sheep.[618] The Christian leader must emulate these actions.[619] The Christian leader, like the shepherd, must also constantly guard those under his care, "Watch out for false prophets. They come to you in sheep's clothing, but inwardly they are ferocious wolves."[620]

In other words, a Christian leader, while he may possess authority, uses his position to become a servant subordinating himself to the care of other. As Pastor John MacArthur put it:

Under the plan God has ordained for the church, leadership is a position of humble, loving service. Church leadership is ministry, not management. Those whom God designates as leaders are

---

[617] John 10:11
[618] See Ezekiel 34:16, for parallels
[619] 1 Corinthians 11:1
[620] Matthew 7:15

called not to be governing monarchs, but humble slaves; not slick celebrities, but laboring servants. Those who would lead God's people must above all exemplify sacrifice, devotion, submission, and lowliness. Jesus Himself gave us the pattern when He stooped to wash His disciples' feet, a task that was customarily done by the lowest of slaves (John 13). If the Lord of the universe would do that, no church leader has a right to think of himself as a bigwig.[621]

Despite the truth of this statement, Christian leaders are human and subject to the same ambitions and temptations of others humans. We strive to move up the leadership ladder; we want the higher paying, the more prestigious job. Our personal desires and the organizational influences we face cannot help to shape our path. This was true even of the disciples:

They were on their way up to Jerusalem, with Jesus leading the way, and the disciples were astonished, while those who followed were afraid. Again he took the Twelve aside and told them what was going to happen to him. "We are going up to Jerusalem," he said, "and the Son of Man will be betrayed to the chief priests and teachers of the law. They will condemn him to death and will hand him over to the Gentiles, who will mock him and spit on him, flog him and kill him. Three days later he will rise."[622]

In verse thirty-three, Jesus is talking about the death that awaits him in Jerusalem. Despite this profound message two of the disciples have other thoughts in mind, "Then James and John, the sons of Zebedee, came to him. "Teacher," they said, "we want you to do for us whatever we ask." "What do you want me to do for you?" he asked. They replied, "Let one of us sit at your right and the other at your left in your glory."[623]

For James and John, the agony and pain of Jesus is not important. They are more interested in securing a well established and recognized position of leadership. They were saying, in effect, "Jesus don't bother us with your pain, just make us the two key leaders."

---

[621] MacArthur, John *"Wanted: A Few Good Shepherds (Must Know How to Wash Feet)*

[622] Mark 10:32-34

[623] Mark 10:35-37

'You don't know what you are asking,' Jesus said. 'Can you drink the cup I drink or be baptized with the baptism I am baptized with?' 'We can,' they answered. Jesus said to them, 'You will drink the cup I drink and be baptized with the baptism I am baptized with, but to sit at my right or left is not for me to grant. These places belong to those for whom they have been prepared.' [624]

When the remaining ten disciples heard this they were indignant.[625] Why were they angry? They were angry because they feared for their own positions. They were in leadership for the wrong reason. The ambition which leads to spiritual lordship is one great cause of animosity in religious societies, and has proved the ruin of even the most flourishing churches.[626] Despite this Jesus replied with gentleness. Jesus made two points, first they have not yet met the qualifications for leadership and proved themselves worthy to "drink the cup I drink" and second, that position in heaven is not achieved in the manner it is achieved on earth, it is for, "those for whom it has been prepared." The others became upset with James and John for asking for seeking a position above them.[627] Jesus was forced to explain what Christian leadership means:

> Jesus called them together and said, 'You know that those who are regarded as rulers of the Gentiles lord it over them, and their high officials exercise authority over them. Not so with you. Instead, whoever wants to become great among you must be your servant, and whoever wants to be first must be slave of all. For even the Son of Man did not come to be served, but to serve, and to give his life as a ransom for many.' [628]

First, he reminded the Twelve of the world's standard of greatness. It is customary for rulers and dignitaries to exercise lordship and authority over the people. In Jesus' world the opposite is true. "Not so with you. Instead, whoever wants to become great among you must be your servant." In contrast to the world the one who would be great must

---

[624] Mark 10:32-41 (NIV)
[625] Mark 10:41 (NIV)
[626] Adam Clarke Commentary
[627] Mark 10:41, NASB
[628] Mark 10:42-45 (NIV)

be a minister to his fellows and "and whoever wants to be first must be slave of all."

As His death would soon establish, Jesus did not talk about this in the abstract; He modeled for their benefit, "For even the Son of Man did not come to be served, but to serve, and to give his life as a ransom for many." Jesus demonstrated the principle in John 13:1-17:

It was just before the Passover Feast. Jesus knew that the time had come for him to leave this world and go to the Father. Having loved his own who were in the world, he now showed them the full extent of his love. The evening meal was being served, and the devil had already prompted Judas Iscariot, son of Simon, to betray Jesus. Jesus knew that the Father had put all things under his power, and that he had come from God and was returning to God; so he got up from the meal, took off his outer clothing, and wrapped a towel around his waist. After that, he poured water into a basin and began to wash his disciples' feet, drying them with the towel that was wrapped around him.

He came to Simon Peter, who said to him, "Lord, are you going to wash my feet?" Jesus replied, "You do not realize now what I am doing, but later you will understand." "No," said Peter, "you shall never wash my feet." Jesus answered, "Unless I wash you, you have no part with me." "Then, Lord," Simon Peter replied, "not just my feet but my hands and my head as well!" Jesus answered, "A person who has had a bath needs only to wash his feet; his whole body is clean. And you are clean, though not every one of you."

For he knew who was going to betray him, and that was why he said not every one was clean. When he had finished washing their feet, he put on his clothes and returned to his place. "Do you understand what I have done for you?" he asked them. "You call me 'Teacher' and 'Lord,' and rightly so, for that is what I am.

Now that I, your Lord and Teacher, have washed your feet, you also should wash one another's feet. I have set you an example that you should do as I have done for you. I tell you the truth, no servant is greater than his master, nor is a messenger greater than the one who sent him. Now that you know these things, you will be blessed if you do them. [629]

Washing feet was a practice deeply steeped in the Old Testament.[630] Washing feet was the first act on entering the tent or house after a journey. Since people wore only sandals, this washing was refreshing as well as hygienic. In the case of ordinary people, the host furnished the water, and the guests washed their own feet, but in the richer houses, the washing was done by a slave. It was looked upon as the lowliest of all services.[631]

On the last evening of His life, Jesus washed the disciples' feet.[632] Their pride, heightened by the anticipation of their place in the Messianic kingdom (the fulfillment of which they immediately expected) prevented them from doing this service for each other. Possibly the same pride had expressed itself on this same evening in a controversy about places at the table. The apostles were refusing to serve one another, and they were jockeying for positions of leadership, but Jesus offered correction as a true leader, by modeling. His simple act was more powerful than ten thousand sermons.

Jesus Modeled Suffering for God

This is another subject that is absent from the books and seminars on leadership. Leaders must be prepared to serve and minister in a fallen world with an enemy who will do all that is within his power to neutralize effective workers. We have not prepared them to face difficulties, disappointments, hurts and organized persecution. Christian leadership development will fail if we do not place appropriate and adequate emphasis on suffering. This point is often made in scripture: "For it has been granted to you on behalf of Christ not only to believe on him, but also to suffer for him." [633] and "If we suffer, we shall also

---

[629] NIV
[630] See e.g. Genesis 18:4; Genesis 19:2; Genesis 24:32; Genesis 43:24; Judg.19:21; 1 Samuel 25:41; 2 Samuel 11:8; Psalms 58:10
[631] 1 Samuel 25:41
[632] John.13:1-16
[633] Philippians 1:29

reign with him…". [634] Scripture also notes that, "…for a little while you may have had to suffer grief in all kinds of trials [not only persecution, but "all kinds" of suffering]. These have come so that your faith…may be proved genuine and may result in praise, glory and honor when Jesus Christ is revealed." [635] and "…those who suffer according to God's will should commit themselves to their faithful Creator and continue to do good." [636]

In particular, suffering is a vital part of *leadership*. Godly leaders know that sufferings produce spiritual maturity, brokenness and genuine faith in God; thus, they do not shy away from the cross in their lives. The Apostle Paul's cry was: "I want to know Christ and the power of his resurrection and the fellowship of sharing in his sufferings, becoming like him in his death, and so, somehow, to attain to the resurrection from the dead." [637] Look closely: Paul said, "I want to know…the fellowship of sharing in His sufferings." Paul actually desired to suffer with Jesus! This was not because he enjoyed pain in some perverse way, but because he knew that the greatest place of union with God is found in the dark shadows of rejection and suffering. Paul knew that we only find God's deep presence when we have been united with Him in His sufferings and death. Paul knew that the cross precedes the crown, darkness precedes glory, brokenness precedes true victory, and death precedes true life. Thus, Jesus showed the way of suffering to the leaders He was building. He personally demonstrated sufferings to them, "He was despised and rejected by men, a man of sorrows, and familiar with suffering. Like one from whom men hide their faces he was despised, and we esteemed him not."[638]

Jesus said, through the suffering of the cross as He was lifted up from the ground and hung before them, "But I, when I am lifted up from the earth, will draw all men to myself." [639] Paul also demonstrated the cross before the men he raised up as leaders, "You, however, know all about my teaching, my way of life, my purpose, faith, patience, love, endurance, persecutions, sufferings - what kinds of things happened to

---

[634] 2 Timothy 2:12
[635] 1 Peter 1:6-7
[636] 1 Peter 4:19
[637] Philippians 3:10-11
[638] Isaiah.53:3, See also Matthew 26:39, Hebrews 5:8
[639] John 12:32

me in Antioch, Iconium and Lystra, the persecutions I endured. Yet the Lord rescued me from all of them." [640] Today, many Christian leaders are offered the temptation of power without suffering, ministry without any pain. When reality hits them, they are unprepared; no wonder many are abandoning ministry early.

I am surprised by a developing theology which claims that Christians need not suffer. Its advocates believe that if you suffer it is because of lack of faith. I wonder whether they have read the life of Job and other heroes of our faith. This view is denied by a discussion between Peter and Jesus in Matthew 16:23, when Peter tried to talk Jesus into such a theology. Peter spoke against Jesus' death on the cross. Jesus responded sternly, "Get behind me, Satan! You are a stumbling block to me; you do not have in mind the things of God, but the things of men."

Jesus refused a "cross-less" leadership. He knew there is no true authority without sacrifice. Faith is what allows us to persevere through trials, because of our knowledge of the character of God and the eternal life that awaits Christians. We are all familiar with the great Christian hymn; "It is well with my soul":

When peace like a river, attendeth my way;
When sorrows like sea billows roll;

Whatever my lot, thou hast taught me to say,
It is well, it is well with my soul.

It is well...with my soul... It is well, it is well, with my soul...[641]

Though Satan should buffet, though trials should come,
Let this blest assurance control,

That Christ hath regarded my helpless estate,
And hath shed His own blood for my soul.

It is well...with my soul... It is well, it is well, with my soul...

I wonder how many realize the suffering that preceded this great statement of faith written by Horatio Gates Spafford. Spafford was a

[640] 2 Timothy 3:10-11
[641] Horatio Gates Spafford, 1873

prominent Chicago attorney who invested heavily in the downtown real estate of the city. In 1871 fire stuck Chicago, wiping out much of Spafford's investments. Spafford, although dealing with the recent death of his son, and staggering over the loss of much of his fortune, dedicated himself to helping those made homeless by the tragedy. After working hard for two years in this effort, he decided to take his family on a vacation. He and his family would join one of Dwight Moody's evangelistic campaigns and then go on to tour Europe. Spafford, delayed by business, sent his wife and four daughters ahead.

They traveled on the ship *Ville de Harve*. Off Newfoundland, it was struck by the English ship *Loch Earn* and sank within twenty minutes. Although his wife Anna was one of the forty-seven survivors, his four daughters, Maggie, Tanette, Annie and Bessie drowned. Spafford immediately boarded another ship to support his wife. When he finally reached her and Moody in Europe Spafford said, "It is well, the will of God be done" Spafford, in the midst of grief that would have broken most men, understood the character of God and His eternal promise well enough to write one of the greatest hymns of faith ever written.

There is no true spiritual maturity without suffering. There is no true leadership without the cross, "If anyone would come after me, he must deny himself and take up his cross and follow me. For whoever wants to save his life will lose it, but whoever loses his life for me will find it." [642] This was the kind of leadership Jesus taught His disciples: a leadership born of brokenness, produced in pain, forged in the fire of suffering. Such leaders have depth. They have been proven by the trials they face. Malachi gives a wonderful picture of this in verse 3:3, "He will sit as a refiner and purifier of silver." A refiner of silver would sit and hold a piece of silver in the middle of the fire, the fire's hottest spot was necessary to purify the silver. His focus was critical; if it were left a moment too long the silver would be destroyed. The test to determine when it was done was a simple one, it was pure when the smith could see his image in it. God will never hold us in the fire to long, but he will use trial to purify us, until He can see His image.

---

[642] Matthew 16:24-25

CONCLUSION

Scripture establishes that Christian leadership is more than technique. It is modeled by those who have the necessary knowledge, experience and relationship with God. These attributes provide a leader with depth. Gordon MacDonald tells the story of the *Vasa* to illustrate the need for a Christian leader to have this depth.[643] In the 17th century, a Swedish king decided that to project influence throughout the Baltic, he needed a powerful fleet. He commissioned four new galleons, the mightiest of which was to be known as the *Vasa*. It would be the greatest ship ever built. The king was so engrossed in this effort, he personally designed the *Vasa*. No one dared argue against the King's blueprint. It took three years to build the *Vasa*, which was not only a weapon of war but a work of art.

Vasa began her maiden voyage on August 10, 1628, sailing on a light breeze from the southwest. A gale wind appeared from nowhere and the *Vasa* sank within one nautical mile of the start of her voyage before she even left the Stockholm archipelago. The sinking was a mystery until the ship was raised from the depths in 1961. The cause was discovered; the ship lacked ballast. For a sailing ship to be stable it must have as much weight below the waterline as above.

The world is infatuated by what is seen, what is above the waterline. The glib tongue, the smooth speaking style and the handsome features are sought in leaders. However, such leaders may lack the depth that comes from having suffered, and like the *Vasa* capsize at the start of their journey.

---

[643] Form an address at Mariners Church, March 7, 2008

CHAPTER 10

Leadership Application

ATTRIBUTES OF A LEADER

YOU will note the tone of the book and the emphasis is on the personal walk of a worker with God. Without a meaningful deep relationship with God, ministry will only be an ego trip. However, for a worker to succeed, he needs to develop his leadership skills; "personal success without leadership ability brings only limited effectiveness."[644] A person's impact is only a fraction of what it could be with good leadership. The greater the impact you want to make, the greater your influence needs to be. Whatever you will accomplish is restricted by your ability to lead others.

Let me give you a picture of what I mean. Let's say that when it comes to success, you're an 8 (on a scale from 1 to 10). But let's also say that your leadership ability is only a 1. Your level of effectiveness would look like this:

---

[644] Developing The Leader Around You, John C. Maxwell

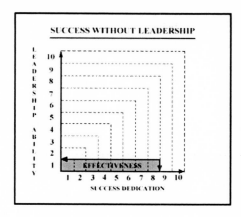

To increase your level of effectiveness, you have a couple of choices. You could work very hard to increase your dedication to success and excellence; you could work toward becoming a 10. But you have another option. Let's say that instead you work hard to increase your level of *leadership*. Over the course of time, you develop yourself as a leader, and eventually, your leadership ability becomes, say, a 6. Visually, the results would look like this:

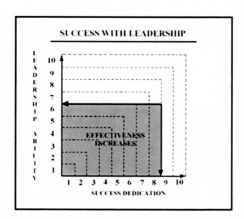

By raising your leadership ability without increasing your success level at all, you can increase your original effectiveness by five hundred percent. If you were to raise your leadership to 8, where it matched your success dedication, you would increase your effectiveness by seven hundred percent. Leadership has an exponential effect.

A Leader Encourages

Henry Ford said, "My best friend is the one who can bring the best out of me. Many leaders expect their people to encourage themselves, but most people require outside encouragement to propel them forward. It is vital to their growth." Physician George Adams found encouragement to be so vital to a person's existence that he called it "Oxygen to the soul".

Researchers are turning up new evidence to support the old truth that encouragement brings out the best in people. In one experiment adults were given ten identical puzzles to solve. They worked on them, turned them in and were given the results. The results however were fictitious. Half of the exam takers were told they had done well, getting seven of ten correct. The other half were told they had done poorly, getting seven of ten wrong. Then all were given another ten puzzles. Again, the puzzles were the same for each person. The half who had been told they had done well with the first puzzles did better with the second set. The other half did worse. Criticism, even though it was given falsely, ruined them.

Victor Frankl said, "If you treat people to a vision of themselves, if you apparently overrate them, you make them become what they are capable of becoming. You know, if we take people as they are, we make them worse. If we take them as they should be, out the best in me." How true. Every leader wants to bring out the best that is in people. And every successful leader knows that encouragement is the correct method.

Sharks grow in proportion to the environment provided. A shark in a pond will be restricted in growth and it will grow in proportion to the pond. If the same shark is allowed to grow in the ocean, the shark will grow to be much bigger. The environment plays a vital role in the growth and the development of the shark. The same is true of your workers. We need to examine the environment we provide. J. C Stachle, after analyzing many surveys found that the principal causes of unrest among workers are actions good leaders can avoid. They are listed in the order of their importance:

1. Failure to give credit for suggestion.
2. Failure to correct grievances.
3. Failure to encourage.
4. Criticizing employees in front of other people.
5. Failure to ask employees to ask for their opinion.
6. Failure to inform employees of their progress.
7. Favoritism.[645]

Avoiding these pitfalls can easily improve one's leadership skills.

A Leader Invests in those with Sound Character

When Paul wrote to Timothy[646] about the qualification of an elder, he was referring to more about the character of the person than his ability. In fact the only ability he referred to was the ability to teach. Apart from character, ministry is only religious activity or even worse, religious business. G Campbell Morgan was riding with D L Moody, when suddenly Moody asked, "What is character anyway" Morgan knew that the evangelist wanted to answer his own question, so he waited. "Character", said Moody "is what man is in dark". General H. Norman Schwarzkof comments "Leadership is a potent combination of strategy and character. But if you must be without one, be without strategy".

Character flaws should not be confused with weaknesses. We all have weaknesses. They can be overcome through training or experience. Character flaws cannot be changed overnight. Change usually takes a long period of time and involves significant relational investment and dedication on the part of the leader. Any person that you hire who has character flaws will be the weak link in your organization. Depending on the nature of the character flaw, the person has the potential to destroy the organization.

---

[645] As quoted from John C. Maxwell., *Developing the Leader within you.*, p.135-136
[646] 1 Timothy 3:1-7

Some of the qualities that make up good character include: honesty, integrity, self-discipline, receptiveness, dependability, perseverance, conscientiousness, and a strong work ethic. The words of a person with right character match the deeds. His reputation is solid. His manner is straightforward.

The assessment of character can be difficult. Warning signs to watch for include: a person's failure to take responsibility for his actions or circumstances and unfulfilled promises or obligations. Also, look at his interaction with others. You can also tell much about a person's character from his relationships. Examine his relationships with superiors, colleagues, and subordinates and ask if appropriate boundaries are maintained.

It is a tragedy when a church looks only to the gifts of individuals and based only on these gifts appoints people into key positions of leadership. If they are gifted but lack in character, sooner or later they will crash, and when they crash they will dishonour the name of God and cause many other innocent believers to stumble. Remember "Apart from character, ministry is only religious activity or even worse, religious business."

A Leader Empowers

To develop leaders, the leader must empower others without fear. Without empowering you cannot develop leaders. When you see the geese heading south for the winter flying along in a "V" formation, you might wonder why they fly that way. Research has revealed that each bird flaps its wings; it creates uplift for the bird immediately behind it. By flying in a "V" formation, the whole flock increases its range compared to birds flying alone, by over seventy percent. People, like geese, get where they are going more quickly and easily when they are traveling on another's lift. Whenever a goose falls out of formation, it suddenly feels the drag and resistance of trying to go it alone. It quickly gets back into formation to take advantage of the lifting power of the bird immediately in front. When the lead goose gets tired, he rotates back into the "V" and another goose flies point. The geese honk from behind to encourage those up front to keep up their speed. Finally, if a goose gets sick or wounded by gunfire and falls out, two other geese fall out of formation and follow it down to help and protect it. They stay with the goose until it is either able to fly again or is dead, and then they start out on their own or with another formation to catch up with their group.[647]

If ministry is to grow, we must empower others. By empowering others we tap into God-given resources that enhance our ministry. "A leader is great, not because of his or her power, but because of his ability to empower others. Success without a successor is a failure. A worker's main responsibility is doing the work himself. A leader's main responsibility is developing others to do the work."[648]

Andrew Carnegie said, "No man will make a great leader who wants to do it all himself or to get all the credit for doing it." Guy Ferguson puts it this way: "To know how to do a job is the accomplishment of labor. To be available to tell others is the accomplishment of the teacher. To inspire others to do better work is the accomplishment of management. To be able to do all three is the accomplishment of true leaders."[649]

In April of 2004, the Rockefeller Institute of Government commissioned a study of the impact of faith based organizations on their communities.[650] The study found that faith based organizations excelled at empowerment, and the results of that empowerment were profound. The study noted that government based programs saw the people they aided as clients and dealt with their problems in piecemeal fashion, the help limited by the confines of the program. Examining some urban programs the study concluded that the persons they served were often disempowered because they were taught:

> [T]he nature and extent of their problems, and the value of services as the answer to their problems. As a result, many lower income urban neighborhoods are now environments of service where behaviors are affected because residents come to believe that their well-being depends upon being a client. They begin to see themselves as people with special needs that can only be met by outsiders.[651]

---

[647] Developing The Leader Around You, John C. Maxwell, p.8
[648] Developing the leader within you, John C. Maxwell, p.9
[649] Quoted from What Every Principal Would Like to Say— and what to Say Next Time ..., by Noah BenShea, pg. 8
[650] Wallace, Meyers & Holly, *The Roundtable on Religion and Social Welfare Policy*
[651] Ibid, pg 7

The effects of such programs are low self esteem, a feeling of worthlessness, dependence and the belief that one's problems can only be solved by others.[652] Contrast this impact with those of a faith based holistic ministry. The study found that such ministries often had empowerment as their chief component. That principle, employed first with the individual, radiates outward through the fabric of the community. The study illustrated this in the table below:

LEVEL OF ANALYSIS	EMPOWERING FAITH-BASED PROCESS	EMPOWERED FAITH-BASED OUTCOMES
	Howfaith empowers individuals and families, organizations, neighborhoods and beyond	The results of empowering faith-based processes
INDIVIDUAL (& FAMILY)	• Relationship building • Opportunities to learn and practiceservice/ ministry skills • Social support • Growth through spiritual disciplines (e.g., study, prayer)	• Strong interpersonal relationships • Sense of mastery and control • Church attendance and participation • Influence on church operations and policy • Spiritual maturity

---

[652] Ibid.

FAITH-BASED ORGANIZATIONS	• Helping members discover spiritual gifts, natural talents, passions, and purpose • Develops members' leadership skills • Provides members social support • Program (i.e., ministry) development • Develop organizational capacity	• Actively involved members • Shared organizational leadership • Increased organizational capacity • Ability to acquire and effectively manage resources, influence public policy and deliver formal services
NEIGHBORHOOD (& BEYOND)	• Collaboration with other faith-based organizations • Community organizing around social issues • Developing linkages across sectors	• Collaboration across sectors • Transformed communities • Political power • Coalitions of organizations [664]

It is apparent that empowering leaders not only aides their growth but also stimulates growth throughout the church and surrounding areas.

Developing leaders for the future is one of the most important functions of any leader. A leader that fails in this area has failed in ministry. He has not invested in others who could continue the ministry

---

[653] Ibid

in the future nor has he increased his productivity by empowering others. He has been out there on an ego trip proving to himself and others that there is no better person than himself. In reality he has been fooling himself and failing to prepare the next generation. Empowering others, however, comes with its traps and barriers.

Barriers to Empowering

Fear of Losing Position

This is one of the most common problems of the church; the leader fearing that others might take his place and ministry, guards his position. A weak leader worries that if he helps subordinates, he will become dispensable. But the truth is that the only way to make yourself indispensable is to make yourself dispensable. In other words, if you are able to continually empower others and help them develop so that they become capable of taking over your job, you will become so valuable to the organization that you become indispensable. That's a paradox of the law of empowerment. Failing to understand this, a weak leader will guard his position even at the expense of destroying and eliminating leaders who may seem to pose a threat, "They came to John and said to him, "Rabbi, that man who was with you on the other side of the Jordan -- the one you testified about -- well, he is baptising, and everyone is going to him." To this John replied, "A man can receive only what is given him from heaven." [654]

The "they" in this text relates to John the Baptist's disciples. Failure to mention Jesus more definitely than to refer to Him as "He", seems like studied depreciation. John's disciples were concerned over the waning position of their leader. The crowds were now gathering in throngs around to Jesus. John answered and said, "A man can receive nothing, except it be given him from heaven."

> The Baptist deplored any thought of rivalry between himself and Jesus. His own place, given by God (from heaven), was not that of the Christ but that of

---

[654] John 3:26-27 (NIV)

the forerunner (v. 28). His position was not that of the Bridegroom, who should take the people of God to himself. This was reserved for another. Rather, he was the friend of the Bridegroom. It was the function of such a man to act as go-between in making the marriage arrangements. His joy was vicarious—participation in the happiness of the groom as a new family was formed.

John's work was done in launching the work of Jesus. He could baptise only with water, not with the Spirit. He could announce the coming of the kingdom but not enter into it himself. His cause had to fade, in the nature of the case, as that of Jesus increased (v. 30). This was God's plan. And so Jesus, in addition to being superior to Judaism, was superior to the movement that centred about John (cf. Acts 19:1-3). [655]

This is true in the case of every individual in ministry; we can have only what God has ordained for us. He loves us and promises to be with us to the end. He does not manipulate us with positions or gifts to attract our attention and draw our love; He loved us even when we were yet sinners. Having forgiven us He has entrusted us with an earthly responsibility and to fulfil this responsibility, He has given us grace and gifts. We need not fear or envy others, because what God has ordained is the best for us and no one can take it away. Only the Lord can; if He does so, it will be for a greater purpose or because we have willingly and consistently disobeyed God. As much as there is security in your call, you cannot prevent another from fulfilling his or her call; if you attempt it, you will destroy your ministry, bringing dishonor to God and disunity in the body.

The Old Testament provides an illustration. When Saul was appointed King of Israel he was also warned that rebellion would result in rejection. [656] Though he was warned, Saul acted foolishly. God therefore rejected him and appointed David in his place.[657] Despite being told David was

[655] Wycliffe Commentary
[656] 1 Samuel 12:13-15
[657] 1 Samuel 13:10-14

the choice of the Lord, Saul tried to keep him from becoming King.[658] Saul's jealousy of David was boundless.[659] Saul spent much of His life in a fruitless attempt to keep David from fulfilling the role ordained to him. His own inability to obey God and walk with him was the cause of the rejection. Rejected by God, he attempts to keep the throne by his own power and ability. The result was tragedy.

Self Image

A self-image based on position is a common problem in the church. If our identity is based on what we do, what we do becomes the most important objective in life. Our security and worth will be determined by it. If it is taken away or there is the threat of it being taken away, it will have devastating effect on us and those around us. God is the object of our faith. He called us to ministry. He gives us grace to serve Him and his people, and He is our security. When we are secure in the Lord, we can do anything. We need not worry about our image, we may simply serve. As we discussed above, Jesus himself proved this concept for us be washing the feet of the disciples.[660]

The foot washing demonstrates the voluntary abasement of our Lord Jesus. Jesus, knowing His own glory as God and His own authority and power as Mediator, might well have risen from supper, laid aside his ordinary garments, called for robes, and told others keep their distance, and do him homage. But, on the contrary, His actions provide us with a great teaching in humanity. As Mathew Henry's Commentary puts it this way, "A well-grounded assurance of heaven and happiness, instead of puffing a man up with pride, will make and keep him very humble." [661]

Failure to See the Need

Some self-made leaders fail to see the need to empower others. Through God's leading they found a relationship with Him and a

---

[658] 1 Samuel 16:12-13
[659] 1 Samuel 18:6-9
[660] See John 13:1-15 and discussion in this chapter
[661] *Matthew Henry's Commentary*

leadership position without being mentored. In most cases, no one was available to help them grow in the Lord. Their commitment and love for God was so intense that they searched for Him in the scriptures, and although they had no role models to follow, they prayed themselves into the ministry. They trusted God, took the biblical promises literally in childlike faith. Willing to suffer any loss, their love for God was greater than any difficulty. God has honored them and blessed their ministry. Leadership development for them is something that flows out of a relationship with God and not something that needs man's assistance. Encouraging others and helping believers in times of discouragement is completely foreign and alien to them. They fail to develop leaders not because they do not want to develop leaders; they see that as the function of God.

We have discussed Henry Ford's vision. He was the revolutionary innovator in the automobile industry and a legend in American business history. In 1903, he co-founded the Ford Motor Company with the belief that the future of the automobile lay in putting it within the reach of the average American. Ford committed to build a car large enough to hold a family but maintainable by one man. Designed to be simple and durable it was low price but high quality. Ford carried his vision with the Model T, and it changed the face of twentieth-century American life. By 1914, Ford was producing nearly fifty percent of all automobiles in the United States. The Ford Motor Company looked like an American success story.

However, Ford's entire story is not about positive achievement, and one of the reasons was that he didn't embrace the law of empowerment. Henry Ford was so in love with his Model T that he never wanted to change or improve it, nor did he want anyone else to change it. One day when a group of his designers surprised him by presenting him with the prototype of an improved model, Ford ripped its doors off the hinges and destroyed the car with his bare hands. For almost twenty years, the Ford Motor Company offered only one design, the Model T, which Ford had personally developed. It wasn't until 1927 that he finally, and grudgingly, agreed to offer a new car to the public. The company produced the Model A, but it was far behind its competitors in technical innovations. Despite its head start and lead over its competitors, the Ford Motor Company's market share kept shrinking. By 1931, it was down to twenty eight percent.

Henry Ford was the antithesis of an empowering leader. He undermined his leaders and looked over the shoulder of his employees. He created a sociological department within Ford Motor Company to check up on his employees and direct their private lives. As time went by, he became more and more eccentric. He once went into his accounting office and tossed the company's books into the street, saying, "Just put all the money we take in [sic] a big barrel and when a shipment of material comes in reach into the barrel and take out enough money to pay for it." He devoted more and more of his time and money to pet projects, such as growing and experimenting with hundreds of varieties of soybeans.

Perhaps Ford's most peculiar dealings were with his executives, especially his son Edsel. The younger Ford had worked at the company since he was a boy. As Henry became more eccentric, Edsel worked harder to keep the company going. If it weren't for Edsel, the Ford Motor Company probably would have gone out of business in the 1930s. Henry eventually gave Edsel the presidency of the company and publicly said that Ford Motor Company's future looked bright with his leadership. Yet at the same time he undermined him and backed other leaders within the organization. Any time a promising leader rose up in the company, Henry tore him down. As a result, the company kept losing its most promising executives. The few who stayed did so because of Edsel. They figured that someday old Henry would die, and Edsel would finally take over and set things right. Instead, in 1943, Edsel died at age forty-nine.

Edsel's oldest son, the twenty-six-year-old Henry Ford II, quickly left the navy so that he could return to Dearborn, Michigan, and take over the company. At first, he faced opposition from his grandfather's entrenched followers. But within two years, he gathered the support of several key people, received the backing of the board of directors and convinced his grandfather to step down so that he could become president in his place.

Young Henry was taking over a company that hadn't made a profit in fifteen years. At that time, it was losing $1 million *a day*! The young president knew he was in over his head, so he began looking for leaders. Fortunately, a group of leaders approached him. It was a team of ten men, headed by Colonel Charles "Tex" Thornton, who had decided they wanted to work together following their service at the War Department during World War II. Their contribution to Ford Motor Company was substantial. In the years to come, the group produced six company vice presidents and two presidents.

The second influx of leadership came with the entrance of Ernie Breech, an experienced General Motors executive and the former president of Bendix Aviation. Young Henry hired him to be Ford's executive vice president. Although Breech held a position second to Henry's, the expectation was that he would take command and turn the company around. And he did. Breech quickly brought in more than 150 outstanding executives from General Motors, and by 1949, Ford Motor Company was on a roll again. In that year, the company sold more than a million Fords, Mercurys, and Lincolns—the best sales since the Model A.

Resistance to Change

Nobel prize-winning author John Steinbeck asserted, "It is the nature of man as he grows older to protest against change, particularly change for the better." By its very nature, empowerment brings constant change because it encourages people to grow and innovate. Change is the price of progress.

A Leader Studies Scripture.

A Christian leader is knowledgabe of the teaching of scripture. One cannot lead without understanding the directions of the "boss." As Timothy wrote:

You, however, continue in the things you have learned and become convinced of, knowing from whom you have learned them, and that from childhood you have known the sacred writings which are able to give you the wisdom that leads to salvation through faith which is in Christ Jesus. All Scripture is inspired by God and profitable for teaching, for reproof, for correction, for training in righteousness; so that the man of God may be adequate, equipped for every good work.[662]

Knowledge of the scriptures is an absolute requirement to be a spiritual leader. It is a weapon to be used in the battle, "For the word of God is living and active and sharper than any two-edged sword, and piercing as far as the division of soul and spirit, of both joints and marrow, and able to judge the thoughts and intentions of the heart."[663] Scripture gives the leader a path to follow. To lead, one must clearly see the destination. Jesus made this clear when speaking of the religious leaders of His day, the Pharisees. Although they had position and authority, Jesus made it clear they could not be trusted to lead. He said, "Let them alone; they are blind guides of the blind. And if a blind man guides a blind man, both will fall into a pit." [664]

The Lord has left his instructions to us in scripture. Without this knowledge we cannot succeed as leaders.

A Leader has Faith

A leader must have absolute confidence in the power of God. He must, along with Paul, be willing to state, "I can do all things through Him who strengthens me."[665] His trust in the Lord must be absolute. A great example of a leader's faith is shown by the life of Gideon. Called to fight the Midianites, he raised an army of 32,000 men. But God said this was too many and Gideon sent 22,000 home. This was still too many to demonstrate the power of God, so Gideon was given a test. Only those who drank in a certain way were allowed to battle for the Lord.

---

662 2 Timothy 3:14-17
663 Hebrews 4:12
664 Matthew 15:14
665 Philippians 4:13

Only three hundred passed this test and that small number prevailed in battle. Imagine the faith shown by Gideon as had faith enough to engage a foe after releasing ninety-nine percent of his army.[666]

The biblical leaders always exemplify great faith. Moses, after initial protestation led his people out of Egypt,[667] Abram left all that he had to journey to Ur,[668] Paul, a persecutor of the church, abandoned a rich life to follow God.[669]

A Leader Leads by Example

In the typical authoritarian model of leadership, the one with the highest position commands by his words. A Christian leader leads by modeling the behavior he wants to see in his followers. Paul described this to Titus, "···in all things show yourself to be an example of good deeds, with purity in doctrine, dignified, sound in speech which is beyond reproach, so that the opponent will be put to shame, having nothing bad to say about us"[670] A leader is to model in all aspects of his life.[671] One cannot be a leader if he does not set the example.

A Leader does not Play Favorites

Paul made this point clear to Timothy, "I solemnly charge you in the presence of God and of Christ Jesus and of His chosen angels, to maintain these principles without bias, doing nothing in a spirit of partiality."[672] In most organizations, the biggest customer, the richest member, the biggest name celebrity receives all the attention. How quickly we, as Christian leaders, fail back into this corrupt model. We favor the rich, calling them differences-makers; we hire family regardless of qualifications saying we can be sure of their loyalty; we give ministry positions to those who help us in our secular lives. None

---

[666] See Judges Chapter six.
[667] Exodus Chapter four
[668] See Romans 4:3
[669] See, e.g. Acts 8:3
[670] Titus 2:7-8
[671] Romans 12:11, NASB
[672] 1 Timothy 5:21, NASB

of these actions may be done by a Christian leader. Those who act in this manner receive a strong rebuke from scripture, "For he who does wrong will receive the consequences of the wrong which he has done, and that without partiality."[673]

A Leader is Steadfast

Christian leaders face all manner of adversity, they must therefore be resolute. James puts it this way, "For that man ought not to expect that he will receive anything from the Lord, being a double-minded man, unstable in all his ways." [674] Corinthians expresses the thought this way, "Therefore, my beloved brethren, be steadfast, immovable, always abounding in the work of the Lord, knowing that your toil is not in vain in the Lord."[675]

A Leader is Wise

When the Apostles needed to choose leaders to serve food to the hungry they looked first for the quality of wisdom, "Therefore, brethren, select from among you seven men of good reputation, full of the Spirit and of wisdom, whom we may put in charge of this task."[676] It is a quality sought in leaders to this day. Wisdom, along with faith and God's word, is what a Christian relies on in times of trouble:

> But you followed my teaching, conduct, purpose, faith, patience, love, perseverance, persecutions, and sufferings, such as happened to me at Antioch, at Iconium and at Lystra; what persecutions I endured, and out of them all the Lord rescued me! Indeed, all who desire to live godly in Christ Jesus will be persecuted. But evil men and impostors will proceed from bad to worse, deceiving and being deceived. You, however, continue in the things you have learned and become convinced of, knowing from whom you have learned them, and that from childhood you have known the sacred writings which are able

---

[673] Colossians 3:25, NASB
[674] James 1:7-8, NASB
[675] 1 Corinthians, 15:58 NASB
[676] Acts 6:3, NASB

to give you the wisdom that leads to salvation through faith which is in Christ Jesus. [677]

Proverbs exalts the importance of wisdom:

Acquire wisdom! Acquire understanding! Do not forget nor turn away from the words of my mouth. "Do not forsake her, and she will guard you; Love her, and she will watch over you. "The beginning of wisdom is: Acquire wisdom; And with all your acquiring, get understanding. "Prize her, and she will exalt you; She will honor you if you embrace her. "She will place on your head a garland of grace; She will present you with a crown of beauty."[678]

If we lack wisdom we are commanded to ask for it from God.[679] Without it we may not serve as leaders.

TRAINING LEADERS

Aesop's Fable

A poor farmer discovers a glittering golden egg in the nest of his pet goose. At first, he thinks it must be some kind of trick. But as he starts to throw the egg aside, he has second thoughts and takes it in to be appraised. The egg is pure gold; the farmer can't believe his good fortune. He becomes even more incredulous the following day when the experience is repeated. Day after day, he awakens to rush to the nest and finds another golden egg. He becomes fabulously wealthy; it all seems too good to be true.

But with his increasing wealth comes greed and impatience. Unable

---

[677] 2 Timothy 3:10-15, NASB
[678] Proverbs 4:5-9, NASB
[679] James 1:5

to wait day after day for the golden eggs, the farmer decides he will kill the goose and get them all at once. But when he opens the goose, he finds it empty. There are no golden eggs, and now there is way to get any more. The farmer has destroyed the goose that produced them. [680] In ministry if you are the leader, your workers are the goose that lay the golden eggs. If they are healthy, well-equipped and happy in the work they do, they will lay more golden eggs.

Part of the equipping process is training people to perform the specific tasks of the jobs they are to do. The approach the leader takes to training will largely determine his people's success or failure. If he takes a dry, academic approach, the potential leaders will remember little of what's taught. If he simply throws the people into the job without any direction, they will certainly crash.

An Approach to Training

The best type of training takes advantage of the way people learn. Researchers tell us that we remember ten percent of what we hear, fifty percent of what we see, seventy percent of what we say, and ninety percent of what we hear, see, say, and do. Knowing that, we must develop a training approach that fully involves the student. A good approach uses a five-step process:

Step 1: Model

The process begins with doing the task while the people being trained watches. We must provide an opportunity to see the whole process. Too often when leaders train, they begin in the middle of the task and confuse the people they are trying to teach. When people see the task performed correctly and completely, it gives them something to duplicate.

Step 2: Mentor

During this next step, continue to perform the task, but this time

---

[680] Stephen R. Covey, The Seven Habit of Highly Effective People, supra, p. 53-54

bring the person being trained alongside to assist in the process. Take time to explain not only the *how,* but also the *why* of each step.

Step 3: Monitor

The next step is to exchange places. The trainee performs the task while the leader assists and corrects. It is especially important during this phase to be positive and encouraging to the trainee to prevent him from abandoning the effort. The leader must continue to work with the trainee until he develops consistency. Once he appears to understand the process, ask him to explain it to you. It will help him to understand and remember.

Step 4: Motivate

The next step is to allow the trainee to perform the task alone. The leader's task is to make sure he knows how to do it without help and to keep encouraging him so he will continue to improve. It is important for the leader to stay with him until he senses success. Success is a great motivator. At this time the trainee may want to make improvements to the process. Encourage him to do it, and at the same time learn from him.

Step 5: Multiply

Once the new leaders do the job well, it becomes their turn to teach others how to do it. As teachers know, the best way to learn something is to teach it. The beauty of this is it frees the original leader to do other important developmental tasks while new leaders carry on the training.

All the training in the world will not help if you don't turn your people loose to do the job. If you get the best people, give them vision, train them in the basics, and then let go, you will get a high return from them. As General George S. Patton once remarked, "Never tell people how to do things. Tell them what to do and they will surprise you with their ingenuity." You can't turn people loose with no structure, but you also want to give them enough freedom to be creative. The way to do that is to give them the big three: responsibility, authority, and accountability. For some people, responsibility is the easiest of the three to give. We all want the people around us to be responsible. We know how important it is. As author/editor Michael Korda said, "Success on any major scale requires you to accept responsibility.... In the final analysis, the one quality that all successful people have ... is the ability to take on responsibility."

What is more difficult for some leaders is allowing their people to keep responsibility after it's been given. Poor managers want to control every detail of their people's work. When that happens, the potential leaders who work for them become frustrated and do not develop. Rather than desiring more responsibility, they become indifferent or avoid responsibility altogether. If you want your people to take responsibility, truly give it to them. With responsibility goes authority. Progress does not come unless they are given together. Winston Churchill, while addressing the House of Commons during the Second World War, said, "I am your servant. You have the right to dismiss me when you please. What you have no right to do is ask me to bear responsibility without the power of action." When responsibility and authority come together, people become genuinely empowered.

There's an important aspect of authority that needs to be noted. When we first give authority to new leaders, we are actually *giving them permission* to have authority rather than *giving them authority* itself. True authority has to be earned. George Davis, in Magic Shortcuts to Executive Success, notes:

> Authority is not something we buy, are born with, or even have delegated to us by our superiors. It is something we earn—and we earn it from our subordinates. No manager has any real authority over his people until he has proved himself worthy of it—in the eyes of his people—not his own, nor those of his superiors. [681]

We must give our people permission to develop authority. That is our responsibility. They, in turn, must take responsibility for earning it.

---

[681] Copyright © 1962 Wiley Periodicals, Inc

Evaluate Performance

One of the most serious errors a leader can make is to let someone continue to hold an important responsibility and carry on that function without evaluating his performance. This harms both the leader and the organization. The leader is harmed because, without an in-depth evaluation, the worker may not be aware of whether he is performing well. He can live in a fool's paradise assuming that he is doing well and contributing to the development of the organization, when in reality he is off target. Wise leaders will evaluate their workers, help them to perform better in weak areas and affirm them in strong areas so that the worker can perform better.

Lack of evaluation harms the organization because the worker may be drifting in continuous activity not contributing to the objectives of the organization. He will continue to be busy without recognizing his failure. Eventually when the organization tires of his failure, the worker is fired. This problem has destroyed many workers and eroded the confidence and potential within them. This could have been avoided if an evaluation was carried out and the worker trained to do better.

Correction is a Leadership Function

Confrontation is very difficult for most people. It may seem less drastic if one substitutes the word "clarify" for "confront". Clarify the issue instead of confronting the person. Then follow these ten commandments of this clarification:

1. Do it privately, not publicly.
2. Do it as soon as possible. That is more natural than waiting.
3. Speak on one issue at a time. Do not overload the person with a long list of issues.
4. Once you've made a point, do not keep repeating it.
5. Deal only with actions the person can change. If you ask the person to do something he or she is unable to do, frustration builds in your relationship.
6. Avoid sarcasm. Sarcasm signals that you are angry at people, not at their actions, and may cause them to resent you.

7. Avoid words like *always* and *never*. They usually detract from accuracy and make people defensive.
8. Present criticisms as suggestions or questions if possible.
9. Don't apologize for the confrontational meeting. Doing so detracts from it and may indicate you are not sure you had the right to say what you did.
10. Don't forget the compliments. Use what I call the "sandwich" in these types of meetings: Compliment – Confront – Compliment.

It is critical that when offering correction the leader maintain a respectful attitude to those that are receiving it. Gene Molway, Pastor of Leadership Development at Mariners Church in Irvine, California, is succinct and emphatic in his opinion:

> Never belittle, humiliate, or threaten a fellow team leader publicly or privately. Never embarrass a leader, or use sarcasm in a hurtful way (is there a non-hurtful way?) Never point your finger at a leader in judgment. Never be disrespectful. Never! Never! Never! [682]

Part of successfully being able to confront the failings of others is being able to recognize and accept one's own failings. As the leader, if you make a mistake, you must be big enough to take responsibility for the mistake. In addition, leaders must not take advantage of their position. Leaders often use their leadership position, knowledge, and speaking skills to break through the defenses of others in order to "win" the argument. They may be are convinced that they won the argument, but in reality they have lost the respect of their followers.

It takes a great deal of character and strength to apologize quickly and from one's heart. People with little internal security cannot do it. It makes them too vulnerable. They feel it makes them appear soft and weak, and they fear that others will take advantage of their weakness. Their security is based on the opinions of other people, and they usually feel justified in what they did. They rationalize their own wrong in the name of the other person's wrong, and if they apologize at all it is superficial. A leader cannot win the argument at the expense of being able to speak to and help the people he leads.

---

[682] Molway, Gene; Pep Talks for Leaders, Ace Ministries, 2007

THE GURU MODEL
OF LEADERSHIP

A guru is a leader who, because of his own hard work and discipline and his extraordinary achievements has been placed in a position of authority. His accomplishments have attracted others to follow him. He is the leader of the movement; others are followers who learn from him. People see him as the authentic leader, and clamor for his attention. When one is a guru, no other person can substitute for him. He is replaced only after retirement or death. This is a common leadership model in Asia. The guru model has infiltrated the church.

An example of this model is found in the life of Moses. During the Exodus, Jethro and the rest of Moses' family joined Moses in the wilderness near Mount Sinai.[683] During this visit, Jethro was quite surprised by the leadership style of Moses; he was burning out and limiting the ability of others to serve. Jethro saw Moses' practice as harmful both to Moses and the people.

Moses was a guru to the people; they stood around him from morning until evening.[684] Jethro is horrified by this act and by how Moses took all responsibility solely on himself.[685] Moses responded with what seems a perfectly reasonable answer,"…"Because the people come to me to inquire of God. When they have a dispute, it comes to me, and I judge between a man and his neighbor and make known the statutes of God and His laws." [686] Even though Moses' response seems right, Jethro sees the danger of his conduct:

> Moses' father-in-law said to him, "The thing that you are doing is not good. "You will surely wear out, both yourself and these people who are with you, for the task is too heavy for you; you cannot do it alone. "Now listen to me: I will give you counsel, and God be with you. You be the people's representative before God, and you bring the disputes to God, then teach them the statutes and the laws, and make known to them the way in which they are to walk and the work they are to do. Furthermore, you shall select out of all the people able men

---

[683] Exodus 18:5
[684] Exodus 18:17-24
[685] Exodus 18:14
[686] Exodus 18:15-16

who fear God, men of truth, those who hate dishonest gain; and you shall place these over them as leaders of thousands, of hundreds, of fifties and of tens. "Let them judge the people at all times; and let it be that every major dispute they will bring to you, but every minor dispute they themselves will judge. So it will be easier for you, and they will bear the burden with you. "If you do this thing and God so commands you, then you will be able to endure, and all these people also will go to their place in peace." [687]

The experience highlighted in Exodus is a common one. It has happened far too many leaders to be ignored. Many leaders have worked themselves to death; others have burned out in ministry. Jethro is genuinely concerned for Moses, so he suggests an alternate strategy, building up leaders to shoulder the burden.

Due to these well known dangers western societies have overreacted and completely rejected the guru model. At times this departure has resulted in inexperienced younger leaders holding station above their abilities. This is very shortsighted. Attempting to correct one problem should not result in replacing it with another. In addition, this approach undermines the values of many cultures where age and experience are greatly valued.

A survey of the Old Testament shows that the leaders were appointed by God to lead the ministries entrusted to them. The older leaders empowered the younger ones, but this does not mean the older leaders were rejected and replaced.

In the New Testament, Jesus continued to lead even to the point of His death on the cross. Peter and Paul continued to lead the ministries entrusted to them. Paul's style of leadership was a guru model. Consider the verses beginning with 2 Timothy 4:9:

Do your best to come to me quickly, for Demas, because he loved this world, has deserted me and has gone to Thessalonica. Crescens has gone to Galatia, and Titus to Dalmatia. Only Luke is with me. Get Mark and bring him with you, because he is helpful to me in my ministry. I sent Tychicus to Ephesus. When you come, bring the cloak that I left with Carpus at Troas, and my scrolls, especially the parchments.

---

[687] Exodus 18:17-23

Alexander the metalworker did me a great deal of harm. The Lord will repay him for what he has done. You too should be on your guard against him, because he strongly opposed our message. At my first defense, no one came to my support, but everyone deserted me. May it not be held against them? But the Lord stood at my side and gave me strength, so that through me the message might be fully proclaimed and all the Gentiles might hear it. And I was delivered from the lion's mouth. The Lord will rescue me from every evil attack and will bring me safely to his heavenly kingdom. To him be glory for ever and ever. Amen.

Greet Priscilla and Aquila and the household of Onesiphorus. Erastus stayed in Corinth, and I left Trophimus sick in Miletus. Do your best to get here before winter. Eubulus greets you, and so do Pudens, Linus, Claudia and all the brothers. The Lord be with your spirit. Grace be with you.[688]

Note the tone of the language and the request he makes. This is the language of a guru as Paul directs his people and requests resources in accordance with his experience.

The problem is not in the guru model, but the failure of the gurus to empower others. We should not replace the guru model because we do not understand it, but instead develop sanctified gurus who will lead ministries entrusted to them while empowering the younger leaders to take their rightful place. The younger leaders also must be encouraged to be faithful to the task the Lord has entrusted to them, knowing that God will honor them for their faithfulnesses though they are not the leader. If we believe that God is sovereign and that He appoints leaders to lead, we can relax and be faithful to that task that the Lord has appointed.

CONCLUSION

The role of the leader is paramount to the success of a ministry. By following the modeling of Jesus, diligently developing the attributes of a leader and effectively training those involved, our organizations become more powerful for the Lord.

---

[688] 2 Timothy 4:9-22, NIV

CHAPTER 11

Giving

INTRODUCTION

STEPHEN King is an American Author who has written more than two hundred stories and fifty bestsellers. His writing is far from the Christian theme; it is based on horror. King writes about evil, mayhem and the dark underside of life.

On June 19, 1999 at about 4:30 p.m., he was walking on the right shoulder of Route 5 in Center Lovell, Maine. Bryan Smith, distracted by his rottweiler, Bullet, struck King with his truck, who landed in a depression in the ground about 14 feet from the pavement. He suffered a collapsed right lung, multiple fractures of the right leg, scalp lacerations and a broken hip. The accident had a profound effect on King, and this author of decidedly non Christian books adopted a decidedly Christian view about our money and resources. This is what he wrote after the accident:

A couple of years ago I found out what "you can't take it with you" means. I found out while I was lying in a ditch at the side of a country road, covered with mud and blood and with the tibia of my right leg poking out the side of my jeans like a branch of a tree taken down in a thunderstorm. I had a MasterCard in my wallet, but when you're lying in a ditch with broken glass in your hair, no one accepts MasterCard.

...We come in naked and broke. We may be dressed when we go out, but we're just as broke. Warren Buffet? Going to go out broke. Bill Gates? Going out broke. Tom Hanks? Going out broke. Steve King? Broke. Not a crying dime.All the money you earn, all the stocks you buy, all the mutual funds you trade—all of that is mostly smoke and mirrors. It's still going to be a quarter-past getting late whether you tell the time on a Timex or a Rolex....

So I want you to consider making your life one long gift to others. And why not? All you have is on loan, anyway. All that lasts is what you pass on. Now imagine a nice little backyard, surrounded by a board fence. Dad—a pleasant fellow, a little plump—is tending the barbecue. Mom and the kids are setting the picnic table: fried chicken, coleslaw, potato salad, a chocolate cake for dessert. And standing around the fence, looking in, are emaciated men and women, starving children. They are silent. They only watch.

That family at the picnic is us; that backyard is America, and those hungry people on the other side of the fence, watching us sit down to eat, include far too much of the rest of the world: Asia and the subcontinent; countries in Central Europe, where people live on the edge from one harvest to the next; South America, where they're burning down the rain forests; and most of all, Africa, where AIDS is pandemic and starvation is a fact of life. It's not a pretty picture, but we have the power to help, the power to change. And why should we refuse? Because we're going to take it with us? Please.

Giving isn't about the receiver or the gift but the giver. It's for the giver. One doesn't open one's wallet to improve the world, although it's nice when that happens; one does it to improve one's self. A life of giving—not just money, but time and spirit—repays. It helps us remember that we may be going out broke, but right now we're doing O.K. Right now we have the power to do great good for others and for ourselves.

So I ask you to begin giving, and to continue as you begin. I think you'll find in the end that you got far more than you ever had, and did more good than you ever dreamed.[689]

Through trauma, King discovered the wisdom available to us through simple obedience, for King clearly stated many of the principles of the Bible. In fact, money, wealth, generosity are some of the most

---

[689] Stephen King, from his graduation address at Vassar College.

frequently discussed topics in Scripture. God understands our attitude regarding money can be a barrier in our relationship with Him:[690]

> But people who long to be rich fall into temptation and are trapped by many foolish and harmful desires that plunge them into ruin and destruction. For the love of money is at the root of all kinds of evil. And some people, craving money, have wandered from the faith and pierced themselves with many sorrows.[691]

God desires an intimate relationship with us. He wants us to experience the abundance He has to offer when we trust Him and place Him first in our life. However, we live in a world which values and honors those who have financial riches. The world demands that we focus on money and solve problems ourselves rather than trusting God with our daily needs. The result is financial bondage. Whether you are poor or successful, without the proper view of God's wealth you are not free. To obtain this freedom we must understand the Bible's view of the wealth entrusted to us.

First, we must understand God is more concerned with ours hearts than our wealth.[692] God has been consistent since the beginning of time regarding our offerings to Him. They are to be proportionate, generous, sacrificial, voluntary, and, most importantly, heartfelt.

GIVING BEFORE MOSAIC LAW

Cain and Abel made the first recorded offering.[693] We are not told what percentage of their harvest they offered as a gift to the Lord. Cain offered some of his crops to the Lord, Abel gave the best and first of his livestock. Upon receiving each gift, God accepted Abel and his gift but rejected Cain and his.

Abram gave an offering to Melchizedek, the King of Salem and Priest of God Most High, as recorded in Genesis 14. Abram's gift was

---

[690] Much of this chapter is taken from a Mariners Church White Paper on giving which was co-authored by one of the authors of this book.

[691] 1 Timothy 6:9-10

[692] Matthew 6:21, "Wherever your treasure is, there your heart and thoughts will also be." NLT

[693] Genesis 4:3-5

ten percent of plunder from war with the remaining ninety percent being returned to the King of Sodom so that the king could never claim he was the one whom made Abram rich.[694] Abram's gift was a voluntary offering in the same proportion that later became a formal part of the Mosaic Law known as the tithe.

Abram's gift was given freely to Melchizedek. A reasonable assumption is that Abram personally sought the heart of God for direction in his action just as he had done so many times before. Jacob promised to give God a tenth of everything God gave to him if God would do certain things for Jacob.[695] Again, it appears the gift was not required by God but a voluntary vow by Jacob.

GIVING UNDER MOSAIC LAW

Giving was defined and regulated under Mosaic Law. Required giving was legislated in Numbers 18. Some of the giving required during this time is detailed below:

Reference	Amount	Description
Leviticus 27:30-33	10%	Levite's tithe
Deuteronomy 12:6-7, 14:22-27	10%	Festival tithe
Deuteronomy 14:28-29	10%	Poor tithe (every three years)
Leviticus 19:9-10		Do not glean the fields so the poor can find food
Nehemiah 10:32-33	One third of a shekel	Temple tax

---

[694] Genesis 14: 21-24
[695] Genesis 28:20-22

VOLUNTARY GIVING

The Old Testament also recounts examples of "free will" giving. The importance of these offerings was not the percentage but the heart or attitude of the giver. Such gifts included first fruits gifts and voluntary offerings. These freewill offerings were given to the Levites but were shared with the poor and needy. Consider these verses:

> The Lord said to Moses 'Tell the people of Israel to bring me their sacred offerings. Accept the contributions from all whose hearts are moved to offer them.[696]

> All must give as they are able, according to the blessings given to them by the Lord your God.[697]

> Then you must celebrate the Festival of Harvest to honor the Lord your God. Bring him a freewill offering in proportion to the blessings you have received from Him.[698]

There are many examples of such voluntary giving in the Old Testament.[699] Required giving was a form of taxation necessary for the social good while voluntary giving always came from the heart.

NEW TESTAMENT GIVING

The New Testament models of giving focus on voluntary action as seen in Luke and first and second Corinthians:

> Give, and it will be given to you: good measure, pressed down, shaken together, and running over will be put into your bosom. For with the same measure that you use, it will be measured back to you.[700]

---

[696] Exodus 25:1-2
[697] Deuteronomy 16:17
[698] Deuteronomy 16:10
[699] See Number 18:12, Proverbs 3:9-10 Exodus 25, 35:21-29ff, 36:5-6, I Chronicles 29.
[700] Luke 6:38

Now concerning the collection for the saints, as I have given orders to the churches of Galatia, so you must do also: On the first day of the week let each one of you lay something aside, storing up as he may prosper, that there be no collections when I come. [701]

Meanwhile, Zacchaeus stood the and said to the Lord, "I will give half my wealth to the poor, Lord, and if I have overcharged people on their taxes, I will give them back four times as much!" Jesus responded, "Salvation has come to this home today, for this man had shown himself to be a son of Abraham.[702]

But this I say: He who sows sparingly will also reap sparingly, and he who sows bountifully will also reap bountifully. So let each one give as he purposes in his heart, not grudgingly or of necessity; for God loves a cheerful giver. And God is able to make all grace abound toward you, that you, always having all sufficiency in all things, may have an abundance for every good work. [703]

There are no references in the New Testament where God requires believers to give a specified percentage of income. Tithing is mentioned only three times in the New Testament.[704] Each of these references is in the context of Israel's obligation to God under the law and is not used as a requirement to believers redeemed by Christ.

Rather than precise instruction, in the New Testament, believers are given values for giving. Believers are asked to give as much as dictated by their hearts and never as a result of pressure.[705] We are also asked to give proportionately as we have been blessed by God.[706] Though we are to give as our hearts require, we are also asked to give regularly[707] and sacrificially.[708]

As was the case with Abel and Abram's giving in the days prior to The First Covenant Law and with offerings given by Israelites over and above the tithe laws, believers today have the pleasure and privilege

---

[701] 1 Corinthians 16:1

[702] Luke 19:8-9

[703] 2 Corinthians 9:6-8

[704] Hebrews 7, Luke 18:9-14, Luke 11:41-42

[705] 2 Corinthians 9:7

[706] 2 Corinthians 8:11-12

[707] 1 Corinthians 16:2

[708] 2 Corinthians 8:2-3

of revealing Christ in their lives by unlimited acts of generosity and obedience as they personally seek to understand and give in ways that will receive the praise and approval of God. Giving is not God's plan for raising money for the church; giving is God's plan to raise disciples of Jesus Christ. Because of this, training in stewardship and giving should be incorporated into church training.

In Philippians, Paul writes:

> I know how to get along with humble means, and I also know how to live in prosperity; in any and every circumstance I have learned the secret of being filled and going hungry, both of having abundance and suffering need. I can do all things through Him who strengthens me. Nevertheless, you have done well to share with me in my affliction. And you yourselves also know, Philippians, that at the first preaching of the gospel, after I departed from Macedonia, no church shared with me in the matter of giving and receiving but you alone; for even in Thessalonica you sent a gift more than once for my needs. Not that I seek the gift itself, but I seek for the profit which increases to your account.[709]

Our motive as leaders is not to raise more money, but to witness the blessings bestowed on believers when they live lives as generous givers. To do this we must teach the tenants of stewardship and giving from the Bible. The role of a steward is shown most clearly in Matthew in the parable of the talents[710] and the parable of the landowner.[711] The parable of the talents makes clear that what we possess is held in trust for its owner, the Lord:

> For it is just like a man about to go on a journey, who called his own slaves and entrusted his possessions to them. To one he gave five talents, to another, two, and to another, one, each according to his own ability; and he went on his journey. Immediately the one who had received the five talents went and traded with them, and gained five more talents. In the same manner the one who had received the two talents gained two more. But he who received the one talent went away, and dug a hole in the ground and hid his master's money.

---

[709] Philippians 4:12-17
[710] Mathew 25:14-30,
[711] Mathew 21:33-46

Now after a long time the master of those slaves came and settled accounts with them. "The one who had received the five talents came up and brought five more talents, saying, 'Master, you entrusted five talents to me. See, I have gained five more talents.' His master said to him, 'Well done, good and faithful slave. You were faithful with a few things, I will put you in charge of many things; enter into the joy of your master.'

Also the one who had received the two talents came up and said, 'Master, you entrusted two talents to me. See, I have gained two more talents.' "His master said to him, 'Well done, good and faithful slave. You were faithful with a few things, I will put you in charge of many things; enter into the joy of your master.'

And the one also who had received the one talent came up and said, 'Master, I knew you to be a hard man, reaping where you did not sow and gathering where you scattered no seed. 'And I was afraid, and went away and hid your talent in the ground. See, you have what is yours.'

But his master answered and said to him, 'You wicked, lazy slave, you knew that I reap where I did not sow and gather where I scattered no seed. 'Then you ought to have put my money in the bank, and on my arrival I would have received my money back with interest. 'Therefore take away the talent from him, and give it to the one who has the ten talents.'

For to everyone who has, more shall be given, and he will have an abundance; but from the one who does not have, even what he does have shall be taken away. "Throw out the worthless slave into the outer darkness; in that place there will be weeping and gnashing of teeth.[712]

This verse makes clear that God had little patience for those who do not understand that what they have is given by him. This principle is reinforced by the parable of the landowner:

Listen to another parable. There was a landowner who PLANTED

---

[712] Mathew 25:14-30, NASB

A VINEYARD AND PUT A WALL AROUND IT AND DUG A WINE PRESS IN IT, AND BUILT A TOWER, and rented it out to vine-growers and went on a journey. When the harvest time approached, he sent his slaves to the vine-growers to receive his produce. The vine-growers took his slaves and beat one, and killed another, and stoned a third. Again he sent another group of slaves larger than the first; and they did the same thing to them. But afterward he sent his son to them, saying, 'They will respect my son.' But when the vine-growers saw the son, they said among themselves, 'This is the heir; come, let us kill him and seize his inheritance.' They took him, and threw him out of the vineyard and killed him. Therefore when the owner of the vineyard comes, what will he do to those vine-growers?" They said to Him, He will bring those wretches to a wretched end, and will rent out the vineyard to other vine-growers who will pay him the proceeds at the proper seasons.[713]

This verse illustrates a fundamental truth, that the world and all that is in it belongs to the Lord,[714] and that we are charged to maintain it on His behalf, "God blessed them and told them, 'Multiply and fill the earth and subdue it. Be masters over the fish and birds and all the animals.' And God said, 'Look! I have given you the seed-bearing plants throughout the earth and all the fruit trees for your food." [715]

It is important to understand that all wealth, however you define it, is from God:

I have no complaint about your sacrifices or the burnt offerings you constantly bring to my altar. But I want no more bulls from your barns; I want no more goats from your pens. For all the animals of the forest are mine, and I own the cattle on a thousand hills. Every bird of the mountains and all the animals of the field belong to me. If I were hungry, I would not mention it to you, for all the world is mine and everything in it.[716]

This principle is echoed in Acts:

---

[713] Mathew 21:33-46 NASD
[714] See e.g. Psalms 24:1, Leviticus 25:23, Haggai 2:8, Deuteronomy 8:18.
[715] Genesis 1:28-29
[716] Psalms 50:8-12

He is the God who made the world and everything in it. Since he is Lord of heaven and earth, he doesn't live in man-made temples, and human hands can't serve his needs-for he has no needs. He himself gives life and breath to everything, and he satisfies every need there is. From one man he created all the nations throughout the whole earth. He decided beforehand which should rise and fall, and he determined their boundaries. His purpose in all of this was that the nations should seek after God and perhaps feel their way toward him and find him-though he is not far from any one of us. For in him we live and move and exist. As one of your own poets says, 'We are his offspring.'[717]

When we understand that everything we have is from God it is easy to understand the attitude toward money and possession that God requires of us. We are to use God's gifts for God's purposes:

Don't store up treasures here on earth, where they can be eaten by moths and get rusty, and where thieves break in and steal. Store your treasures in heaven, where they will never become moth-eaten or rusty and where they will be safe from thieves. Wherever your treasure is, there your heart and thoughts will also be.[718]

When we ignore God's design for use of our wealth, we inadvertently make the decision not to serve Him, as shown in these verses:

No one can serve two masters. For you will hate one and love the other, or be devoted to one and despise the other. You cannot serve both God and money."[719]

Stop loving this evil world and all that it offers you, for when you love the world, you show that you do not have the love of the Father in you. For the world offers only the lust for physical pleasure, the lust for everything we see, and pride in our possessions. These are not from the Father. They are from this evil world.[720]

Often we feel we cannot follow God's teaching because we lack

---

[717] Acts 17: 24-28, NIV
[718] Matthew 6:19-21
[719] Luke 16:13
[720] 1 John 2:15-16

gifts of significance, but God does not need our money, he requires our hearts. A large gift will not please God if given without a joyful heart; a small gift will delight Him if given with joy.[721] God will always perceive our heart.[722] As Ananias learned, we can't deceive God concerning our attitude:

> There was no poverty among them, because people who owned land or houses sold them and brought the money to the apostles to give to others in need...There was also a man named Ananias who, with his wife, Sapphira, sold some property. He brought part of the money to the apostles, but he claimed it was the full amount. His wife had agreed to this deception. Then Peter said, 'Ananias, why has Satan filled your heart? You lied to the Holy Spirit, and you kept some of the money for yourself. The property was yours to sell or not sell, as you wished. And after selling it, the money was yours to give away. How could you do a thing like this? You weren't lying to us but to God.' As soon as Ananias heard these words, he fell to the floor and died. Everyone who heard about it was terrified.[723]

Money is often a barrier in our relationship with God. We focus on the money as our source of security rather than trusting God. Church should be a place where people are taught about the joys of being a giving person. True fulfillment comes not from hoarding resources, but from using resources to honor God and to reflect our trust in Him to meet our needs.

It is difficult as a church leader to focus on the true definition of Biblical giving. We need funds; funds to pay salaries, funds for maintenance of church structures, funds to care for the poor. The temptation is to focus on the good that could be done with the funds rather than the attitude of the giver that is required by God. We can inadvertently find ourselves pressuring others for money, secure in the knowledge that the funds will be well spent. Proper use of funds is important, but it does not justify obtaining them through pressure.

All giving should be done with a proper attitude and heart. Gifts should be given out of love for God and in appreciation for all He provides and not as the result of guilt or undue pressure. Giving is a

---

[721] See e.g. Mark 12:43-44
[722] James 4:3, see also Hebrews 13:5
[723] Acts 4:34-35, 5:1-5

way of showing our obedience to God because we are commanded to give. We must lead others not only to give, but to Biblically give, with a joyful heart and pure motives.[724] Here are some of the motives and characteristics required of us by scripture when dealing with money:

Characteristic	Principle	Reference
Cheerfulness	God loves a cheerful giver	2 Corinthians 9:7
Honesty	Be honest with money in thoughts and deeds	Proverbs 28:6
Humility	...do not be egotistical	Romans 12: 16-17
Forgiveness	forgive the debts and wrongs of others	Matthew 18:23-35
Thankfulness	Always show an attitude of gratefulness	1 Thessalonians 5:18
Obedience	be doers of God's Word	James 1:22
Contentment	be satisfied with what God provides	Philippians 4:11
Trust	place your confidence in God	Luke 12:29-31

We must teach that the giver should ensure his motives are pure. Is he giving to do good and to show his love, trust and obedience? Or is he giving in the hope of obtaining something in return; i.e. recognition, selfish gain, release from feelings of guilt, etc.? It is the responsibility of the leadership of the church to ensure that all teaching and requests for giving are completed in a way that encourages pure motives.

When we claim to serve God, people look for the proof of His love in our lives. We are God's representative on earth. We are His reflection. Therefore, we are to represent Him well. This does not mean we are required to be highly successful, renowned, wealthy or exceptionally

---

[724] Proverbs 16:2, "All the ways of a man are clean in his own sight, but the Lord weighs the motives."*NIV*

brilliant people. We are to follow His precepts without compromise and seek to glorify Him. Since money and possessions are highly valued in the world our actions in these areas we have great impact on how others see the Lord through us. Those who handle their wealth and possessions well receive special favor with the Lord.[725]

THE PRINCIPLE OF SOWING

God does not need our help or our gifts to bring about His plan for the world. The good news for us is that God has chosen to work with and through us as we have faith and are obedient to Him. Moreover, God guarantees us a good return for our gifts. To illustrate we will use the example of the sowing of seeds as did the Lord himself. The apostle Paul uses this example in his second letter to the Christian church in Corinth, where he writes about their generosity to believers in Jerusalem. Paul writes that there is a direct link between how much we plant (give) and how much we harvest (receive). In examining this principle we must be careful. The Bible does not suggest giving as an easy vehicle to obtain more wealth. The return promised by God, is to His eternal plan, and His kingdom, not to the profit of any individual. Let us examine the principle extolled by Paul.

We reap only IF we sow, "Remember this--a farmer who plants only a few seeds will get a small crop. But the one who plants generously will get a generous crop."[726] Consider this example: One kernel of corn contains all the potential to reproduce. If a kernel is planted, it will reproduce itself and bring forth many times the original kernel; each new kernel containing the potential to be planted and yield even more kernels. That cycle can go on and on producing countless millions of kernels. However, if that kernel of corn is taken and cherished, placed in a frame or jar on a table so that it may be admired, it will never grow or multiply. The only way the kernel of corn can be valuable is if it is planted. As long as we hold onto the things God has given us,

---

[725] Matthew 24:45-46, "Who is a faithful, sensible servant, to whom the master can give the responsibility of managing his household and feeding his family? If the master returns and finds that the servant has done a good job, there will be a reward." *NIV*

[726] 2 Corinthians 9:6

refusing to sow them back into the harvest field, we will never see any increase.

We reap only WHAT we sow, "Those who live only to satisfy their own sinful desires will harvest the consequences of decay and death. But those who live to please the Spirit will harvest everlasting life from the Spirit." [727] If we plant corn, we will harvest corn. We cannot plant corn and expect to harvest watermelon. We reap exactly what we sow. If we sow anger and discord, life will be filled with anger and discord. The only way to have friends is to sow friendship. The same principle applies to our use of money.

We reap MORE than we sow, "For God is the one who gives seed to the farmer and then bread to eat. In the same way, he will give you many opportunities to do good, and he will produce a great harvest of generosity in you."[728] Returning to our example of planting corn, if we planted a kernel of corn, nourished it, waited six months, and harvested only one kernel of corn, there would be no reason to sow. There is no gain if there is no increase. God has assured us that our gifts will grow and multiply in His kingdom. In explaining this concept to the Corinthian believers, Paul used the Greek word for abundance several times, "And God is able to make all grace **abound** toward you, that you, **always** having all sufficiency in all things may have an **abundance** for **every** good work." [729] And what sort of return should we expect? According to Matthew our return we be a hundredfold.[730]

We reap LATER than we sow, "So don't get tired of doing what is good. Don't get discouraged and give up, for we will reap a harvest of blessing at the appropriate time."[731] When we plant, we must wait for the harvest. If we plant corn one day, we cannot expect to harvest more corn the next day. No matter how anxious or upset we become, we cannot harvest the corn until the proper time. It takes time for a crop to grow into maturity, "So, my dear brothers and sisters, be strong and immovable. Always work enthusiastically for the Lord, for you know that nothing you do for the Lord is ever useless." [732]

---

[727] Galatians 6:8
[728] 2 Corinthians 9:10
[729] 2 Corinthians 9:8
[730] Matthew 19:29
[731] Galatians 6:9
[732] 1 Corinthians 15:58

Our giving must not be done for self-glorification. God clearly instructs us to give to an audience of one, and, as a church, we should not take any action contrary to the intent of God's direction to the individual members of our church body.

THE PRINCIPLE OF HUMILITY

"Take care! Don't do your good deeds publicly, to be admired, because then you will lose the reward from your Father in heaven. When you give a gift to someone in need, don't shout about it as the hypocrites do – blowing trumpets in the synagogues and streets to call attention to their acts of charity! I assure you, they have received all the reward they will ever get. But when you give to someone, don't tell your left hand what your right hand is doing. Give your gifts in secret, and your Father, who knows all secrets, will reward you." [733]

We must sow with humility. The Bible often cautions against hypocrisy. This word appears frequently in scripture primarily signifying "one who sets himself apart"; one who either pretends to be what he is not or dissembles what he really is.[734] Our giving is for the Lord and not to improve our social standing. In Matthew 3, Jesus not only says that we should not boast, but we should also move so far from making a display that we do not dwell on it even in our own thoughts as it may contribute to spiritual pride:

And when you pray, do not be like the hypocrites, for they love to pray standing in the synagogues and on the street corners to be seen by men. I tell you the truth, they have received their reward in full. But when you pray, go into your room, close the door and pray to your Father, who is unseen. Then your Father, who sees what is done in secret, will reward you. [735]

Although it seems Jesus is condemning public prayer, this is not the case. Jesus is not concerned with public prayer but with vanity. Jesus is dealing with the intent and desire of the person rather than the

[733] Matthew 6:1-4
[734] See Luke 12:1-2
[735] Matthew 6:5-6 NIV

act. If the intent is self-glorification or public acknowledgement, it is wrong. Jesus' concern is with the actor not the act. As leaders we must be cautious not to provide a stage for such actions. This is not as easy as it appears because scripture provides many examples of the public disclosure of gifts. Consider this example:

Now I want to tell you, dear brothers and sisters, what God in his kindness has done for the churches in Macedonia. Though they have been going through much trouble and hard times, their wonderful joy and deep poverty have overflowed in rich generosity. For I can testify that they gave not only what they could afford but far more. And they did it of their own free will. They begged us again and again for the gracious privilege of sharing the gift for the Christians in Jerusalem. Best of all, they went beyond our highest hopes, for their first action was to dedicate themselves to the Lord and to us for whatever directions God might give them [736]

Here Paul publicly celebrates giving. He is free to do so because the gift was made according to Biblical principle, and he has a Godly motive in celebrating.

PAUL'S PRINCIPLES

Paul, as leader in the church, publicly extols the giving of the church in Macedonia as a way to excite and encourage the Corinthians in their giving. Paul goes further:

There is no need for me to write to you about this service to the saints. For I know your eagerness to help, and I have been boasting about it to the Macedonians, telling them that since last year you in Achaia were ready to give; and your enthusiasm has stirred most of them to action. But I am sending the brothers in order that our boasting about you in this matter should not prove hollow, but that you may be ready, as I said you would be. For if any Macedonians come with me and find you unprepared, we-not to say anything about you-would be ashamed of having been so confident. So I thought it necessary to urge the brothers to visit you in advance and finish the arrangements

---

[736] 2 Corinthians 8:1-5, NIV

for the generous gift you had promised. Then it will be ready as a generous gift, not as one grudgingly given...[737]

Paul actually boasts about the Corinthians' eagerness to give. The generous giving of one church is made an important example for other churches. We should note however how Paul did this. First, he acknowledges a group of believers rather than honoring an individual; second, he had a purpose, to show that the gift was received and was important in helping thankful hearts to grow:

> Yes, we will be enriched so that you can give even more generously. And when we take your gifts to those who need them, they will break out in thanksgiving to God. So two good things will happen – the needs of the Christians in Jerusalem will be met, and they will joyfully express their thanksgiving to God [738]

Paul also sees the result that God is praised:

> You will be glorifying God through your generous gifts. For your generosity to them will prove that you are obedient to the Good News of Christ. And they will pray for you with deep affection because of the wonderful grace of God shown through you. Thank God for His Son – a gift too wonderful for words![739]

These verses establish that we are to give generously to model Christ giving to us. We are to give sacrificially as Christ gave to us recognizing we could never give as much as He did, "You know how full of love and kindness our Lord Jesus Christ was. Thou He was very rich, yet for your sakes He became poor, so that by His poverty He could make you rich"[740]

Although we are instructed not to showcase piety for praise, we are also told to let God's love be seen through are good deeds, "In the same way, let your light shine before men, that they may see your good deeds and praise your Father in heaven."[741] For our actions to reflect glory on God and for our deeds to be a light to the world, they must be known.

---

[737] 2 Corinthians 9:1-5, NIV
[738] 2 Corinthians 9:11-12
[739] 2 Corinthians 9:13-15
[740] 2 Corinthians 8:9
[741] Matthew 5:16 NIV

But God also cautions to abstain from doing our acts publicly in order to find praise. How then do we proceed? Once again, we return to the heart for understanding. We must speak primarily through our actions serving God, and not so that we will be *seen* serving God. Only by reflecting God's heart can we paint a true picture of His grace.

To do this, when we feature good deeds, we must have a purpose of glorifying Christ. These works should be highlighted to encourage others and bring praise to God but for not for any personal purpose. Note King David's action in building the temple:

> Then King David said to the whole assembly: "My son Solomon, the one whom God has chosen, is young and inexperienced. The task is great, because this palatial structure is not for man but for the LORD God. With all my resources I have provided for the temple of my God-gold for the gold work, silver for the silver, bronze for the bronze, iron for the iron and wood for the wood, as well as onyx for the settings, turquoise, stones of various colors, and all kinds of fine stone and marble-all of these in large quantities. Besides, in my devotion to the temple of my God I now give my personal treasures of gold and silver for the temple of my God, over and above everything I have provided for this holy temple: three thousand talents of gold (gold of Ophir) and seven thousand talents of refined silver, for the overlaying of the walls of the buildings, for the gold work and the silver work, and for all the work to be done by the craftsmen. Now, who is willing to consecrate himself today to the LORD? [742]

Here David features his own generosity, but his intention was to encourage and be a model to the people regarding their giving. His actions were effective, next his leaders stepped forward to enforce the example set by David, "Then the leaders of families, the officers of the tribes of Israel, the commanders of thousands and commanders of hundreds, and the officials in charge of the king's work gave willingly."[743] As a result of David's public announcement of his giving and demonstration of his commitment, the leaders, officers, and commanders all gave willingly and the example carried forward. We can conclude that acknowledging generosity is appropriate when done for a Godly purpose; to provide testimony, encouragement, modeling

---

[742] 1 Chronicles 29:1-5
[743] 1 Chronicles 29:6

and praise and thanksgiving to God. Paul in his writings is always clear on the need to set an example:

> For you know that you ought to follow our example. We were never lazy when we were with you. We never accepted food from anyone without paying for it. We worked hard day and night so that we would not be a burden to any of you. It wasn't that we didn't have the right to ask you to feed us, but we wanted to give you an example to follow.[744]

And careful to acknowledge those who provided support:

> You yourselves also know, Philippians, that at the first preaching of the gospel, after I left Macedonia, no church shared with me in the matter of giving and receiving but you alone; for even in Thessalonica you sent a gift more than once for my needs. Not that I seek the gift itself, but I seek for the profit which increases to your account. But I have received everything in full and have an abundance; I am amply supplied, having received from Epaphroditus what you have sent, a fragrant aroma, an acceptable sacrifice, well-pleasing to God. And my God will supply all your needs according to His riches in glory in Christ Jesus.[745]

He followed his own teaching by modeling principles of stewardship[746] and required the principles be followed by others.[747] He fortified the importance of his actions by reminding those who relied on him:

> As apostles of Christ we certainly had a right to make some demands of you, but we were as gentle among you as a mother feeding and caring for her own children. We loved you so much that we gave you not only God's Good News but our own lives, too.

> Don't you remember, dear brothers and sisters, how hard we worked among you? Night and day we toiled to earn a living so that our

---

[744] 2 Thessalonians 3:7-10
[745] Philippians 4:15-19
[746] Acts 18:3
[747] 2 Thessalonians 3:10

expenses would not be a burden to anyone there as we preached God's Good News among you.[748]

***

This should be your ambition: to live a quiet life, minding your own business and working with your hands, just as we commanded you before. As a result, people who are not Christians will respect the way you live, and you will not need to depend on others to meet your financial needs.[749]

Paul constantly extolled the importance of giving in his epistles. To the Corinthians, he wrote, "On every Lord's Day, each of you should put aside some amount of money in relation to what you have earned and save it for this offering. Don't wait until I get there and then try to collect it all at once."[750] He followed these instructions by sending Titus to meet with them personally to reinforce what he had written, "So we have urged Titus, who encouraged your giving in the first place, to return to you and encourage you to complete your share in this ministry of giving."[751] In his second letter he answered questions about giving by referring to the Macedonian model:

Now I want to tell you, dear brothers and sisters, what God in his kindness has done for the churches in Macedonia. Though they have been going through much trouble and hard times, their wonderful joy and deep poverty have overflowed in rich generosity. For I can testify that they gave not only what they could afford but far more. And they did it of their own free will. They begged us again and again for the gracious privilege of sharing in the gift for the Christians in Jerusalem. Best of all, they went beyond our highest hopes, for their first action was to dedicate themselves to the Lord and to us for whatever directions God might give them. [752]

He elaborated regarding the importance of the ministry of giving and following through on giving commitments:

---

[748] 1 Thessalonians 2:7-9
[749] 1 Thessalonians 4:11-12 NLT
[750] 1 Corinthians 16:2
[751] 2 Corinthians 8:6
[752] 2 Corinthians 8:1-5

Since you excel in so many ways—you have so much faith, such gifted speakers, such knowledge, such enthusiasm, and such love for us—now I want you to excel also in this gracious ministry of giving. I am not saying you must do it, even though the other churches are eager to do it. This is one way to prove your love is real. You know how full of love and kindness our Lord Jesus Christ was. Though he was very rich, yet for your sakes he became poor, so that by his poverty he could make you rich. I suggest that you finish what you started a year ago, for you were the first to propose this idea, and you were the first to begin doing something about it. Now you should carry this project through to completion just as enthusiastically as you began it. Give whatever you can according to what you have. If you are really eager to give, it isn't important how much you are able to give. God wants you to give what you have, not what you don't have. Of course, I don't mean you should give so much that you suffer from having too little. I only mean that there should be some equality. Right now you have plenty and can help them. Then at some other time they can share with you when you need it. In this way, everyone's needs will be met. Do you remember what the Scriptures say about this? Those who gathered a lot had nothing left over, and those who gathered only a little had enough. [753]

Paul even dedicated leadership to help assure the task was completed sending Titus and two others to help with follow through:

I am thankful to God that he has given Titus the same enthusiasm for you that I have. He welcomed our request that he visit you again. In fact, he himself was eager to go and see you. We are also sending another brother with Titus. He is highly praised in all the churches as a preacher of the Good News. He was appointed by the churches to accompany us as we take the offering to Jerusalem—a service that glorifies the Lord and shows our eagerness to help. By traveling together we will guard against any suspicion, for we are anxious that no one should find fault with the way we are handling this generous gift. We are careful to be honorable before the Lord, but we also want everyone else to know we are honorable.

And we are also sending with them another brother who has been thoroughly tested and has shown how earnest he is on many occasions.

[753] 2 Corinthians 8:7-15

He is now even more enthusiastic because of his increased confidence in you. If anyone asks about Titus, say that he is my partner who works with me to help you. And these brothers are representatives of the churches. They are splendid examples of those who bring glory to Christ. So show them your love, and prove to all the churches that our boasting about you is justified. [754]

Paul sensitively reminded the Corinthians that they had motivated the Macedonians to give in the first place and probably to avoid embarrassment, he informs the Corinthians that some Macedonians will come with him to receive the gift the Corinthians had promised:

I really don't need to write to you about this gift for the Christians in Jerusalem. For I know how eager you are to help, and I have been boasting to our friends in Macedonia that you Christians in Greece were ready to send an offering a year ago. In fact, it was your enthusiasm that stirred up many of them to begin helping. But I am sending these brothers just to be sure that you really are ready, as I told them you would be, with your money all collected. I don't want it to turn out that I was wrong in my boasting about you. I would be humiliated—and so would you—if some Macedonian Christians came with me, only to find that you still weren't ready after all I had told them! [755]

Giving is always near to Paul's heart and present in his instruction. Paul tells Timothy, as a young minister of the gospel to:

Tell those who are rich in this world not to be proud and not to trust in their money, which will soon be gone. But their trust should be in the living God, who richly gives us all we need for our enjoyment. Tell them to use their money to do good. They should be rich in good works and should give generously to those in need, always being ready to share with others whatever God has given them. By doing this they will be storing up their treasure as a good foundation for the future so that they may take hold of real life. [756]

It is apparent that Paul expected Timothy to take an active role in

---

[754] 2 Corinthians 8:16-24, see also 2 Corinthians 9:5
[755] 2 Corinthians 9:1-4, NLT
[756] 1 Timothy 6:17-19, NLT

mentoring those who were blessed with wealth. However, here we must be clear. There is a difference between mentoring those with wealth and showing them favoritism. The latter is forbidden by scripture, "The poor is hated even by his neighbor, but those who love the rich are many."[757] James makes this point:

> My brethren, do not hold your faith in our glorious Lord Jesus Christ with an attitude of personal favoritism. For if a man comes into your assembly with a gold ring and dressed in fine clothes, and there also comes in a poor man in dirty clothes, and you pay special attention to the one who is wearing the fine clothes, and say, "You sit here in a good place," and you say to the poor man, "You stand over there, or sit down by my footstool," have you not made distinctions among yourselves, and become judges with evil motives?[758]

There is no doubt that Paul's teaching on giving was intense and persistent, however this was for a good reason. The Holy Spirit knew how difficult a topic this would be for spiritual leaders and wanted to reinforce the need and level of intensity for this type of communication.

Paul expresses to his congregation the joy that comes from a life of giving as well as the obligation to give. Paul takes no responsibility for any guilt that the reader might experience as a result of his challenge because he knows he is merely sharing the words the Holy Spirit has placed on his heart. In the remainder of his letter, he establishes a series of principles for giving. Some of Paul's principles are summarized below:

Paul's Values	2 Corinthians
Pray-Generous, sacrificial giving is prompted by God's power in people hearts.	8:1
Stories of giving may be shared for proper purposes.	8:1,8
Lead people to seek God's will; He will lead them to give	8:1,5,6

---

[757] Proverbs 14:20
[758] James 2:1-4, NASD

God will lead people to give.	8:5,11
Leaders need to model and encourage giving.	8:6
One may be encouraged to follow through with their intentions	8:6
People should be challenged in giving as with other gifts.	8:7
Work to develop generous givers and a generous church.	8:7,11,15
Encourage full participation regardless of amount;it is the heart that benefits from giving.	8:11
Take the highest care in financial matters; involve others to verify.	8:20
In addition to being right before God, we must work to be honorable in the sight of man.	8:21
Accept gifts only from those with a willing heart.	9:3-5
God multiplies generous giving to His kingdom.	9:6
Do not seek a gift from one who feels under pressure.	9:7
Mature believers are consistent givers, less mature givers believe giving as an event.	9:10
Encourage generosity	9:13

THE PRINCIPLE OF GENEROSITY

We note that we are often instructed to give generously, but why? It is because only by generous giving can we reflect God's gift to us. We must always remember God's gift, "For God so loved the world that he gave his one and only Son, that whoever believes in him shall not perish but have eternal life."[759] God gave His only Son; He lends us the fruits of His world and provides for our needs, "He who did not spare his own Son, but gave him up for us all—how will he not also, along with him, graciously give us all things?" [760] Simply put, anything less than generous giving neglects the character of God to which all Christians ascribe. We must give as we have received, and follow god's example, for He promises to provide for us, "If you, then, though you are evil, know how to give good gifts to your children, how much more will your Father in heaven give good gifts to those who ask him!"[761]

GOD'S AGENDA FOR GIVING

In addition to demonstrating God's attitude for giving we most follow God's agenda in giving. Not every generous act done in the name of the Lord reflects his desires. In another chapter we have discussed working among the poor and its importance to God. It is no surprise then that giving to the poor is a frequently mentioned part of God's agenda for giving, ""He who is kind to the poor lends to the LORD, and he will reward him for what he has done."[762] Such service is service to the Lord:

> [Cornelius] and all his family were devout and God-fearing; he gave generously to those in need and prayed to God regularly. One day at about three in the afternoon he had a vision. He distinctly saw an angel of God, who came to him and said, 'Cornelius!' Cornelius stared at him in fear. 'What is it, Lord?' he asked. The angel answered, 'Your prayers and gifts to the poor have come up as a memorial offering before God ...' [763]

Providing for the needs of one's family is a Godly use of funds,[764] as is meeting the needs of the church and its leaders:

---

[759] John 3:16
[760] Romans 8:32-33
[761] Matthew 7:11
[762] Proverbs 19:17
[763] Acts 10:2-4, See also Galatians 2:9-10, Matthew 25:34-40
[764] 1 Timothy 5:8

Who at any time serves as a soldier at his own expense? Who plants a vineyard and does not eat the fruit of it? Or who tends a flock and does not use the milk of the flock?

I am not speaking these things according to human judgment, am I? Or does not the Law also say these things? For it is written in the Law of Moses, "YOU SHALL NOT MUZZLE THE OX WHILE HE IS THRESHING." God is not concerned about oxen, is He? Or is He speaking altogether for our sake? Yes, for our sake it was written, because the plowman ought to plow in hope, and the thresher to thresh in hope of sharing the crops. If we sowed spiritual things in you, is it too much if we reap material things from you? [765]

This purpose was reinforced later in the chapter, "In the same way, the Lord has commanded that those who preach the gospel should receive their living from the gospel."[766]The Bible also implies support for giving to spread God's word:

···for"WHOEVER WILL CALL ON THE NAME OF THE LORD WILL BE SAVED." How then will they call on Him in whom they have not believed? How will they believe in Him whom they have not heard? And how will they hear without a preacher? How will they preach unless they are sent? Just as it is written, "HOW BEAUTIFUL ARE THE FEET OF THOSE WHO BRING GOOD NEWS OF GOOD THINGS! [767]

Jesus himself used this support in spreading the Word, "After this, Jesus traveled about from one town and village to another, proclaiming the good news of the kingdom of God. The Twelve were with him, and also some women who ... were helping to support them out of their own means." [768]

THE EFFECT OF GIVING

From the verse above, we know giving will rebound to the

---

[765] 1 Corinthians 9:7-11, See also 1 Timothy 5:17
[766] 1 Corinthians 9:14
[767] Romans 10:13-15
[768] Luke 8:1-3

Kingdom's credit, but it also impacts the giver, clearing the way to a proper perspective:

> But godliness with contentment is great gain. For we brought nothing into the world, and we can take nothing out of it. ... Command those who are rich in this present world not to be arrogant nor to put their hope in wealth, which is so uncertain, but to put their hope in God, who richly provides us with everything for our enjoyment. Command them to do good, to be rich in good deeds, and to be generous and willing to share. In this way they will lay up treasure for themselves as a firm foundation for the coming age, so that they may take hold of the life that is truly life.[769]

Jesus recognized the barrier caused by an improper view of money. He commended his followers to relinquish all when wealth interfered with their service.[770] We can only enjoy the benefits of understanding God's character when we manifest His generosity.

CONCLUSION

Jesus often told stories about handling money. Jesus knew spirituality is connected to our generosity.[771] Paul also frequently discussed attitudes towards money and giving.[772] The New Testament church set the example for us.[773] The Old Testament also has sage advice on giving and stewardship.[774]

Many church leaders, perhaps concerned with favoring the wealthy, or being seen as valuing money as the world does, shy away from their obligation to actively encourage, model, acknowledge and develop generosity in their churches. How many ministries have suffered because leaders confused personal reluctance with piety? The failure to engage in developing generous givers is disservice to one's ministry

---

[769] 1 Timothy 6:5, 17-19
[770] Mark 10:21
[771] Luke 16:10-13; Luke 12:13-21; Matthew 6:19-21, 24-34
[772] 1Timothy 6:8-10, 17-19
[773] Acts 2:42-47, Acts 4:32-37
[774] See e.g. Deuteronomy 8:10-18, Proverbs 6:6-11, Proverbs 28:20, Proverbs 21:25-26, 22:7, Proverbs 22:26-27

and is not in accord with scripture. Scripture compels us to develop the gift of generosity along with the other gifts of the body.

CHAPTER 12

The Church

INTRODUCTION

C HURCH is probably the universal icon for Christians. Ask someone to envision a Christian, and they will probably think of a gathering at a church, complete with a culturally relevant structure. Tell someone you are a Christian, and if the statement does not anger them, he will probably immediately ask you which church you are from. The Bible however, does not present the common picture of Christians and their relationship with a church structure. In fact, it is surprising vague on the subject of church.

The doctrine of the church was not mentioned in Old Testament prophecy. Nor is the word found in the Old Testament at all.[775] It was a called a mystery and mentioned only twice in the Gospels.[776] It fares better in the rest of the New Testament; the word "*ekklesia*" which is translated as "church" is mentioned more frequently in the rest of the New Testament. It means, "a called out assembly, meeting, congregation. A community of members on earth, saints in Heaven, or both." As can be seen from the definition, the word does not always relate to a body of believers but can be applied to a secular group [777] or Jewish gathering.[778] Even when referring to believers, it can connote a local gathering, an assembly of local churches, or all those who are saved by Christ, living or dead.[779]

---

[775] However, the people Moses led through the wilderness were mentioned as a group like a church, See Acts 7:38

[776] Matthew 16:18; Matthew18:17

[777] Acts 19:32,39

[778] Acts 7:38

[779] See Discussion in Chapter Five

Perhaps the lack of precision concerning God's church is not so surprising after all. As we have seen in this book, Christians are set to the task of accomplishing God's mission on earth; spreading the word of his sacrifice and salvation and restoring his creation by assuring justice and dignity. We do this not only because we are instructed to but because it is in the very nature of God, His *imagio dei,* that salvation is offered and his creation restored. But technically God has no mission for His church; he left no instruction for "the church" to accomplish His mission, only His followers. The church is a concept created by God to fortify and support His believers in achieving that goal. For that reason, God ordained the church and its three main functions: to glorify God,[780] to evangelize,[781] and to edify the believers.[782] It must therefore be designed for that purpose and its "mission" must be to aid the believers in the accomplishment of theirs.

The New Testament defines the word church as an assembly of believers called to service of the Lord and refers back to the calling of God's people in the Old Testament:

> But you are A CHOSEN RACE, A royal PRIESTHOOD, A HOLY NATION, A PEOPLE FOR God's OWN POSSESSION, so that you may proclaim the excellencies of Him who has called you out of darkness into His marvelous light; for you once were NOT A PEOPLE, but now you are THE PEOPLE OF GOD; you had NOT RECEIVED MERCY, but now you have RECEIVED MERCY.[783]

The church makes believers "one people" for the purpose of reflecting God's image in the world. There are different members who have different gifts, but are one body, and have one mission.[784] It would be wonderful if scripture simply laid out a road map of organization for His church so churches could be perfectly unified, but nothing of the sort can be found in scripture. Instead, to determine the role of the church, we must examine Biblical themes and apply them in light of the overarching obligation to be the worldly embodiment of the *imagio*

---

[780] See, Ephesians 1:6, Ephesians 1:12, Ephesians 1:14, Ephesians 3:10, 1 Corinthians 10:31

[781] Matthew 28:19-20

[782] Matthew 28:19-20, Ephesians 4:7-16

[783] 1 Peter 2:9-10

[784] Romans 12:4-5

dei of the Lord. Christ revealed the content of the truth that the church is to proclaim through His incarnation, "We have seen his glory, the glory of the One and Only, who came from the Father, full of grace and truth" [785]

IMAGES OF THE CHURCH

The Bible refers to the church only through images, duties and hallmarks. That is, the Bible provides representative pictures and defining attributes but no blueprint for the Christian church. In Ephesians, Paul writes:

> So then you are no longer strangers and aliens, but you are fellow citizens with the saints, and are of God's household, having been built on the foundation of the apostles and prophets, Christ Jesus Himself being the corner stone, in whom the whole building, being fitted together, is growing into a holy temple in the Lord, in whom you also are being built together into a dwelling of God in the Spirit. [786]

One hallmark of the church is unity. We were aliens, but God's church makes us citizens, we are members of a family, part of a household; we are fitted together as a temple to the Lord. The cornerstone of the temple is Christ.[787] The image is one of disunity becoming united,[788] through the salvation of Jesus.[789] This unity is not only required of individuals joining together within one church, but also to separate churches working together.

Another attribute is faith. In response to Peter's expression of faith in Jesus, He replied that is was *upon this rock*, which is faith, that Christ would build his church.[790] Christ could not build His church without men of faith. Christians are often identified in the Bible as those who believed (had faith) in the Lord. [791]

---

[785] John 1:14
[786] Ephesians 2:19-22
[787] Ephesians 2:21
[788] Ephesians 4:4
[789] Colossians 1:18
[790] Matthew 16:18
[791] See e.g. Acts 2:44, Acts 4:32, 1 Timothy 4:12

A third attribute is fellowship:

They devoted themselves to the apostles' teaching and to the fellowship, to the breaking of bread, and to prayer. Everyone was filled with awe, and many wonders and miraculous signs were done by the apostles. All the believers were together and had everything in common. Selling their possessions and goods, they gave to anyone as he had need. Every day they continued to meet together in the temple courts. They broke bread in their homes and ate together with glad and sincere hearts, praising God and enjoying the favor of all the people. And the Lord added to their number daily those who were being saved.[792]

It is through fellowship that the gifts and resources are shared to accomplish the church's mission. We could go on to list additional attributes of the church, but that is not the point of this chapter. Rather we will explore the need to seek balance in formulating a church to incorporate these attributes and achieve God's goals.

The most frequent picture of the church is as a group representing the body of Christ, "For just as we have many members in one body and all the members do not have the same function, so we, who are many, are one body in Christ, and individually members one of another."[793] To come to Christ is to be incorporated into his body, the church. The local church is the tool employed in the process of building up the disciple's life. The different gifts of the body of Christ are intended for the complete discipleship of the believers.[794] Church members in their unity to each other mirror the unity of God with the universal church. In fact, unity is so important that the same images are often used for both Christ and Christ's church. Discussing Christ, "Jesus answered them, "Destroy this temple, and in three days I will raise it up.""[795] Concerning His church, "having been built on the foundation of the apostles and prophets, Christ Jesus Himself being the corner stone, in whom the whole building, being fitted together, is growing into a holy temple in

---

[792] Acts 2:42-47
[793] Romans 12:4-5
[794] Hull, Bill. 1990. *The Disciplemaking Church*. Old Tappan: Fleming H. Revell.
[795] John 2:19

the Lord, in whom you also are being built together into a dwelling of God in the Spirit."[796]

Jesus was referred to as the high priest, "Therefore, holy brethren, partakers of a heavenly calling, consider Jesus, the Apostle and High Priest of our confession."[797]

His believers were described as a priesthood, "you also, as living stones, are being built up as a spiritual house for a holy priesthood, to offer up spiritual sacrifices acceptable to God through Jesus Christ."[798]

Jesus and His church are so entwined that the Bible says that the church extends form the vine that is Christ:

> I am the true vine, and My Father is the vinedresser. "Every branch in Me that does not bear fruit, He takes away; and every branch that bears fruit, He prunes it so that it may bear more fruit. "You are already clean because of the word which I have spoken to you. "Abide in Me, and I in you. As the branch cannot bear fruit of itself unless it abides in the vine, so neither can you unless you abide in Me. "I am the vine, you are the branches; he who abides in Me and I in him, he bears much fruit, for apart from Me you can do nothing. "If anyone does not abide in Me, he is thrown away as a branch and dries up; and they gather them, and cast them into the fire and they are burned. "If you abide in Me, and My words abide in you, ask whatever you wish, and it will be done for you. "My Father is glorified by this, that you bear much fruit, and so prove to be My disciples. "Just as the Father has loved Me, I have also loved you; abide in My love. "If you keep My commandments, you will abide in My love; just as I have kept My Father's commandments and abide in His love.[799]

The church grows out of Christ and must reflect His nature. It is this relationship that allows us to bear fruit. It is an intimate relationship likened to the relationship between a husband and wife.[800] The church, called to be the worldly image of God, is intimately related to Christ and His mission:

> Wives, be subject to your own husbands, as to the Lord. For the

---

[796] Ephesians 2:20-22
[797] Hebrews 3:1
[798] 1 Peter 2:5
[799] John 15:1-10
[800] Ephesians 5:22-32

husband is the head of the wife, as Christ also is the head of the church, He Himself being the Savior of the body. But as the church is subject to Christ, so also the wives ought to be to their husbands in everything.

Husbands, love your wives, just as Christ also loved the church and gave Himself up for her, so that He might sanctify her, having cleansed her by the washing of water with the word, that He might present to Himself the church in all her glory, having no spot or wrinkle or any such thing; but that she would be holy and blameless. So husbands ought also to love their own wives as their own bodies. He who loves his own wife loves himself; for no one ever hated his own flesh, but nourishes and cherishes it, just as Christ also does the church, because we are members of His body. FOR THIS REASON A MAN SHALL LEAVE HIS FATHER AND MOTHER AND SHALL BE JOINED TO HIS WIFE, AND THE TWO SHALL BECOME ONE FLESH. This mystery is great; but I am speaking with reference to Christ and the church.[801]

This relationship, called a mystery, may never be fully understood in this world, but it certainly involves transferring the grace received from Christ to the world by modeling and advocating His love and forgiveness. We are also called to understand and follow His commands.[802] The issue confronting His believers is how to find a church framework that that matches these images and supports God's mission on earth.

A CHURCH FRAMEWORK

Having been created in the *imagio dei* we are to reflect our creator and to engage in God's mission, the *missio dei*. Since, as discussed above, the church exists to aid God's followers in pursuit of that mission, it must be designed to accomplish that goal. As noted there in no specific design for God's church on earth, so instead we must look to a framework for its operation. This is a critical exploration. Paul who

---

[801] Ephesians 5:22-32

[802] "*The man who says, 'I know him,' but does not do what he commands is a liar, and the truth is not in him*" 1 John 2:4

claimed to be an "an expert builder" laying the "foundation of Jesus Christ" cautions other believers to "be careful" how they build.[803]

The article, *Missional Helix*,[804] provides such a foundation, recognizing four important elements in church formation each with its own weight. Theological reflection is the first and most important element. This requires a local church to be organized in support of the Biblically mandated elements that form the nature of God. Christ's life, the crucifixion, His ascension and the forgiveness it brought, as well as His mission on earth must be identified and supported within the church. Paul Hiebert writes:

> Too often we choose a few themes and from there build a simplistic theology rather than look at the profound theological motifs that flow through the whole of Scripture. Equally disturbing to the foundations of mission is the dangerous potential of shifting from God and his work to the emphasis of what we can do for God by our own knowledge and efforts. We become captive to a modern secular worldview in which human control and technique replace divine leading and human obedience as the basis of mission. [805]

A full scriptural framework must support the church. Absent this framework, the structure fails. We must not assume that past founders have already fulfilled this requirement:

> Christianity has . . . consistently reduced or distorted the gospel. Many of the problems with which non-Western churches struggle have to do with the versions of the gospel that the missionary evangelists brought them, and much of the spiritual health of those churches may be attributed to their willingness to struggle afresh with the basic challenge of the gospel. We simply may not assume that our formulations of the gospel, as familiar and time-tested as they may be, exhaust the fullness and the scope of God's great good news, culminating in the life, death, resurrection, and mission of Jesus Christ. Every judgment we will make about the methodologies of evangelism will depend upon our answer to the questions: What is

---

[803] 1 Corinthians 3:10-11

[804] Monthly Missiological Reflection #25 *"From Theology to Practice: The Helix Metaphor"* from missiology.org

[805] Hiebert, Paul. 1993. De-theologizing missiology: A response. *Trinity World Forum* 19 (Fall):4

the gospel? What is the fullness of the apostolic message? What is salvation? What does the church's gospel mission intend? What is the missio Dei ("mission of God") that defines the identity, purpose, and the way of life of the church?[806]

The issue for a church is whether its scriptural support is based on a thorough Biblical understanding or whether it is based upon finding support for preconceived concepts of ministry. The failure to conduct this research will result in a church that drifts from theory to theory, perhaps based on what church surveys reveal or the support of donors dictates.

After the Biblical foundation is in place, a cultural analysis must be made. As discussed more fully in chapter one, a cultural analysis is needed to understand the people who will form the church, learn the barriers that separate them from ministry and intersect the scripture with cultural aspects of their lives, such as weddings, funerals, and our key celebrations.

Historical perspective, the third element, acknowledges the historical forces at play, the character of the nation, whether colonial vestiges are an issue and other important information. In addition, how the church is perceived whether as a family, a business, or an assembly of resources, will depend on its regional history and demographics. Finally, historical perspective provides learning from outside our own sphere of experience. For example, such a perspective taken from early missionaries could provide needed background for avoiding synchronism.

Strategy formation, the final element, is the child of the first three elements. As the author of Missional Helix notes, "Based on these understandings, I will define "strategy" as the practice of model formation for ministry shaped by theological reflection, cultural analysis, and historical perspective and by the continued practice of ministry."[807]

As such strategy cannot exist alone, its success will depend on the quality of the exploration and implementation of the first three

---

[806] Guder, Darrell L. 1994. *Evangelism and the debate over church growth. Interpretation* 47 (April):145-155
[807] *The Missional Helix: Example of Church Planting* taken from www.missiology. org, Monthly Missiological Reflection #26

elements. It will be effected by experience, but still be ever subject to the first three elements. When this constraint is ignored, strategy will fail. Instead of asking, "what is God's goal?" we may ask, "will this make the church grow?" "what will other churches think of this approach?" "how will this effect funding?"

No one can tell you the proper strategy to employ to reach your community, the people God trusts you to develop. Your strategy will be the DNA that makes your church uniquely suited to minister to your people, your culture. As the earlier chapters suggest, some elements are mandated by scripture. Paul Kaak and Neil Cole summarize the main requirement using the metaphor of DNA:

D - Divine Truth: Truth is the foundation for everything. By Divine Truth, we mean the dynamic and living presence of Christ and His Word. A recent variation refers to the "D" as "Divine Connection" and views the Word of God and prayer as two primary means of maintaining that connection with God. The DNA metaphor is thus extended to include four overarching values instead of only three.

N - Nurturing Relationships: Healthy relationships are what make up a family. Love for one another is to be a constant pursuit of the family of God. This is the most basic of Christ's commands.

A - Apostolic Mission: Apostolic means, simply, "sent." Just as Jesus was sent on a mission, so we are sent out on a mission for Him. Our mission is to go into the world and disciple the nations for their good and God's glory.[808]

With these keys concerns as reminders, certain processes will help you think through the proper strategy. The initial framework to consider is described above. Scripture provides your goals and your calling. From these elements you develop your strategy. At this point, what remains is to effectively employ that strategy. So how do we effectively put our strategy into play?

To begin we should return to another Biblical imagine of the

---

[808] Niel Cole and Paul Kaak, "Organic Church Planters Greenhouse: The First Story" (CMAResources. Long Beach, 2004) pg. 1-6.

church. God calls the church to build up the body.[809] The word "build" is used as it is in construction. The church and its member are called to construct more mature believers, "Therefore as you have received Christ Jesus the Lord, so walk in Him, having been firmly rooted and now being built up in Him and established in your faith, just as you were instructed, and overflowing with gratitude."[810]

Other verses also compare developing believers to building a home.[811] We are commanded to build and to build with care.[812] How then are we to build? The strategy will be determined by the culture and opportunities, as noted above, but employing that strategy will have common themes. Thomas Rainer and Eric Geiger in *Simple Church*,[813] suggest that a church must: define, illustrate, measure and discuss.

By "define" we mean a church must have a process that is clearly articulated. Mariners Church in Irvine, California, seeks to develop its members into fully devoted followers of Christ. Toward this end, they define their strategy using a concentric circle which is divided into areas of development. Mariners' circle describes the stages of this development as follows: reach, belong, grow, serve and lead. Each area has programs designed to move the believer to the next part of the circle until a person reaches the "lead" stage, where he becomes part of training the next person to advance through the circle. The leaders and members know exactly what the church is trying to accomplish.

It is important to note that a clear definition does not mean the process should be rigid or compartmentalized. Instead the process should be implemented holistically without the rigid ministry divisions that inhibit effective ministry. But clarity of goals is essential to implementing ministry. As the authors of Simple Church note:

Without definition, people are uncertain about how the church is making disciples. Without definition, people are clueless about how the church is designed to bring people to spiritual maturity. Without definition, there is room for ambiguity. Most churches are ambiguous

---

[809] Ephesians 4:11-12
[810] Colossians 2:6-7, NIV
[811] See 1 Peter 2:5, Ephesians 2:2
[812] Corinthians 3:14
[813] B & H Publishing Group, 2006

about their ministry process, either because they do not have one, or it is loosely defined.[814]

Defining is the strength of the western church. Western churches tend to excel in the description and teaching areas of building believers. Eastern and African Churches tend to excel in incarnational training. Unfortunately, each is also weak in the corresponding area of building believers. For some reason, despite the shrinking of the world brought about by technology, they seem unable to learn from each others strengths. This reminds me of Rudyard Kipling's, "The Ballad of East and West", " Oh, East is East, and West is West, and never the twain shall meet/ Till earth and sky stand presently at God's great judgment seat..."

To be successful and to conform to scripture, churches must have both an educational and an experiential aspect of preparation. Imagine a house built by a person who never learned how to handle electricity or understood the structural support necessary to hold up a roof. Now imagine one built by someone versed in engineering, who had never hammered a nail. As builders, we should accept neither. Think of a pilot. The pilot begins solely in the classroom, understanding both the physics and the mechanics of flying. Next he is put at the controls beside an experienced instructor. Finally he is licensed for certain kinds of flight. But before he can move to the next level of licensing, he must accumulate hours of actually experience. No amount of classroom or simulator work will earn him the right to progress. Are we preparing our brothers to fly? We are if we include both education and experiential training in developing our members.

Next, a church must effectively "illustrate" its defined process. Referring back to the Mariners model, its process is easily presented by a simple circle. Illustration can be done visually through a drawing such as Mariners uses or through illustration by stories and by examples. God instructed Hosea to marry a prostitute[815] to illustrate to his community that they had lost their love of the Lord. When they looked to Hosea, they saw a picture of their own spiritual prostitution.

After Jesus said he was the bread of life, he illustrated the point by

---

[814] Simple Church, supra, pg 113
[815] Hosea 1:2; See Simple Church pgs. 118-119

feeding five thousand.[816] After claiming to be the light of the world He restored a blind man's sight.[817] After announcing He was the resurrection and the life, He called Lazarus from the tomb.[818] We must constantly seek ways to illustrate our process so that leaders and members are clear on the strategy of the church.

Next a church must "measure." It must find a creative way to measure progress toward it goals. This is not as easy as it seems. The measurement must fit the methods. Let's return to the example of Mariners and its *reach, belong, grow, serve, lead* model. Let's assume that in one year they measure and find that they have two hundred members in each part of the circle. The following year they measure again and find they have four hundred at each stage. What have they learned? Well, the overall ministry would have grown, which is always a good thing. But to truly understand how their model is doing, they would have to measure how members had progressed through the circle. Growth in numbers alone might suggest that more members are stagnating in one area without progressing to another. To understand, Mariners would (and does) measure laterally rather than using a bottom line business measurement.

Finally the church must "discuss" the strategy. Strategies can be defined, illustrated, measured and then lost. The strategy and it effectiveness must be a constant conversation within the church, especially at the leadership level. Constant discussion will make it part of the church DNA.

PRESENT DAY MODELS

Inward and Outward Looking Churches

It will easier to discuss present church models if we first establish critical definitions "inward ecclesiology" and "outward ecclesiology":

---

[816] John 6
[817] John 8-9; See Simple Church pgs. 118-119
[818] John 11; See Simple Church pgs. 118-119

With the term "inward ecclesiology," I connote the church view that is concerned largely on the members inside the church, while the term "outward ecclesiology" is the view that focuses on those outside of the church. The former is focused mostly on strengthening the church itself, while the latter on serving the world.[819]

Inward ecclesiology results from the reformation, when, reacting to the strictures of existing church, the reformers found so much liberation from the grace of the scripture that they tended not to focus on God's children in need:

> The ecclesiology of the Reformers and their heirs, which can be called the "inward ecclesiology," emphasized the holiness of the Christians as the people called out of the world. It tended to look at the church as the Noah's ark rather than a rescue boat for lost people. Then as this aspect is accentuated, the church can become a people who escape from the world rather than challenge and change the world according to God's will. Its focus is personal godliness, and not so much on serving the world.[820]

An inward looking church will focus on its pastoral role and tend to neglect its apostolic role. With the rise of missionary influences, the inward facing model began to be questioned.[821] Outward ecclesiology was a reaction to the deficiencies of inward ecclesiology and was established to cure those ills rather than as a holistic approach. As Lesslie Newbigin put it:

> The church has its existence in relation to the salvation which has been wrought at Christ's coming into the world and is to be consummated at His coming again. Since that consummation concerns the whole world, the Church's existence is in the act of being the bearer of that salvation to the whole world.... We must say bluntly that when the Church ceases to be a mission, then she ceases to have any right to the titles by which she is adorned in the New Testament. [822]

---

[819] Seung-Oh An, Toward A Holistic Ecclesiology for Effective Kingdom Ministry, *JAM* 4:2 (2002), pp. 163-178

[820] Ibid at 166

[821] See for examples, Charles Van Engen, *God's Missionary People: Rethinking the Purpose of the Local Church* (Grand Rapids, MI: Baker, 1991),

[822] Newbigin, *The Household of God*, pp. 162-63

As a reactionary concept, outward facing ministry suffered from it origins. Ministry which addresses the needs of an unredeemed mankind is draining and dangerous because it does not give adequate consideration to the needs of the believers to be restored and edified. Churches with this approach also tended to emphasize social and political needs at the expense of the requirements and ordinances of scripture. Rather than serving the world because of God's agenda, they tended to set their agenda based solely on the needs of the world. Furthermore its proponents tended to rely on the strengths on man, rather than trusting God for results.

Jesus' ministry demonstrates the needs for balance between theses extremes. His arrival harkened the advent of God's kingdom on earth, He Himself proclaimed this, "Now after John had been taken into custody, Jesus came into Galilee, preaching the gospel of God, and saying, "The time is fulfilled, and the kingdom of God is at hand; repent and believe in the gospel."[823]

He proved the truth of His kingdom by performing miracles.[824] He established its power by casting out demons.[825] Having begun the work of establishing the Kingdom he called the people to it. They were requested to leave everything and follow him.[826] Having called people to His kingdom, he showed the nature of the kingdom by His aid and concern for the poor and needy.[827] After the death of Jesus, the church became the custodian of God's kingdom. We therefore, as the custodians of Christ, need only to look to His example which models both the salvation of man through grace and the care of man though works in God's name.[828]

Other Church Models

There are literally hundreds of articles and books about church models. The subject is worthy of a book of it own. For our purposes, we can paint in broad stokes. After looking at inward and outward

---

[823] Mark 1:14-15

[824] See e.g. Mark 5:23-43

[825] Matthew 12:28

[826] Matthew 10:34-38; Luke 9:57-62

[827] See Chapter Four

[828] See 1 Corinthians 1:17 and Chapter Two

facing churches, we need only to examine a few more basic theories for our focus on balancing ministry. Toward this end, we will look at church theories which missiologist Dr. Ed Stetzer calls Relevants, Reconstructionists, and Revisionists.

Relevants spend less time exploring theology and more time updating existing music, preaching and leadership structures to fit with their conception of current culture. The church's goal is constant-to be relevant. In these churches one is as likely to see the pastor carrying the latest book on pop management techniques as the Bible. Because relevance is not by itself a meaningful scriptural anchor, the trap for such churches is to flutter in the wind, blowing from trend to trend measuring success only by how current their latest strategy appears. Staff members, unless independent minded and strong, can learn to exist without contribution simply by celebrating the latest change, becoming cheerleaders rather than players.

It may also be difficult for these churches to set effective success measurements. They may adapt business models without adequate conversion of the principle to fit the goals of God's mission. Often they will adopt numeric goals that are artificial, easy to obtain but unrelated to true progress. Mission success, for example, might be measured by the total number of people who go on a trip, without regard to how they progress after that travel or how the trip served the foreign ministry. Leadership development may be measured by attendance at seminars or distribution of leadership tracts rather than true discipleship. For Relevants, proof of relevance is found solely in church growth. This is a dangerous measurement for this model church. Since the church is specifically designed to be acceptable to the temporal styles of the community, measuring by growth will only demonstrate success in this one area. Numbers say nothing about how the church is doing internally.

This model can fail in the balance because relevance, although a key component of any ministry, is given too much weight. When the relevance of the church is given so much attention, the changes made tend to be superficial: adaptations of music, decoration, media, without becoming truly relevant to the physical and spiritual needs of the community. The church adopts a relevant style without adopting a relevant character.

Reconstructionists are evangelical and concerned with the current forms of church. They lament that the lives of today's Christian vary little from non-Christians. They will move to organic incarnational models for church. They seek the informal and would support house churches as the essence of ministry. The risk for these churches is to become an accumulation of Christians whose sole bond is dissatisfaction with other churches. Often their membership is composed of those negatively reacting to the mega-church trend.

Revisonists, according to Stetzer, "are theologically liberal and question key evangelical doctrines, critiquing their appropriateness for the emerging postmodern world." These efforts often simply rehash debates of prior years, and the effort and constant refining of doctrine can inhibit conversion growth. In addition, the focus on differences in doctrine makes it difficult for these churches to partner with others church and faith based organizations.

The point of reviewing these models is not to be critical. Instead, it is to point out that each may be trapped by turning a virtue into a vice. The Christian church has a powerful enemy. As Martin Luther wrote, "... where God built a church, there the Devil would also build a chapel."[829] We must constantly monitor a churh's journey to keep it vibrant. There is nothing wrong with the defining factors of each model discussed above, in fact, they are commendable. It is only the failure to achieve balance that can lead to difficulties.

Indeed, instead of copying successful pastors or adopting particular models, church leaders should seek a model of their own, unique to the particular body they seek to serve. Ed Stetzer puts it this way:

Every time I read a book from a church health pastor ... he warned "Don't copy me. You are not in [my community]." I didn't listen very well. As I look around me, I see that lots of other pastors didn't listen either, as clones of successful mega-churches popped up across the continent. The temptation was too great—we really wanted to reach as many people as they did, so we copied their models and hoped for the same results. Unfortunately, it didn't work in most places.

Now, instead of importing styles and models, more pastors are genuinely asking the same questions as international missionaries:

---

[829] Martin Luther; *Table Talk, lxvii*

What style of worship/music will best help this group to worship in spirit and truth?, What evangelism methods should I use here to reach the most people without compromising the gospel?, How can this church be God's missionary to this community?

If we simply replace the Church Growth Movement with a rush to copy innovative pastors, we will fail to engage effectively with the lost in our community. God didn't call your church to reach Southern California, so it shouldn't look like Saddleback or Mosaic (prominent … churches in So Cal). Instead, every church needs to ask what God is calling them to be and to do. [830]

As Stetzer makes clear God has appointed church leadership to reflect His image and carry out His mission to the particular community they serve. We can certainly learn from church models, but we are entrusted to effectively accomplish the mission in our local community with its local culture and local world views. Simply replicating what others do will not work. As Paul noted, "…but you will receive power when the Holy Spirit has come upon you; and you shall be My witnesses both in Jerusalem, and in all Judea and Samaria, and even to the remotest part of the earth."[831]

We design our methods to fit our mission. We design our church to be "missional." Stetzer writes:

The missional church is not just another phase but a full expression of who the church is and what it's called to be and to do. The missional church builds on the ideas of Church Growth and Church Health and brings the lessons learned to their mission focus—their local mission field. As a result, such churches are truly missional as they take up the Acts 1:8 challenge.[832]

CONCLUSION

Our methods of forming churches should be rigorously reviewed and tested; we are called to, "contend for the faith that was once for

---

[830] Stetzer, Ed; *Church Growth: When the Formulas Don't Work.* Pg 5
[831] Acts 1:8, NASB
[832] Stetzer, Ed; *Church Growth: When the Formulas Don't Work.* Pg 6

all entrusted to the saints"[833] The truth is meant for all people, but the methods are entrusted to us. The stakes could not be higher, "... the manifold wisdom of God might now be made known through the church to the rulers and the authorities in the heavenly places."[834]

We should be worthy of this trust.[835] The importance placed upon us is best illustrated by Jesus' prayer before he went to the cross:

> Jesus spoke these things; and lifting up His eyes to heaven, He said, "Father, the hour has come; glorify Your Son, that the Son may glorify You, even as You gave Him authority over all flesh, that to all whom You have given Him, He may give eternal life. "This is eternal life, that they may know You, the only true God, and Jesus Christ whom You have sent. "I glorified You on the earth, having accomplished the work which You have given Me to do. "Now, Father, glorify Me together with Yourself, with the glory which I had with You before the world was.
>
> "I have manifested Your name to the men whom You gave Me out of the world; they were Yours and You gave them to Me, and they have kept Your word. "Now they have come to know that everything You have given Me is from You; for the words which You gave Me I have given to them; and they received them and truly understood that I came forth from You, and they believed that You sent Me. "I ask on their behalf; I do not ask on behalf of the world, but of those whom You have given Me; for they are Yours; and all things that are Mine are Yours, and Yours are Mine; and I have been glorified in them. "I am no longer in the world; and yet they themselves are in the world, and I come to You. Holy Father, keep them in Your name, the name which You have given Me, that they may be one even as We are. "While I was with them, I was keeping them in Your name which You have given Me; and I guarded them and not one of them perished but the son of perdition, so that the Scripture would be fulfilled.[836]

Facing the cross, His last thoughts were of us and the mission He left us. He left us a guide through the scriptures and the support though

---

[833] Jude 3

[834] Ephesians 3:10

[835] Ephesians 1:22-23; "And He put all things in subjection under His feet, and gave Him as head over all things to the church, which is His body, the fullness of Him who fills all in all."

[836] John 17:1-12

the Holy Spirit.[837] He prayed for our safety and left us the church so that we could be equipped to do God's call in accordance with God's wish.[838]

It is our submission that the approaches outlined in our book reflect both the scriptural images of God's church and a proper framework for banding together to effect God's mission. To be effective, each church must seek the balance called for in God's word. There is no royal road to a Godly church because each church must, in part, be influenced by its relevant culture and history. Its strategy for ministry is primarily shaped by scripture, but cannot work without adapting to the circumstances that affect the local body of believers. We must constantly work to be effective and balance the mission of salvation for God's created with the mission of restoring God's creation to His will. Ministry lies in the balance.

---

[837] John 16:13

[838] Hebrews 13:20, "Now the God of peace, who brought up from the dead the great Shepherd of the sheep through the blood of the eternal covenant, even Jesus our Lord, [21]equip you in every good thing to do His will, working in us that which is pleasing in His sight, through Jesus Christ, to whom be the glory forever and ever. Amen."

About the Authors

ADRIAN de Visser, M.A., is President and Senior Pastor of Kithu Sevana Ministries, Colombo, Sri Lanka. He also serves as International Deputy Director for South Asia of the Lausanne Committee for World Evangelization and is currently on the Board of Directors of Colombo Theological Seminary. In addition to developing churches in Sri Lanka Adrian has in instrumental in planting dozens of churches through out South Asia. Adrian resides in Sri Lanka with his wife Ophelia, his son Prashan and his daughter Thelini.

Dave Sprowl, is an AV rated attorney (Martindale Hubble's highest rating) and a former partner at the law firm McDermott, Will & Emery. He is an Elder at Mariners church where he served on three occasions as chairman of the board of Elders. He also served as Associate Pastor for the global outreach ministry of Mariners before resigning in 2006 to devote more time to Resplendent Hope, a non profit foundation. Dave has served on many other Church and non profit boards during his thirty-five year history of ministry. He resides in Newport Beach, California, with his wife Dale, his son Barrett and his daughters Brooke and Bayley.

Printed in the United States
203995BV00002B/541-570/P

9 781589 615915